Alexander at the Battle of the Granicus:
A Campaign in Context

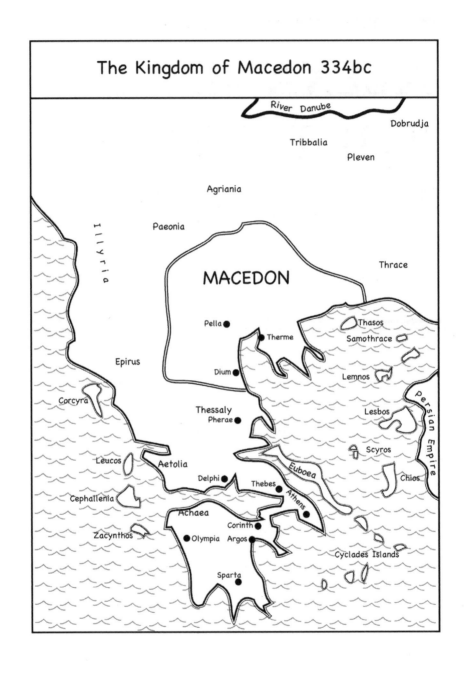

The Kingdom of Macedon 334bc

River Danube

Dobrudja

Tribbalia

Pleven

Agriania

Illyria

Paeonia

Thrace

MACEDON

Thasos

Pella

Therme

Samothrace

Epirus

Dium

Lemnos

Corcyra

Persian Empire

Thessaly
Pherae

Lesbos

Leucos

Aetolia

Scyros

Euboea

Delphi

Thebes

Chios

Cephallenia

Athens

Achaea

Zacynthos

Corinth

Olympia   Argos

Cyclades Islands

Sparta

ALEXANDER AT THE BATTLE OF THE GRANICUS:

A CAMPAIGN IN CONTEXT

by

Rupert Matthews

SPELLMOUNT

British Library Cataloguing in Publication Data:
A catalogue record for this book is available
from the British Library

Copyright © Rupert Matthews, 2008
Maps Copyright © Rupert Mathews

ISBN 978-1-86227-448-8

First published in the UK in 2008 by
Spellmount Publishers
The History Press Ltd
The Mill, Brimscombe Port,
Stroud, Gloucestershire GL5 2QG

1 2 5 7 9 8 6 4 2

Printed in Great Britain

Contents

List of Maps

Preface

Alexander the Great is one of the few figures from the ancient world who is widely known today. His reputation as a military genius was established by defeating armies far larger than his own with relentless consistency. His exploits in conquering most of the known world were stupendous. And yet it is easy to forget, looking back on his lifetime, that there was a time when Alexander was an untried and relatively inexperienced youth, and that time is the subject of this book.

Alexander unexpectedly inherited the Kingdom of Macedon when his father, Philip II, was murdered. At the time Alexander was only 20 years old. He had fought alongside his father on several campaigns, but had never held an independent command. Outside the Macedonian royal family he was known only as a good-looking boy who could be charming when he wanted to be, who read Homer's heroic verses with passion but who drank more than was good for him. Those opposed to Macedonian power caricatured him as a beardless boy who dreamed of the deeds of ancient legend. Time would show that Alexander was far more than that, but at the time the view was widely held and had much evidence to support it. The Granicus Campaign would establish Alexander as a capable and talented commander, though it also revealed him as one liable to make mistakes by getting carried away with excitement.

The story of Alexander's career is relatively well known. The events were dramatic, exciting and far-reaching in their importance so they were well recorded at the time and have been much explored by historians since. Hollywood has made two biopics about Alexander the Great.

What marks all these accounts is that they tend to concentrate on the political side of the conflict. Although battles and campaigns are often dealt with in some detail, they are seen as background to and results of the intrigues and machinations of the rulers and politicians who fill the pages of these writings. This is understandable, for the ancient sources that we have focus on pretty much the same things.

For a military historian, this can all be rather frustrating. The reasons for battles are given clearly enough and who won them, but only very rarely is there any discussion about how the battles were fought. We read almost nothing about weapons, tactics or logistics. But how were the armies kept supplied with food? How did a Macedonian soldier fight? Why were Alexander's cavalry so devastating in battle?

This book is an attempt to explain to the general reader the reality of warfare in the year 334BC. It seeks to give a plausible recreation of the tactics used in the Granicus Campaign and to put them into the context of the time. It explains what the weapons were like and how they were used in action. It describes the usual tactics of the different military units involved and how these would have had an impact on each other in battle. I handled replica weapons at some length. I have then used this information to put together an account of the campaign itself.

It is usual for an historian to explain something of the way in which he has treated his sources. Footnotes are the usual academic way of doing this, but I find that the constant flicking and back and forth can spoil the flow of a work for a reader. Instead, I have mentioned my sources in the body of the work and how I have interpreted them. But I have done so only when dealing with a contentious issue or when I felt it necessary for one reason or another. I shall make some more general points here.

The career of Alexander was dramatic not only in itself but because of the effects that it had on the political world of the time. The Persian Empire had been the world superpower for centuries, but suddenly it was gone. In its place were created a number of states, each led by one of Alexander's Macedonian officers leading an army equipped and trained in the Macedonian fashion. The Greek city states had likewise been swept away. They were no longer independent, but were subject to one or other of Alexander's successors.

At the time most people recognised the profound change that had come over the world because of Alexander. There was a huge appetite for books about him and his career. Several of the men who had served Alexander wrote their memoirs. Among the most important of these was Ptolemy, son of Lagos, who later became Pharaoh of Egypt. He wrote a long, detailed account of his experiences with Alexander. Nearchus, another senior officer, also wrote up his memoirs as did Oneiscritus.

Nor was Alexander himself retiring about his exploits. He employed the historian Callisthenes to travel with the Macedonian army and write up its exploits in suitably heroic style. The resulting book was entitled *The Deeds of Alexander*. Alexander also employed a geographer named Aristobulous to accompany the army, and he too later wrote a book based on his experiences. Eumenes, the head of the army staff, kept a daily diary. This was not intended for publication and only parts of it ever became public.

All these men were either employed by Alexander or were friends with him and undoubtedly this coloured their work. They are all complimentary about Alexander. Good deeds are emphasised and treated at length whilst events that do not reflect so well on Alexander are either skated over or blamed on somebody else.

Another contemporary book was published by a Greek historian named Cleitarchus. He was from Colophon, but lived most of his life in Egypt. He had travelled to Babylon during Alexander's lifetime, but seems to have begun his work only after Alexander's death. He spoke to many men who had served with Alexander, but also to men who had been involved in politics, some of them opponents of Alexander. Crucially for this book he spoke to at least one of the Greek mercenaries who had fought on the Persian side during the Granicus Campaign. All these accounts were included in his biography of Alexander.

But the real problem when it comes to writing about Alexander is that none of these books has survived to the present day. All these books were lost when the Roman Empire collapsed. Instead we have to rely on the works of men who lived later, but who quoted from the contemporary sources or relied on them.

Of these later sources the most important are Arrian, Plutarch and Diodorus. Arrian was an admirer of Alexander who drew mostly on the books by Ptolemy and Aristobulous. He also had other sources, some of which were probably official government records. Arrian's *Life of Alexander* is long and detailed. Arrian was a Greek who rose to be governor of Cappadocia in the Roman Empire. He wrote his book around the year AD110.

Plutarch was another admirer of Alexander. He wrote a shorter biography, but he put more effort into looking behind events to assess character and intentions. He based the outline of events on the work of Ptolemy, but also quoted from a host of other sources that are now lost. Many of the human interest anecdotes known about Alexander come from Plutarch's work.

Writing around the year 50BC, Diodorus Siculus is the oldest surviving source on Alexander. Diodorus actually wrote a 40 volume *History of the World*, of which the exploits of Alexander form only a part of one volume. Diodorus preserves much of the work of Cleitarchus, and so is the main source for any stories that do not portray Alexander in a favourable light.

All these sources share a common problem when read today. They assume that their readers will know things that, today, we don't. They did not need to set down detail on the weapons of the time, for their readers would have seen them for themselves, in the same way that a modern writer need not explain the nature of a tank or aircraft. They also did not need to explain how troops formed up for battle, as their readers would already have known.

For details of how battles were fought we need to look further than the biographies of Alexander. There are two main sources for Macedonian warfare. The first is Polybius, a Greek writer born in 204BC who later moved to Rome and wrote a *History of Rome*. Polybius also wrote a detailed work on military history, but this has not survived. Other writers quoted extensively from Polybius, and some of these books have survived. By picking and choosing excerpts from a dozen later books it is possible to reconstruct much of what Polybius had to say.

The second main source for military matters is Asclepiodotus, who was writing about a century after Polybius. His works have survived and include some very detailed information on weapons and tactics. Unfortunately for us, Asclepiodotus is writing about how the Macedonian system worked some 200 years after Alexander. By that time terminology and practice had both changed and it is not always easy to decide which bits of what Asclepiodotus tells us are relevant to Alexander's time.

It is not often that the ancient authors actually contradict each other. More often they give different information. It is the role of the historian to compare the different accounts and try to match them together to present a coherent and credible account of what really happened.

There are many deductions that I have made in this book, some of which I explain in detail and others that I do not. No doubt some readers and scholars will disagree with me, but for better or worse, this is my interpretation of events. It is based on what I believe to be sound logic, on an understanding of how war was organised and fought in that distant age and on my understanding of how men thought back then – which was very different from how they think today.

I have done my best to produce a readable and yet well researched account of a military campaign that took place some 2,300 years ago. Reader, it is over to you.

Cast of Characters

It must be admitted that the names of the Macedonians, Greeks, Persians and others that will be encountered here will be unfamiliar to many readers. To aid the reader – especially with the confusions caused by more than one person having the same name – I give a cast of characters.

Achilles	Legendary Greek hero. He was the bravest of the Greek warriors in the Trojan wars. He was killed in the final attack on the city.
Ada	Carian royal lady and aunt of a former king.
Aeschylus	Greek poet and dramatist. Aeschylus fought at the Battle of Marathon against the Persians in 490BC. He wrote ninety plays, of which only seven survive. He is generally credited with having created the technique of having more than one actor on stage at the same time, and having the characters engage in conversation.
Agamemnon	Legendary Greek king of Mycenae. He led the Greek alliance in the Trojan wars.
Agathon	Macedonian nobleman. The son of Tyrimmas. At the Battle of the Granicus he commanded the cavalry units drawn from tribes allied to Macedon.
Ajax	Legendary Greek hero. In the Trojan wars he was second only to Achilles in terms of bravery and courage.
Alexander	King of Macedon. Alexander III or Alexander the Great. At the time of the Granicus Campaign Alexander was aged just 22 years old and had been on the throne for less than two years.
Alexander the priest	Chief priest of a temple of Athene passed by the Macedonian army after it landed in Asia Minor.
Alexander the Prodromoi	Macedonian army officer. This Alexander was killed when engaged in looting, which led to a famous legal case being presented to Alexander.

Amyntas IV	King of Macedon. As an infant king he was ousted from power by his uncle, who became Philip II. Amyntas was reduced to the status of royal prince and continued to live at court under the watchful eye of the new king.
Amyntas	Macedonian nobleman. Son of Andromenes. During the Granicus Campaign he commanded a lochos of the Foot Companions.
Anonymous Greek mercenary	The name usually given to the source used by the historian Cleitarchus when describing events on the Persian side during the Granicus campaign. He is generally believed to have been an officer in the force led by Memnon. He was certainly at the siege of Harlicarnassos, but may not have been at the Battle of the Granicus itself. This figure may have been more than one man.
Apollo	Greek god. Apollo presided over the arts and over law, order and government. He also spoke directly to humans through his oracle at Delphi.
Arbupales	Persian nobleman and nephew of Darius.
Ariobarzanes	Persian nobleman. A satrap of Phrygia he was executed for mounting a failed rebellion in 361BC.
Aristoboulos	Greek geographer. He accompanied the invasion of Persia as part of Alexander's army to write up geographical notes about the places visited.
Ariston	Son of the King of Paeonia. He commanded the forces from Paeonia that served with Alexander during the Granicus Campaign.
Aristotle	Greek philosopher. Born in 384 at Stageira, a Greek city that was later annexed by the Kingdom of Macedon, Aristotle lived most of his life in Athens. He was hired by Philip II to be the tutor to Alexander, a post he held for about three years.
Arrhidaeus	A son of Philip II. Our sources about Arrhidaeus are vague, but he seems to have been mentally retarded in some way. Certainly he never played a role as great as he should have done as a royal prince.
Arrhidaeus	Macedonian nobleman. During the Granicus Campaign he commanded the Paeonian cavalry.
Arrian	Greek historian, properly Flavius Arrianus. Born in about 96 and became a citizen of Rome in 124. He wrote many books, including a biography of Alexander.
Arsamenes	Persian nobleman. During the Granicus Campaign he was Satrap of an area of Asia Minor.

Arses	Persian monarch. Son of Ochus, Arses died in 336BC in mysterious circumstances, allegedly murdered by his chief minister Bagoas.
Arsites	Persian nobleman. During the Granicus Campaign he was Satrap of Phrygia.
Artaxerxes III	Persian Emperor. In the original Persian the name was Artakhshatra. He died in mysterious circumstances in 338BC.
Artemis	Asian goddess, also worshiped in Greece. She was a fertility goddess who was also linked to hunting.
Asander	Macedonian nobleman and brother of Parmenio.
Asclepius	Greek god. Asclepius was the god of doctors and of healing.
Athene	Greek goddess and patron deity of Athens. She was a virgin goddess of wisdom, but was also considered to be a warrior deity.
Attalus	Macedonian nobleman. Under Philip II Attalus had occupied a number of important government and army positions. His niece, Eurydice, married Philip in 337BC.
Bagoas	Chief minister of the Persian Empire. A eunuch of Egyptian origins, Bagoas rose to the highest level in Persian government. He allegedly murdered the monarchs Arses and Ochus, and perhaps Artaxerxes III, though the allegations were never proven.
Callas	Macedonian nobleman. He commanded the advance guard that wintered in Asia Minor before Alexander's army arrived. During the Granicus Campaign he commanded the Thessalian cavalry.
Callisthenes	Greek historian. Sometimes written Kallisthenes. He established a reputation as a scholar and popular historian and was hired by Alexander to accompany the army on the invasion of Asia to write an account of the war.
Cassandra	Legendary Trojan prophetess.
Cleitus the Black	Macedonian nobleman. Veteran officer in the Companion cavalry and perhaps a squadron commander.
Cleitarchus	Greek historian. He wrote a biography of Alexander based on the memories of men who had served in his army and of men who had fought against him.
Coenus	Macedonian nobleman. During the Granicus Campaign he commanded a lochos of the Foot Companions.
Corrhagus	A Macedonian foot companion who took part in a famous duel with Dioxippus.

Craterus	Macedonian nobleman. During the Granicus Campaign he commanded a lochos of the Foot Companions.
Darius II	Monarch of the Persian Empire. In the original Persian he was Daryavaush. Gaining power in 425BC, he ruled until 404BC.
Darius III	Monarch of the Persian Empire. He came to power in mysterious circumstances in 336BC. He occupied the Persian throne during the Granicus Campaign.
Diodorus Siculus	Greek historian. Born around 90BC. He wrote a vast *History of the World* in 40 books.
Dionysius II	Ruler of the Greek city of Syracuse in Sicily. Dionysius ruled from 357BC to 343BC. He had a great interest in science and technology, which led him to develop new engines of war.
Dioxippus	A Greek athlete who took part in a famous duel with Corrhagus.
Ephialtes	Athenian general. During the Granicus Campaign he served with the Persians.
Erigyos	Greek soldier from Mitylene. He initially commanded the allied Greek cavalry that set out on the Granicus Campaign, but was absent from the battle itself for some unexplained reason.
Eumenes	Greek bureaucrat from the city of Cardia. He was employed by Philip II to be the chief administrator of the Macedonian army, a position he retained under Alexander for the Granicus Campaign.
Eurydice	Macedonian noblewoman, in full Eurydice Cleopatra. Niece of the senior nobleman and army officer Attalus. She married Philip II in 337BC and quickly gave birth to a daughter and a son.
Glaucippus	A Greek resident of Miletus.
Hector	Legendary Trojan warrior. The greatest hero of the Trojans, Hector was killed by Achilles.
Hegelochus	Macedonian nobleman. On the Granicus Campaign he commanded the prodromoi, the mounted scouts.
Hegistratos	Greek mercenary. During the Granicus Campaign he commanded the garrison of the city of Miletus.
Hephaistion	Macedonian nobleman. Boyhood friend and close companion of Alexander. Hephaistion's formal role during the Granicus Campaign is unknown, but he was close to Alexander throughout. Many modern scholars believe him to have been Alexander's lover.

Heracles	Legendary Greek hero. Heracles was said to be the son of Zeus by a human mother and was considered to be a minor deity. He was the special protector of humans in times of trouble and was thought to intervene on behalf of humans to mitigate the anger of the gods.
Homer	Greek poet. Though to have lived around 800BC and to have composed the great epic poems the *Iliad* and the *Odyssey*, that tell of the Trojan War and the journey of Odysseus.
Khabash	Egyptian nobleman. In 338BC he declared himself to be pharaoh under the royal name of Senensetepenptah. Initially successful at ousting the ruling Persians, Khabash was defeated and killed sometime in 335BC.
Kheperkare	Egyptian nobleman. In 380BC he ousted Persian rule over Egypt and declared himself to be pharaoh under the royal name of Nectanebo.
Lityerses	Legendary tyrant of Miletus who was defeated by Heracles.
Lysippus	Greek sculptor. Born in Sicyon, Lysippus was hired by Alexander as his official sculptor to undertake commissions for the Macedonian state. He produced a famous statue of Alexander, now lost, which served as the model on which most other portraits of the king were based.
Mausolos	King of Caria. He died in 353BC and his magnificent tomb, the Mausoleum, became one of the Seven Wonders of the World.
Meleager	Macedonian nobleman. During the Granicus Campaign he commanded a lochos of the Foot Companions.
Memnon of Rhodes	Greek mercenary. By the time of the Granicus campaign he had already been in Persian service for some years. At the Granicus he commanded the Greek mercenaries on the Persian side. After the battle he was promoted to have overall command of the war against Alexander.
Menoitios	Legendary Greek king and father to Patroclus.
Menoitios	Macedonian sailor. The fact that he had a name identical to that of the legendary king led to him having a role in Alexander's visit to Troy.
Mithridates	Persian nobleman. As a senior nobleman and son in law of Darius, Mithridates was man of great power and influence. His precise role in the Granicus Campaign is, however, unclear. He was probably commander of

15

the units drawn from the royal Persian army and sent to fight Alexander, though this is not certain.

Mithrines — Persian nobleman. During the Granicus Campaign he was governor of the city of Sardis.

Mithrobuzanes — Persian nobleman.

Nectanebo II — Pharaoh of Egypt. He ruled from 360BC to 341BC when Egypt was invaded and conquered by the Persians.

Neoptolemus — Legendary Greek hero. Son of Achilles and killer Priam.

Nerieds — Mythical water nymphs.

Nicanor — Macedonian nobleman. Son of Parmenio. During the Granicus Campaign he commanded the Hypaspists.

Niphates — Persian nobleman. During the Granicus Campaign he was Satrap of an area of Asia Minor.

Ochus — Persian monarch. Son of Artaxerxes III he succeeded his father in 338BC, but died within months in mysterious circumstances.

Olympia — Queen of Macedon. Wife of Philip II and mother of Alexander. Her marriage to Philip seems to have been a genuine love match, but after a tempestuous marriage she was passed over when Philip married a new bride named Eurydice. She withdrew to her native Epirus. After Philip's murder, which she may have organised, she resumed a role in public affairs. During the Granicus Campaign she was in Macedonia.

Orontobates — King of Caria. He commanded the forces defending Halicarnassos.

Parmenio — Macedonian nobleman. Of relatively humble origins, Parmenio rose to high office in the Kingdom of Macedon. Philip II admired Parmenio as a general and made him second in command of the Macedonian army. Parmenio retained this position under Alexander for the Granicus Campaign. Sometimes written Parmenion.

Patroclus — Legendary Greek hero. Childhood friend and constant companion of Achilles, Patroclus was killed when wearing the armour of Achilles by Hector.

Pausanias — Macedonian nobleman. A young member of the royal guard, he murdered King Philip II, but was himself killed moments later.

Pausanias — Macedonian nobleman. During the Granicus Campaign he commanded one of the squadrons of the Companion Cavalry.

Pelagon — A son of Syrphax of Ephesos.

Perdiccas II	King of Macedon. Elder brother of Philip II and father of Amyntas IV. Perdiccas inherited the throne from his father Amyntas III in 364, and died in 359BC.
Perdiccas	Macedonian nobleman. A close friend of Alexander and of about the same age. During the Granicus Campaign he commanded one of the lochus of the Foot Companions.
Petines	Persian nobleman. During the Granicus Campaign he was Satrap of an area of Asia Minor.
Pharnaces	Persian nobleman and brother in law of Darius.
Philip II	King of Macedon, father of Alexander. He ruled from 359BC to 336BC. It was Philip who reformed the Macedonian army, planned the invasion of Persia and subdued the Greek states into becoming his allies. He was murdered before he could lead the invasion, a task that fell to his son and successor Alexander.
Philip V	King of Macedon. Inheriting the throne in 221BC, ruled until 179BC. Despite his catastrophic defeat by Rome in 198BC he retained his throne, but the power of Macedon was broken.
Philip	Macedonian nobleman. During the Granicus Campaign he commanded a lochos of the Foot Companions.
Philip, son of Menelaos	Deputy to Erigyos. He commanded the Greek cavalry allied to Alexander at the Battle of the Granicus.
Philotas	Macedonian nobleman. A son of Parmenio. During the Granicus campaign, Philotas commanded the companion Cavalry.
Plutarch	Greek writer. Born around 46, Plutarch wrote a number of books, the best known of which are 50 biographies, including one of Alexander. He died in about 130.
Priam	Legendary King of Troy. He was the ruler of the city during the Trojan wars.
Priapos	Asian fertility deity, later worshiped in Greece and Rome.
Protesilaus	Legendary character from the Trojan Wars. He was the first Greek to land on Trojan territory, and the first to be killed.
Ptolemy of the Thracians	Macedonian nobleman. This Ptolemy seems to have commanded the Thracian troops serving under Philip II. On the Granicus Campaign he commanded all the allied tribes serving with Alexander.

Ptolemy, son of Lagos	Macedonian nobleman. According to the story spread by Ptolemy himself in later years he was not the son of Lagos at all. His mother was Arsinoe, who was a mistress of King Philip of Macedon. When she fell pregnant, Philip hurriedly married her off to Lagos, a wealthy man of humble birth. Arsinoe got a rich husband and Lagos got a king who owed him a favour. Ptolemy was, therefore, the illegitimate half-brother to Alexander. Not everyone took this story very seriously, especially after flatterers added the colourful detail that Lagos had tried to kill the newly born baby Ptolemy but had been attacked by an eagle – an animal sacred to the god Zeus. What is certain is that Ptolemy was a close friend and associate of Alexander.
Rheomithras	Persian nobleman. During the Granicus Campaign he was Satrap of an area of Asia Minor.
Sitalkes	Prince of of Odrysia. Sitalkes commanded the men recruited from the Odrysians, a Thracian tribe, to serve with Alexander in the Granicus Campaign.
Spithridates	Persian nobleman. During the Granicus Campaign he was Satrap of Lydia.
Syrphax	Rich Greek man who ruled Ephesos on behalf of the Persians.
Teos	Pharaoh of Egypt, son of Kheperkare. He died in 360BC.
Timocleia	Theban noblewoman who killed Alexander the Prodromoi.
Titus Quinctius Flamininus	Roman general. In 198BC he defeated King Philip V of Macedon at the Battle of Cynoscephalae. The defeat marked the effective end of the Macedonian army.
Xenophon	Greek mercenary. Born in Athens about 430BC, Xenophon served as a mercenary employed by the Persian Empire for a number of years. His writings were, and are, a key source for much knowledge about the Persian military systems.
Xerxes	Monarch of the Persian Empire. Ruling from 485BC to 465BC, it was Xerxes who had led the great invasion of Greece in 480BC that led to the razing of Athens and other cities. His invasion was ultimately defeated.
Zeus	Greek god. The king of the gods, Zeus was believed to have the power to intervene in human events.

Alexander's March to the Hellespont

The Satrapies of Asia Minor

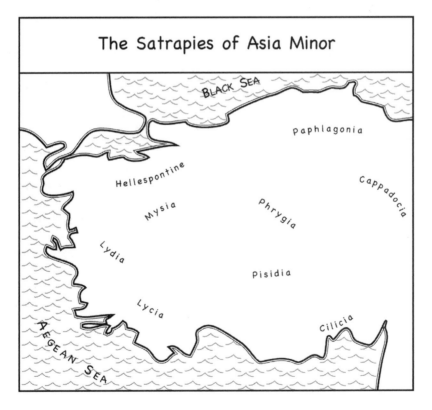

CHAPTER ONE

The Outbreak of War

The Granicus Campaign was the first campaign in Alexander the Great's invasion of the Persian Empire. It was the first major campaign involving a large scale battle in the open field that Alexander had fought since he became King of Macedon, and so was the first real test of his military skills.

The campaign was not however, either Alexander's first nor the opening move in the war between Macedon and the Persian Empire. Both of those had already taken place while Alexander's father, Philip II was King of Macedon. And even Philip was a relative newcomer to the generations-old enmity between Persia and the Greeks.

The trouble had begun two centuries before the time of Alexander when Cyrus, the ruler of the Persian Empire, defeated King Croesus of Lydia. The conquest of Lydia in 546BC brought within the reach of the Persian Empire a number of Greek city states along the coast of Asia Minor that had accepted that Lydia had a vague sort of lordship over them. Cyrus and his successors moved quickly to transform that loose arrangement into a firm rule that made the cities no more than properties of the Persian emperor. That in itself was enough to annoy the Greek cities, but the fact that the Persian empire was based on agricultural wealth meant that neither the Persian monarchs nor their agents understood how Greek commerce worked. That led to disputes over tax and tribute, and to a general decline in the prosperity of the cities.

In 499BC a crisis was reached and several of the Greek cities along the shore of Asia Minor rose in revolt. Their forces burned the Persian provincial capital of Sardis and defeated the local armies of the Persian satraps, or local governors. This was achieved partly with help sent from the states of mainland Greece. However, the Persians put down the rebellion. Determined to exact revenge against those Greek states that had aided the rebels, Darius sent an army by sea to attack Athens in 490BC. That invasion achieved some success, but was defeated at the Battle of Marathon. Darius's son Xerxes tried again ten years later when he personally led a vast army overland to attack Greece. The story of that campaign is told in the book *The Battle of Thermopylae: a Campaign in Context,* which is a companion volume to this. The Persian invasion ultimately failed, but not until several Greek cities had been captured and others destroyed.

Warfare between Persia and the Greek states had been endemic through the decades that followed. The conflict was intermittent and neither side was ever strong enough to defeat the other decisively. The Greek city states spent much of their time fighting each other, while Persia was wracked by civil wars.

Meanwhile the Kingdom of Macedon had been growing in size, wealth and importance. Under King Amyntas II (reigned 389–364BC), the kingdom had enjoyed years of peace and commercial growth. He firmly established the rule of the kings over the hills of Upper Macedonia, as well as over the lowland plains that his forebears had ruled. The upland areas had formerly owed allegiance to the kings, but had been largely in the hands of their own nobles. Amyntas ensured that his rule ran over all Macedonia.

The Macedonians were a people who spoke Greek, albeit with a strong accent that was the cause of many jokes among the Greeks further south. They had not, however, adopted much of the culture that was widespread among the Greek city states. The Macedonians were a wild and rough lot who enjoyed hunting more than philosophical debate and were inclined to run a race rather than engage in a poetry competition. The southern Greeks scorned the Macedonians for the fact that they lived under the rule of kings rather than in a self-governing city state with some degree of democracy. Despite the differences, on which the southern Greeks loved to put emphasis, the Macedonians were Greeks who spoke Greek and worshipped Greek gods.

Amyntas did much to introduce Greek culture to Macedon, importing artisans and scholars. He aimed not only to boost Macedonian levels of civilisation, but also to improve its prosperity by establishing merchants and craftsmen who could be taxed. When Amyntas died he left the throne to his son Perdiccas III. Perdiccas died in 360BC, leaving his infant son Amyntas IV as his heir. It was only months before Philip, a younger brother of Perdiccas, ousted the boy and became king.

Philip II was more ambitious that either his brother or father. He extended Macedonian rule over much of Thrace and tribes to the north and west of Macedonia proper. He used the wealth this brought him to revolutionise the economy and army of Macedon. With his new, professional army and using wily diplomacy, Philip managed to conquer

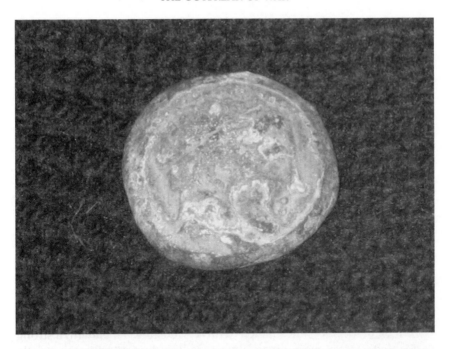

A bronze coin issued by Philip II, father of Alexander the Great. The obverse (top) shows a head of the god Apollo, while the reverse shows a youth riding a prancing horse. Both symbols were traditional for the coins of Macedon.

or ally himself to all the Greek city states. In 338BC Athens and Thebes mustered an alliance against Macedonian power. Philip hurried south with his army and crushed the alliance at the Battle of Chaeronea. Thereafter his grip on the various Greek states was firm.

It was at Chaeronea that Philip's young son Alexander first came to the notice of people outside Macedonia. Aged 18, Alexander commanded a cavalry unit and was credited with saving Philip's life at a critical moment in the battle. He was subsequently sent, along with the veteran commander Parmenio, to treat for peace with Athens. The young, good looking prince made a great impression on this mission. He had been educated for some years by Aristotle and showed a great interest in Athenian arts and culture. Alexander offered lenient terms to Athens, so long as the city was willing to send delegates to a great Congress of the Greeks being organised by Philip at Corinth. The Athenians agreed.

The Congress of Corinth was a masterstroke of diplomacy by Philip. At it he created a League of the Greeks. In reality this was little more than a means by which he could issue his instructions to the states that lay under his thumb. But it was set up in such a way that there was a veneer of democracy and choice involved, and the delegates from the various city states were given almost endless opportunities to debate matters as they wished. So long as they ended up agreeing with Philip all would be well. The avowed purpose of the League was to wage war on Persia in order to avenge past damages and to free from Persian rule the Greek city states of Asia Minor.

Only one major state in Greece neither attended the Congress nor joined the League. That state was Sparta. The Spartans had the finest army in Greece and had not yet been defeated by the Macedonians. When the Congress was over, Philip sent an ambassador to ask the Spartans if they would send a force to join his great invasion of Persia. The Spartan reply was proud and haughty, 'Spartans are accustomed to lead, not to follow'.

In fact, Philip was content. Sparta had a track record of bullying the smaller states around her borders. Philip had posed as the friend of these states, using Macedonian armed might to protect them against Sparta. It would help him to keep these states on side if Sparta stood aloof.

Philip then returned to Macedon to prepare for the great invasion. As well as military preparations, Philip engaged on a round of diplomacy with the tribes and kingdoms to the north of his lands. Two key moves involved marriages: Philip himself married Eurydice from the Upper Macedonian nobility, while his daughter married the King of Epirus. The latter marriage was unremarkable, but the former had involved Philip putting aside his first wife, Olympia the mother of Alexander.

On the day of the wedding of the King of Epirus, Philip organised a week long succession of banquets, sports meetings and artistic performances at the royal palace at Aigai. As Philip was walking into the theatre to make a speech he was suddenly stabbed by one of his own bodyguards, a Macedonian noble named Pausanias. Philip died within seconds. The murderer fled toward the gate, but tripped over a vine as he ran and was quickly overpowered by a mob who butchered him. It was widely believed at the time that the killer had been acting with the encouragement of Olympia, though this was never proved.

The murder paralysed Macedon for there was no obvious heir to the throne. First there were Philip's three sons. Alexander was a grown man, albeit young. Philip's son by Eurydice was only a few months old, but his great uncle was Attalus one of the most powerful nobles in Macedon. Attalus began manoeuvring to get himself appointed regent for the infant. The third son was Arrhidaeus. Like Alexander Arrhidaeus was fully grown, but there was something wrong with him. We don't know quite what this was, but he appears to have been mentally defective in some slight way. Finally, there was Amyntas IV, the boy who Philip had ousted so many years before. He was now a fully grown and apparently capable young man.

Civil war threatened and the other Greek states began to think about throwing off Macedonian control.

Inside Macedon, things moved quickly. The noble families of Upper Macedonia declared for Alexander almost at once. Soon afterwards Parmenio, Philip's trusted second in command, also came out for Alexander. Amyntas was murdered on Alexander's orders, while Eurydice and her son were killed by men working for Olympia. Nobody took Arrhidaeus very seriously. Alexander was acclaimed by the army as King of Macedon and the nobles followed suit. It was all over in less than two months.

Alexander sent messengers to Thessaly, where Philip had been recognised as leader of the Thessalian League. The nobles there instantly accepted Alexander as Philip's successor. The League of Corinth followed suit within weeks when Alexander himself came to ask for their loyalty. Alexander appeared secure. He went back to Macedon in that autumn of 336BC to prepare to invade Persia.

On his way north, Alexander stopped at the great oracle sanctuary of Delphi. This was one of the most famous and important religious sites in Greece. It was protected by sacred rules and hedged about with divinity so profound that no state ever dared violate the sanctuary or its enormous wealth until Christianity rendered the old gods powerless. It was believed that at Delphi the great god Apollo spoke directly to mankind through the agency of his priestess.

Humans could attend the temple. After complex rituals and the payment of an offering, they were allowed to put a question to Apollo. The priestess then performed various rites and fell into trance during which she would give the answer. These answers were sometimes clear and concise, at other times vague or ambivalent. When Alexander arrived he asked 'What does Apollo say to me?'

The priestess replied 'Hail to Alexander the Invincible.'

In the spring of 335BC, Alexander was faced by trouble on his northern border. Instead of marching on Persia, he headed north to defeat the Getae and Triballians before heading west to put down trouble among the Illyrians. While he was campaigning, Darius of Persia sent huge bribes in gold bullion to anti-Macedonian politicians in various Greek states. With this money they began stirring up trouble and encouraging their fellow citizens to rebel.

When a rumour arrived that Alexander had been killed in Illyria, the city of Thebes rose in rebellion against the League of Corinth. The Macedonian garrison that Alexander had left in Thebes fled to the Cadmea, a fortress inside the city, where they were put under siege. Athens did not openly rebel, but it did begin mustering its army for war. Various smaller states followed the lead of Athens, gathering for war, but not yet declaring war on Macedon.

But Alexander was not dead. When he got the news that Thebes was in arms, he was 300 miles away. He did not hesitate for a second, but at once displayed the ability to think and move quickly that was to become his hallmark. He sent gallopers riding south to announce that he was alive and calling on all states still loyal to the League to send their armies to meet him at Onchestus, a small town 15km north of Thebes. He then led his army south. So quickly did Alexander drive his men that they reached Onchestus before the news had reached Thebes that he was on his way.

Next day Alexander appeared before the gates of Thebes with his army and demanded to know if Thebes was loyal to the League or not. He got no reply. Alexander was keen to preserve the League and the fiction of voluntary association if he could. Next day he again asked the Thebans if they would accept the League's authority. This time he got his answer when the Theban army marched out to attack him.

The attack was met by a force led by the general Perdiccas, who was driven back until Alexander came up with the rest of the army. The Thebans began to fall back, but their formation collapsed in the rush for the gates. Perdiccas sent a spearhead of men racing forward with orders to stop the gate being closed. This they did, allowing the Macedonians to burst into the city.

Alexander allowed his men free rein to loot, rape and kill as they liked for the rest of the day. Then he called them to order. By this time the armies of the loyal League states had begun to arrive, and were camped outside the walls of the captured city. Alexander summoned their leaders and asked them to vote, as befitted free members of the League, on how Thebes should be punished. Those on the spot came mostly from states around Thebes which had, in years gone by, suffered invasion and tyranny from Thebes. They voted for the harshest of the alternatives that Alexander gave them.

The city was put to the torch and the defensive walls demolished. All Theban citizens, their wives and children, who could not prove that they had opposed the rebellion were sold into slavery. Over 30,000 people were sold off in this way. All Theban state property was divided up among League members. The city was utterly destroyed and its people dispersed. Thebes was no more.

This brutal act appalled all of Greece. But it did have the desired effect. Athens and all the other states promptly sent ambassadors to Alexander to pledge their loyalty. Alexander was pleased to accept, but he imposed conditions. Certain named men who were known opponents of Macedon were ordered to be handed over, or thrown into prison.

Alexander then returned once again to Macedon to prepare to invade Persia. He recalled the veteran Parmenio, who had been in Asia Minor with a small army of mercenaries on the orders of Philip. Parmenio arrived that autumn and was at once confirmed as second in command by Alexander. The men, ships and supplies for the expedition were ordered to muster at Therme early the following spring.

The invasion was on.

CHAPTER TWO

The Macedonian Army: Infantry

The invasion force that Alexander and Parmenio were mustering at Therme in the spring of 334BC would prove itself to be devastatingly effective. To understand why Alexander's army was able to achieve what it did, it is necessary to appreciate just what it was that made this a revolutionary force that was to change the face of war completely, and set a pattern that would be followed for centuries to come.

As we have seen, Alexander was taking with him large numbers of troops from the Greek city states. These men would prove to be invaluable for all sorts of reasons on the Granicus campaign, but the core of the force setting off to invade the Persian Empire was the Macedonian army. This was a unique force in the ancient world. There had never been anything like it. Although Alexander was undoubtedly a military genius of huge talent, it is doubtful that even he could have achieved half of what he did if he had not been leading the army that he did.

There were two key elements to the success of the Macedonian army in the hands of both Alexander and his father Philip. It was professional and it was integrated. Both were aspects that were rare in the ancient world. To have both features together in one army was unheard of.

The vast majority of armies in the ancient world were composed of men who earned their livings as farmers, potters, merchants or through other trades. A state might hire a full time army commander and staff – or it might rely upon its richer citizens and nobility to fill such a role – but the bulk of the troops were amateurs. They were, no doubt, strong and fit, but they were not full-time soldiers.

Inevitably this affected both the training and the motivation of the men. Most men in Greek states underwent some months of intensive military training as they approached manhood. In some it was a condition of becoming a citizen that a boy should undertake such training. Throughout Greece at this time only men could be citizens.

As a citizen of a state, a man had the sorts of rights that we today take for granted, but which were then seen as a privilege. Conditions varied from state to state, but generally speaking it was only citizens who could own land, who could vote or speak at government meetings and who could have access to the law courts. The rest of the population was composed of the women and children within the families of citizens. There were usually also a large number of freemen. These men might be foreigners resident in a state – perhaps as merchants or exiles – or locals who for one reason or another did not qualify as citizens. There were also slaves, often in surprisingly large numbers.

With citizenship went duties as well as rights. One of these was to serve in the army during war time. Each man was responsible for bringing his own weapons and equipment on campaign. This led to an informal, but strict social hierarchy within the army.

Only the very richest men could afford a horse. As a consequence most Greek armies had very small cavalry forces. Typically they numbered less than 5% of the army and were used mostly for scouting or carrying messages rather than actually fighting. The bulk of the citizens came equipped as heavy, armoured infantry: the hoplite. These men formed the solid formation known as the phalanx which was the main force of any Greek army. The poorest citizens came without armour, carrying javelins or slings, knives or daggers. They were used as skirmishers and light infantry. Only very rarely were men other than citizens summoned to join a Greek army, though mercenaries could usually be hired readily.

At best the men in a typical army would train for a few days each year once their initial training was over. Most men merely practiced once the army was mustered for war, to remind themselves what they were supposed to do. In such conditions it was inevitable that the men would be able to carry out only the simplest of manoeuvres, tactical moves or battlefield formations.

The part time status of the soldiers also affected their morale and their willingness to campaign. Most men were proud of their state, especially if they were citizens with all the rights and duties that that entailed. They were willing to fight, even to die, for their state. But because they had families and businesses to worry about they rarely wanted to be away from home for very long. They served without pay, indeed it cost them money to go on campaign.

Greek states, therefore, tended to fight short, sharp campaigns. This usually involved both sides marching out to find the other's main force with the aim of fighting a battle as quickly as possible so that, win or lose, everyone could get back to their real jobs as soon as possible. Not only were tactics fairly basic, but strategy was minimal as it was never really needed.

A hoplite soldier from a Greek vase made some years before Alexander's time. Apart from the greaves, which most hoplites did not wear by this date, the equipment gives a good idea of the appearance of the Greek hoplites who served both in Alexander's army and with the Persians.

A group of re-enactors in hoplite gear march in open order. By this date the designs painted on shields often identified the city state from which the owner came. The inverted V carried by the man on the left, for instance, identifies him as a Spartan. The mixed designs shown here indicate that this is a mercenary unit. (with thanks to the Hoplite Association)

A further consequence of this was that sieges were rare and unusual events. Before about 350BC they had almost never happened in the Greek world, even after that date they were rare and rudimentary affairs. If an attacking army could not get in quickly, they tended to give up and go home. In such a world, city defences did not need to be particularly strong. Most Greek cities relied upon natural crags and cliffs, augmented when necessary by walls of wood, mud brick or stone. As we shall see, things were improving by Alexander's time but even so most cities had defences that were only as good as they needed to be.

The only exception to this amateur status was the city state of Sparta in the Peloponnese of southern Greece. Sparta had a society that had been transformed centuries earlier to be geared totally for war. The vast bulk of the population was of non-citizen status. Most of these people were expected to work to produce crops and cash to support the state. The small elite of citizens, called the Lacedaemonians, did not need to work as they lived entirely off the labours of others.

Instead they were full time soldiers who trained incessantly. They were famous in Greece both for their hardiness and their skill. As a rule of thumb it was thought that an army had to outnumber a Spartan force by at least three to one to stand even a chance of winning a battle. At least one Greek army simply took to their heels and fled when confronted by a Spartan force.

The only real weakness of the Spartan army was that it was composed only of infantry. Superb though it was, the Spartan army was designed for the type of warfare then usual in Greece. It lacked cavalry, siege engineers and other specialists. In short, it was professional but it was not a properly integrated military machine.

Before Philip II came to the throne, the army of Macedon was little different from that of other states. The men served part time with only rudimentary training. They were called out when needed to serve without pay and at their own expense, then went home when the emergency was over. As we have already seen, Macedon was rather different from other states in the Greek world. Not only was it a kingdom with an established nobility, but its economy was largely agrarian and pastoral rather than urban and based on craft industries. This had a profound effect on the army that the Macedonian kings had been able to raise.

The wide open plains of south-eastern Macedonia meant that there was plenty of grazing ground. Horses were, correspondingly, easier and cheaper to keep than in Greece proper. Men of even relatively modest means could afford a horse, and so rode to war. These men were present in such numbers that they were formed up as bodies of cavalry on the field of battle.

Moreover, Macedon did not have a large body of citizens as such, all men being subjects of the king. Adult men were liable to be called up and, as elsewhere, came with what weapons they could afford. Most infantry came as hoplites, but there were also large numbers of shepherds and goatherds who could not afford such equipment. The men who served as infantry marched to war in units based on the area from which they came and commanded by the local noblemen. There are a few hints that the noblemen may have made some financial contribution to the local war effort, though whether this was buying weaponry, paying wages or supplying food is unclear.

It was Philip's stroke of genius to take this rather unpromising and, in some ways rather backward, army system and transform it. To do that he needed money. Philip was to become notoriously ruthless in his pursuit of money. He conquered Thrace largely to get his hands on the gold mines of the region, and imposed tributes on many of the smaller states and tribes that surrounded his kingdom. With this cash, Philip created his army. And it was that army that Alexander inherited and which he led on the Granicus campaign.

In attempting to recreate an image of the Macedonian army that set off from Therme on the Granicus campaign of 334BC, we are faced with a number of difficulties. The most glaring of these is that we do not have a single, contemporary source which gives a detailed description of the Macedonian army at this date. There is a mass of references to the army in various works, letters and speeches that have survived, but these all take it for granted that the reader already knows about the army. They make some frustratingly vague remarks, and go into detail only rarely. It was not until some years after Alexander's death that anyone thought to sit down and write a description of the Macedonian army. It is not always easy to distinguish between later practice and what was true in Alexander's day.

Nevertheless, the key features of Alexander's army are clear.

The first point of importance is that the army was made up of full-time, professional soldiers. It is not clear how the men were recruited, they may have been volunteers or conscripts, but it is clear that they served full time and for as long as the king needed them. There is some evidence that when campaigning close to Macedon leave was granted during the winter months, presumably on some sort of a rota system as the army remained in being.

That the men were free to be away from home for months and years on end implies that they were paid in some way. We know that by 323 at the latest Alexander was paying his Macedonian men. A rank and file infantryman was receiving 2 drachma a day, senior infantrymen were receiving 4 drachma a day, while rank and file cavalrymen got 6 drachma. It is to be assumed that other men received different levels of pay depending on their rank and position in the army – though the noblemen who made up the higher levels of command may have been serving out of duty or to achieve glory and still served unpaid. It is likely that Philip introduced pay at the same time that he made his army full-time. Otherwise, it is difficult to see how men could serve him without financially ruining themselves and their families.

It is also clear that Philip provided his men with their equipment. Several examples have been found stamped with the letters MAK, indicating that they were issued by and belonged to the Macedonian state. This had a great impact on his army and how it fought. Instead of each man in a unit bringing along his own war gear, every man now had standardised equipment manufactured to the same specification. Instead of units being composed of men with a variety of helmets, shields and weapons, Philip now had formations equipped and, it would seem, dressed identically.

The standardisation of equipment made it possible for the men to adopt a variety of formations and to undertake a series of complex manoeuvres. The full time training that they received gave them the skills to perform these moves and the confidence to do so in the face of the enemy. Needing to both pay and equip his men, it is no wonder that Philip and then Alexander found the army a massive expense and a huge drain on the resources of Macedon. In the year before the Granicus campaign began it is thought that the army consumed the entire income of the royal government, forcing Alexander to go into debt to cover the expenses of his court and civilian government.

Philip was not content merely to have superbly trained men with fine equipment. He also wanted to create an army with a balanced proportion of the various arms then available. At the time he undertook his reorganisation of the Macedonian army, Philip was already an experienced soldier. He had lived in Thebes as a hostage for a number of years and had taken the opportunity to study the equipment and tactics of the contemporary Theban army, then the most powerful in Greece. He had lived among the wilder hill tribes of the Kingdom of Macedon and was, of course, fully familiar with the skills and defects of the traditional Macedonian army. All this knowledge and experience he brought to bear on the composition of his army. By the time that Alexander set off to invade Persia, the Macedonian army was composed of a number of troop types, each with its own place and role in the army as a whole.

The bedrock of the army was the main infantry phalanx. This could be used offensively or defensively, its impressive mass when stationary and momentum when moving made it effectively invincible, though as we shall see it did have its weaknesses if handled badly. Many historians refer to these men as phalangists, as they fought in the main phalanx. The Macedonians called them pezhetairoi, which translates as 'companions on foot', to distinguish them from other types of infantry who could also adopt a phalanx formation when necessary. The word phalangist should properly refer to all infantry able to fight in a phalanx, and is used in this way here. The title of pezhetairoi seems to have been an innovation of Philip to raise the status of these men from that of conscripts to being companions of the king.

The secret to the success of the pezhetairoi was their main weapon, the sarissa. This was a pike about 5.5 metres long. The head of the pike was made of iron and measured 50cm in length. It had an elegantly tapering, leaf-shaped blade that came to a wickedly sharp point. The butt end ended with a shorter, but bulkier metal shoe. This had a short, broad spike behind which was a four-flanged knob. When at rest the sarissa was planted in the ground, the butt spike sticking into the earth while

The foot companions, or pezhetairoi, formed the massive phalanx that was the centre of any Macedonian army. Each man carried a round shield and a sarissa pike of great length. The men were also equipped with helmets and with greaves. This man wears a phrygian style helmet, which seems to have been standard. The latter were probably worn to avoid injury from the but end of the sarissa held by the men in front. Most men seem to have worn the light, flexible linothorax style of body armour.

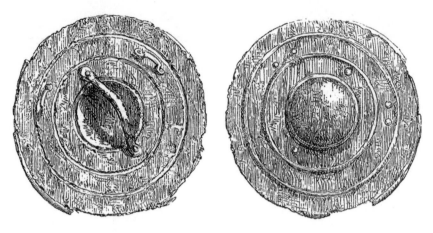

A bronze shield found in what is now Iraq. The shield matches descriptions of those used by the phalangists in the Macedonian army. It is thought that this example may date to about a century after Alexander's time, but its precise dating is obscure.

the flanged knob stopped it going in so far that it could not be lifted free with ease. If the sarissa head broke off in combat, the weapon could be turned around and the butt spike used as an improvised replacement.

The shaft of the sarissa was of wood and was made in two sections. These had a diameter of about 3cm at the extremities and around 4.5cm at the centre, where they were joined together by being slotted into a metal sleeve some 15cm long. The making of the shaft in two parts had a number of advantages. It meant that the sarissa could be split into two more manageable lengths when being carried on the march. It meant that if it broke it could be repaired more easily. It also made its original manufacture cheaper as two medium length shafts are easier to find than one long one. The shaft was made of cornel wood, which is a very rigid wood that has the added advantage of being capable of being coppiced so that it grows in the form of a large number of slim, straight stems. This meant that in action the sarissa remained straight, rather than wobbling about. In all the sarissa weighed around 6kg. Combined with its great length this made it impossible to wield with only one hand. The two-handed grip in turn dictated much of the remaining equipment of the pezhetairoi.

The shield was designed to be strapped to the left arm in such a way that the hand remained free to hold the sarissa. Known as a pelte, this type of shield was about 60cm across which made it much smaller than was usual in Greek armies. There were two arm loops through which the forearm was pushed, one at the centre of the shield for the elbow and one at the rim for the wrist. The shield had a distinctive flattish profile to allow for this grip arrangement.

The pelte also had a strong leather strap that ran from the shield over the shoulder of the pezhetairoi. This strap could be used to carry the shield when on the march, but its true purpose was for combat. When the sarissa was held horizontally, its main weight was carried by the left hand, the right hand being used to control its direction and elevation. The weight of the sarissa was in turn carried by the shoulder strap, so that the left arm did not tire quickly.

Each man also had a sidearm, for use at close quarters if the formation broke up or the sarissa broke completely. It is not entirely clear what this weapon was at the time of Alexander, though a couple of generations later the long double-edged dagger called the machaira was used. It may have been the same in Alexander's day.

Helmets were made of metal, usually bronze, padded inside both to make them more comfortable to wear and to cushion the force of any blow received. The standard helmet for a pezhetairoi in Alexander's army was of the Thracian type. This helmet is usually thought to have originated in Thrace, which by this date formed part of the Kingdom of Macedon. It was made of bronze, the better examples being beaten out of a single sheet, though cheaper examples were of two or three pieces fixed together. The helmet sat on the head like a hat, rising to a point that tipped forward in a bulbous bulge. The smooth, rounded shape of the helmet served to deflect the points of metal weapons, especially those coming from above or the front. Some examples were fitted with a face visor, often decorated with embossed beard and moustache. These were not common, however, and certainly not standard issue.

Some helmets also had fittings into which could be inserted feathers or crests of dyed wool. It is generally thought that the feathers, crests and plumes were used to denote rank. It is possible, however, that they were used to denote the unit to which a soldier belonged.

All pezhetairoi wore metal greaves, again usually of bronze, on their shins. This piece of equipment had generally fallen out of use by this date among Greek infantry. It is thought that Philip reintroduced it to protect his men's legs against accidental injury by the buttspike of the sarissa being carried by the man in front.

That the pezhetairoi wore body armour is beyond doubt, but what form it took is open to question. The sources are vague or contradictory on the subject. Some distinguish between lightly armoured pezhetairoi and those with heavier armour. On balance it would seem that most pezhetairoi wore what was called the linothorax. This was a piece

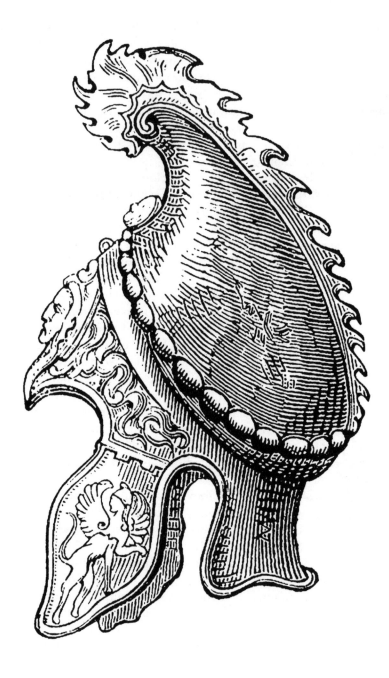

A thracian helmet of the type favoured by the phalangists in Alexander's army. This example with its embossed details and crest must have belonged to an officer.

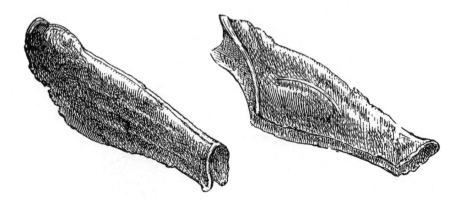

A pair of greaves dating to before Alexander's time. The use of leg armour had fallen out of use in most of Greece, but was revived by Philip II of Macedon.

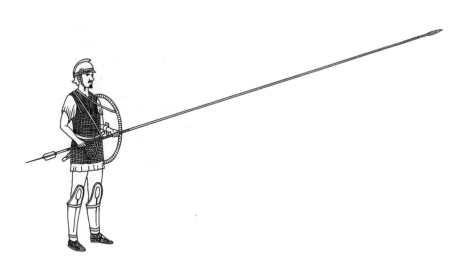

There are references to a type of pezhetairoi soldier described as being more heavily armoured than most of the men in these units. Although no detailed description of how these men were equipped in Alexander's time, we do know more about them as they were a century later. This man wears the more robust thracian helmet and has a chain mail shirt in place of the linothorax.

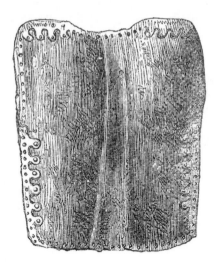

A bronze muscled cuirass of uncertain date. This sort of expensive armour would have been for officers only. Ordinary soldiers wore cheaper versions of body armour.

of armour that consisted of a front piece and separate back piece, each of which covered the body from waist to shoulders. The two sections were tied at the sides, while separate shoulder sections joined the main pieces and were laced into place. From the base of the linothorax a series of rounded straps, called pteruges, hung down to protect the groin area.

The distinguishing feature of the linothorax was that it was made out of linen. This was not as ineffective as it sounds. The garment was made up of as many as 14 or more layers of rough, coarse linen cloth glued to each other. The layers of linen could not stop a determined thrust by spear or sword, but could turn aside a glancing blow and was proof against the lightweight arrows of the day. Many examples of linothorax are known to have been strengthened by having metal plates sewn on to them at key places, such as around the upper chest and on the pteruges, which were less likely to be protected by the shield.

The type of organic glue used in ancient times was stiff and hard when cool. When it was put on, however, the glue was warmed by the wearer's body and soaked by his sweat so that it became softer. The linothorax thus became flexible without losing any of it strength.

The more heavily armoured pezhetairoi probably wore a metal cuirass, almost certainly of bronze plate though iron mail was also entering service at about this time. Metal body armour of this type would have offered greater protection than the linothorax, but would have weighed more than twice as much. In the case of the bronze type, it would also have been less flexible and so restricted the movements of the man wearing it.

Several of the sources refer to another type of pezhetairoi, the ashtetairoi. They are mentioned in contexts that make them part of the pezhetairoi but somehow superior to them. The word translates as 'closest companions', but that phrase has led to more academic debate than decision. It may be that the ashtetairoi were an elite group of pezhetairoi, or they may have been whichever group of them happened to be closest to the king on the field of battle. It is one of those cases where the ancient writers felt that they did not need to explain what they meant because everyone at the time knew what they meant – but we do not.

What is not clear is how the heavier and lighter pezhetairoi differed in action. It is possible that they formed distinct units of heavy and light pezhetairoi. Alternatively it may be that the front two or three ranks of a formation had the heavier armour, and those towards the middle and rear the lighter armour.

It was usual for Greek infantry to go into battle barefoot. This gave them a more secure grip on the ground, and most Greeks habitually went barefoot in their ordinary lives. On the march, however, there is evidence that at least some men wore sandals. The men all wore a short sleeved tunic of linen or wool that reached to just above the knee. For the pezhetairoi, this garment was most probably red. There was also a large cloak, used as a blanket when sleeping or worn in cooler weather.

Philip inherited a decimal organisation for his army, with men grouped in units of ten. He changed that to a system based on sixteen, though he kept the old name of dekas to describe each of these units – a fact that has caused great confusion. This dekas was the basis of pezhetairoi organisation both on the march and in battle. In camp, each dekas shared a camp fire, cooking utensils and rations. The tents of the dekas were pitched close to each other in two rows facing the fire.

Each dekas was led by a man called a dekadarch, who was paid twice as much as the others. He seems to have been responsible for ensuring that his men kept their equipment in good condition and for reporting any lapses of discipline to an officer. There was also a man called a dimoirites and two called dekastateros, whose duties seem to have been restricted to the battlefield.

Each dekas also had a slave and, at least some of the time, a mule or packhorse. This man and his animal were responsible for transporting the equipment needed by the 16 men. This included the tents, the cooking gear, a bowl and cloak for each man, an earthenware pot in which was

Foot Companions
A dekas with ranks.

All men are unranked, except for the dekas
commander (Dekadarch), the deputy
commander (Dimoirites) and the two file closers
(Dekastateros).

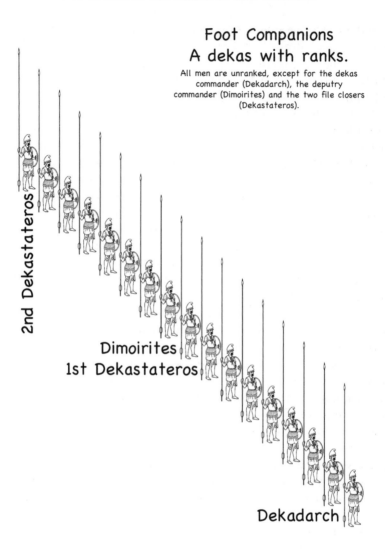

2nd Dekastateros

Dimoirites
1st Dekastateros

Dekadarch

Foot Companion Ranks

This shows a 16 man dekas unit of the Foot Companions drawn up as it would be if in a phalanx in close order. The commander of the unit, termed the Dekadarch, stands at the front. In action it was the task of the Dekadarch to keep closed up with the files on either side and to stay alert for orders. Behind him stand six ranks of ordinary soldiers. The eighth man is a Dekastateros, or file closer. His task was to keep the dressing of the six men in front of him firm and accurate. The ninth man was the Dimoirites, the second in command of the unit. He is followed by six more ordinary soldiers while the 16th and rear rank is taken by the second of the Dekastateros. If the formation was ordered to adopt the locked shield formation the Dimoirites would step to the left and march down to stand alongside the Dekadarch. He would be followed by the men behind him. The front rank would then be composed of alternating Dekadarchs and Dimoirites, while the rear rank would be composed of Dekastateros.

carried smouldering embers to light the campfire and enough food for up to 10 days.

The pezhetairoi were organised into units, known as lochos, each of which was composed of 32 dekas, or 512 men plus a trumpeter, a signaller and four or more officers. The senior officer is thought to have been mounted so that he could see over the heads of his men.

This lochos was the smallest formation available to the pezhetairoi phalanx. On an administrative level it was the basis for the issuing of pay and supplies and was the smallest unit over which a nobleman had command. The lochos were brigaded together in threes, each three lochos forming a taxis of 1,536 men plus officers and others. Each taxis was raised from one particular area of Macedon, and the units were commanded by the local nobility. No doubt there was an element of local, or tribal, loyalty at work here though the exact way it worked is not very clear in our sources. We know of one taxis which was taken over by the brother of its commander when that man went back home to raise fresh recruits.

There were, in all, twelve taxis of pezhetairoi in the Macedonian army. Taking into account officers and other supernumaries, that gives a total of around 19,000 men. Of these, Alexander took six taxis with him on his invasion of Persia. The remainder were left in Macedonia as part of the army under the command of Antipater.

In action the dekas formed the basis of the pezhetairoi formation, the phalanx. When advancing to take up position, and when action was not imminent, the lochos formed up across a frontage of about 30 metres. The dekas were put one behind the other, with a gap of 2 metres between each file. This was termed the Deep Order, or bathos. The gaps between each line of soldiers allowed them to step around bushes, rocks or other obstacles and gave them the space needed to clamber over walls or jump ditches.

Each dekas was led by its dekadarch who set the pace, maintained formation on neighbouring files and kept his eyes and ears open for orders from the officers. The eighth man back was one of the dekastateros. Immediately behind him came the dimoirites. The second dekastateros brought up the rear as the 16th man in line. The main tasks of these senior soldiers as the lochos marched was to ensure that the men kept their positions in the formation.

As soon as the lochos drew close to the enemy, the men adopted the close order, or pyknos. This involved the rear deka of each pair moving forward to fill the gap between two forward ones. This gave a formation sixteen men deep and thirty-two men wide, with each man occupying about a metre of frontage and a metre of depth. This was

Foot Companions
A Lochos in Close Order

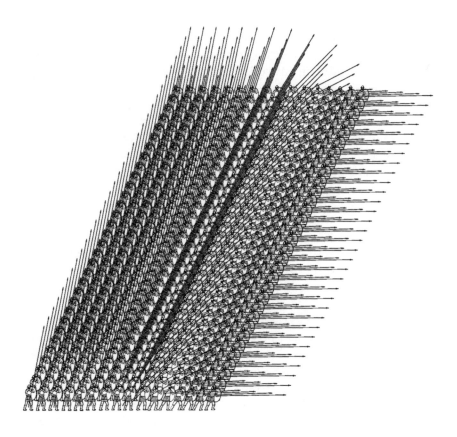

Foot Companions Lochos

This illustration shows a Lochos of Foot Companions in battle order. There are 32 files of 16 men each, a total of 512 men. Each Lochos was led by a Lochoi, who stood on the extreme right of the front rank. Although not shown here, each Lochos also had a herald, a trumpeter, a signaller and a staff officer attached to it. The numbers of these supernumeraries tended to vary, but Alexander tried to keep them to a minimum. The Lochos was the smallest unit of the Foot Companions that operated independently and was the base unit for purposes of administration, rations and pay.

Foot Companions
A Taxis in Close Order

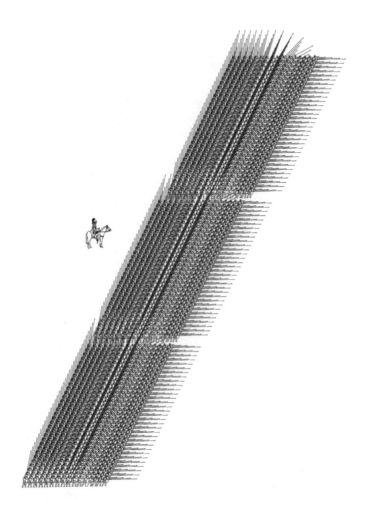

Foot Companion Taxis

It was usual for each area of the Kingdom of Macedon to provide recruits for three Lochos, which were then brigaded together as a Taxis under the command of a nobleman from that area. Alexander took six of these Taxis of Foot Companions with him on the invasion of Asia. In battle the three lochos were drawn up abreast as shown here. The commander of the Taxis and his immediate entourage of about four or five officers and trumpeters would usually take up position behind the Taxis. They were mounted so that they could see over the heads of the men to observe what was happening in the front ranks and in front of the formation. At the Granicus all six Taxis were formed up in line abreast at the centre of the battle line. This created a phalanx about 16 metres deep and 900 metres wide.

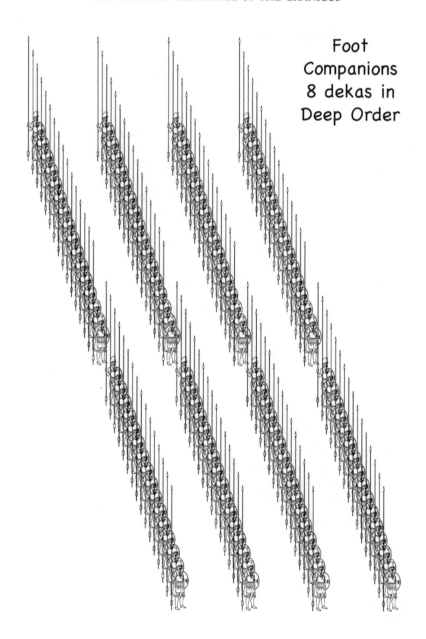

Foot
Companions
8 dekas in
Deep Order

Foot Companions in Deep Order

This illustration shows eight dekas formed up in Deep Order. This was the usual formation for the Foot Companions when advancing in battle order. There is a gap of about 2 metres between the files. The men are drawn up so that one dekas is followed by another, making the formation 2 dekas deep. This open order allowed the men to swerve around stones, bushes and other small obstructions without breaking their ranks, as would be the case in a denser formation.

46

a fairly tight formation, but was looser than was normal for a Greek phalanx. The extra space was needed for the effective use of the extremely long sarissas.

In a few rare instances the lochos is known to have adopted a formation called the shield-lock, or synaspismos. This involved each half dekas moving forward to squeeze into the small space between the files in front. Thus the front rank would be made up of alternating dekadarch and dimoirites, while the rear rank was made up exclusively of dekastateros. In this formation each man occupied only 50 cm of frontage. They were, therefore, packed shoulder to shoulder, with their shields overlapping – hence the name of the formation. It seems that the shield-lock was adopted only when the lochos was on the defensive against overwhelming numbers.

All these manoeuvres and evolutions were carried out with the sarissas carried in a vertical position. If they were held in any other fashion they would have got in the way of the men and made marching and changing formation impossible. As the moment for action approached, however, the sarissas were finally brought into action.

First the dekadarch brought his weapon down so that it projected horizontally from the front of the formation, taking care not to jab his butt spike into the man behind him. The shield hand was positioned about a metre from the butt, meaning that the sarissa tip would have projected forward of the shield by about 4.5 metres. The man in the second rank then lowered his sarissa so that it projected forward immediately to the right of the dekadarch. The third rank then lowered their sarissas so that they too projected forward, again just to the right of the man in front. The fourth and fifth ranks adopted a similar stance. Each rank was successively slightly to the right of the one in front, so that the sarissa of the fifth man touched the left side of the shield of the dekadarch leading the file to his right.

This meant that the pezhetairoi phalanx presented a solid wall of sarissa points to the enemy. The heads of the sarissas were stepped back with each rank, but with only a metre between each blade in each rank and a metre between each rank, the obstacle was effectively impassable to infantry advancing to meet it.

The men in the sixth rank had, meanwhile, lowered their sarissa to an angle of about 30 degrees from the horizontal. This meant that their points hovered about two metres above heads of the front rank dekadarch. The men in the seventh rank likewise angled their sarissa forward, at about 45 degrees and those in the eighth rank, the first of the dekastateros, did so at around 70 degrees. Those in the rear eight ranks kept their sarissas in the vertical position.

Foot Companions
8 dekas in Close Order

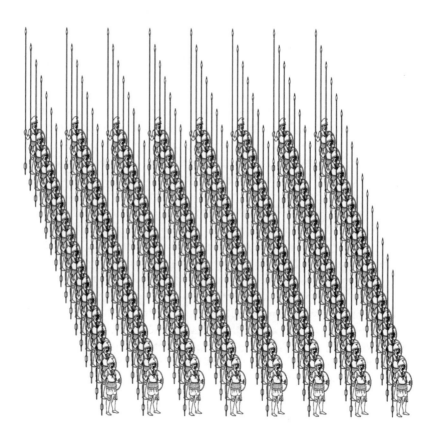

Foot Companions in Close Order

The Close Order was the usual formation adopted by the Foot Companions when going into battle. There was a frontage of about 1.5 metres per man. This gave the men enough space to wield their long sarissa pikes, but kept them close enough together so that they phalanx was a reasonably tight formation that was difficult for the enemy to break up or infiltrate. The Foot Companions stayed in this Close Order throughout the Battle of the Granicus.

Foot Companions
8 dekas in Shield Lock Order

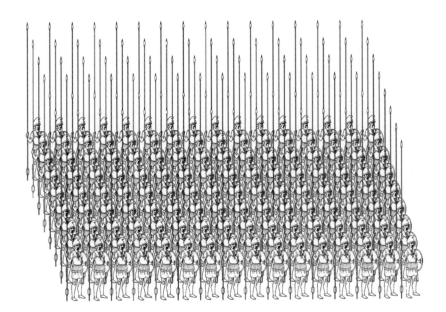

Foot Companions in Shield Lock

On a few, rare occasions, the Foot Companions would adopt the very dense Shield Lock forma-
tion. The rear eight men from each dekas would advance down the gaps between the files to pro-
duce a formation that was eight men deep and very dense. Each man had a frontage of only about
75cm. This order seems to have been adopted only when the Foot Companions were facing a
direct and heavy attack, usually from cavalry. Alexander is known to have used it only once.
That was some years after the Granicus when he fought the Battle of the Hydaspes. His phalanx
adopted the Shield Lock formation when attacked by the war elephants of the Indian army.

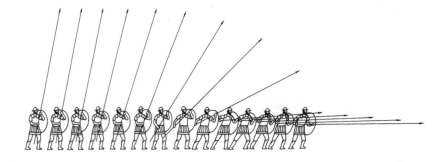

Dekas in Battle Order

Once the pezhetairoi were in close order they would rest with their sarissa pikes upright and resting on the ground. When the enemy approached, the men would lift their pikes and adopt the full battle formation. The front five ranks of men lowered their sarissa so that they were horizontal. The weight of the pike was held in the left hand, which also carried the shield and was supported by a leather strap around the shoulder. The right hand was used to keep the weapon level, or to move it from left to right if required. The great length of the pike meant that the spear head of that held by the man in the fifth rank projected forward of the man in the front rank. This created a solid hedge of pike heads facing the enemy. The pikes held by the rear nine ranks were held upright, but sloping forward at various angles. This provided some cover from incoming missiles and also meant that the pikes could be lowered quickly if required.

The purpose of this layering of sarissas over the heads of the front ranks was to provide cover from missile weapons. Incoming javelins or arrows were likely to catch on shafts of the angled sarissas. They would therefore be deflected, or at least lose some of their momentum and so become less dangerous.

The rear eight ranks, from the dimoirites to the second dekastateros, could in theory about face and level their sarissas to face an enemy coming from the rear. In practice they were unlikely to do this, and there is no record of their doing so, as their main role was to concentrate on what was going on to their front. If an assault by an enemy approaching from behind was considered likely it was more usual to station a second lochos behind the first. This rear lochos could face to the rear to drive off such an attack if it developed, or move up to support that in front if not.

The primary role of the rear ranks was to add momentum to the advance of the pezhetairoi phalanx. Unlike those at the front of the formation, they could not see the enemy very clearly and were more likely to continue to advance. With those rear ranks marching forwards, those in the front had no choice but to go forward themselves.

When they were thus advancing, the men in the pezhetairoi phalanx chanted what was to become the distinctive Macedonian war cry 'ala la la la la lai'. This was a chant sacred to Ares, god of war, in his guise known as the Enyalios – the war rage. This was Ares at his most violent and destructive, his most brutal and merciless. The cry was designed to strike fear into the enemy, not only by its volume and intensity but also through its well known religious links to utter destruction and death. There was even more to the war cry than that. The rhythmic chant of the repeated 'la la la' sound allowed the men in the pezhetairoi phalanx to keep pace with each other, preserving the all important formation and neatly dressed ranks. So long as it maintained its formation, the pezhetairoi phalanx was unstoppable. Again and again the slow, steady and remorseless advance of the foot companions simply crushed its way through or over any opposition.

No other troops on earth had weapons with the reach of the sarissa. The pezhetairoi could skewer their opponents before they could get their weapons to bear. The steady advance of the hedge of sarissa heads pushed an enemy formation back step by step. As men fell, the enemy formation lost its cohesion and eventually crumpled.

The experience of facing up to the advance of a Macedonian pezhetairoi phalanx was summed up by the Roman general Titus Quinctius Flamininus after his battle against Philip V of Macedon at Cynoscephalae in 197BC. Flamininus was a highly experienced soldier who had fought every kind of barbarian that could be mentioned and most of Rome's enemies in Italy and Spain. When asked to describe the pezhetairoi phalanx he replied simply, 'I have never been so terrified in my entire life.'

Although it was immensely strong, and formed the foundation for Macedonian success, the pezhetairoi phalanx had its weaknesses. The first of these was its inflexibility. The front five ranks were locked together by their overlapping sarissas in such a way that none of the men could step to either side, turn around or even move forward or back – unless all of them did so. Given that the lochos was thirty-two men wide it would take a great degree of discipline and effort to do so. Effectively those five ranks could march straight forward, but were incapable of any other manoeuvre unless they were to lift their weapons to the vertical. The following three ranks, with their sarissas angled forward, were not much better off.

And this reveals the second and more alarming weakness of the pezhetairoi phalanx. It was terribly vulnerable to a flank attack. With their extremely long sarissas, the pezhetairoi found it very difficult to turn around, and even more so for the formation itself to change direction. The sarissa was effective only so long as it was presented to the enemy in serried ranks. On its own it was useless.

This fact was shown in stark fashion at a banquet some years after the Granicus campaign was over. A Macedonian pezhetairoi named Corrhagus had been honoured at the banquet for his bravery in battle and, under the influence of drink, became rather boastful. Among those he challenged to a duel was an Athenian athlete named Dioxippus. Far from being put off, Dioxippus calmly stripped naked, picked up a club and accepted the challenge. Likening the two men to Ares with his spear and Herakles with his club, the assembled Macedonians gathered to watch.

Corrhagus advanced with his sarissa levelled and ready. Dioxippus edged about warily as the spear point approached his naked chest. When Corrhagus lunged, Dioxippus sidestepped, grabbed the sarissa in one hand just behind its head and brought his club smashing down to break the pike in half. The Athenian then ran forward at high speed, reaching Corrhagus just as he had dropped his now useless sarissa and was trying to draw a knife. Dioxippus knocked the Macedonian to the ground, put his foot on the prone man's neck and raised his club as if to batter the man's brains out. He then paused, grinned at his audience and, after just long enough to ensure the humiliation of Corrhagus, dropped his club and returned to his seat.

If the formation of the foot companions could be disrupted by an attack from flank or rear, the individual soldiers would be as helpless as was Corrhagus. The sarissa, the key to their success, would then be their undoing.

Both Philip and Alexander were, of course, well aware of the weaknesses of the pezhetairoi phalanx. It was to protect the vulnerable flanks of the pezhetairoi that the hypaspists were formed. The name of this unit means 'shield-bearers'. The phrase may refer to the type of shield that these men carried, or it might refer to the unit's origins as a group of men who carried the shields of the king's closest companions. Either way, this was an elite unit in the Macedonian army. There is reason to believe that they were recruited from among richer families than the peasants who served among the pezhetairoi.

The hypaspists were armed and equipped in a very similar fashion to the contemporary hoplites of the main Greek states. They carried the aspis – the large, metre diameter shield which was heavily domed and was the distinctive feature of the hoplite. They carried the shorter dory spear, about 2.5 metres in length, which was usually wielded overhead in phalanx. They seem to have been equipped with the linothorax and with metal greaves. Alone among the infantry these men are sometimes shown wearing boots, an item of footwear usually reserved for horsemen at this date. It is thought, from fragmentary and uncertain references, that the hypaspists may have worn purple tunics under their armour and full red cloaks over it.

The helmets of the hypaspists distinguished them from the pezhetairoi. Some of them wore chalcidian helmets. This style had a round crown,

This hypaspist carries the weaponry typical of a heavy hoplite. He has a dory spear and an aspis shield as well as linothorax body armour strengthened with metal scales. His shield is decorated with the Macedonian star, a symbol of the kingdom for some generations before the time of Alexander. He wears a thracian style helmet with a trailing crest to indicate the elite status of his unit.

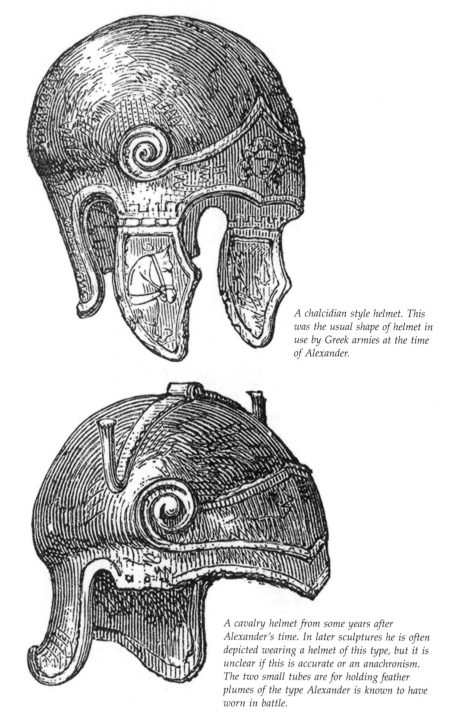

A chalcidian style helmet. This was the usual shape of helmet in use by Greek armies at the time of Alexander.

A cavalry helmet from some years after Alexander's time. In later sculptures he is often depicted wearing a helmet of this type, but it is unclear if this is accurate or an anachronism. The two small tubes are for holding feather plumes of the type Alexander is known to have worn in battle.

a bar coming down to protect the hose and large cheek pieces. Others wore what has become known in modern times as the vergina type. This was similar to the chalcidian, though it had a peak over the eyes in place of a nasal bar. It also had a detachable metal crest that rose some 15 cm from the top of the helmet and on to which could be fixed a horsehair or wool crest. Both types of helmet seem to have carried crests, shaped so that they flowed down over the back of the neck. Although the evidence is not entirely clear, it seems that the hypaspists helmets may have been painted blue with gold insignia of some kind.

Although they could, and did, fight in a phalanx formation, the hypaspists were far more flexible in training and skill than that. On the field of battle the hypaspists formed up in phalanx on the right flank of the pezhetairoi. With their smaller spears, larger shields and light armour, the hypaspists seem to have been given the task of being a mobile blocking force to protect the right flank of the more cumbersome main phalanx if the army was on the defensive. As an elite force the hypaspists would have been able to change formation quickly, alter their front to face a flank or march rapidly to cover a threatened area with speed and certainty.

On the attack, their role was even more dynamic. They had the task of keeping up with the Companion cavalry as they advanced. This demanded speed and stamina from the hypaspists, so it comes as something of a surprise to find that they are described in some sources as including the oldest and most experienced veterans, some of them over 60 years of age.

The precise tactical role of the hypaspists when attacking in conjunction with the Companion cavalry is never described by the ancient sources. Again they seem to take it for granted that their readers would know without being told. From scraps of information in various accounts of the battles of Philip and Alexander, however, it is possible to see them undertaking various tasks.

The first of these is mopping up enemy troops and formations left behind by the advance of the Companions. If any enemy troops remained in formation, or were in the process of reforming, they could pose a danger both to the rear of the cavalry and to the Macedonian infantry. It was clearly the task of the hypaspists to disperse and defeat any such enemy units.

The hypaspists also had a more defensive role. Cavalry charges, even those of Alexander's Companion cavalry, did not always succeed. If a charge failed, or at least was brought to a brief halt, the horsemen needed a temporary refuge where they could reform while being protected from any enemy counterattack. The hypaspists can be glimpsed in this role. Those light troops seem to have advanced at a jog behind the cavalry. If the horsemen got into trouble, the hypaspists would form a solid defensive phalanx to hold the ground already won and act as a defensive screen behind which the cavalry could regain formation. If the cavalry were to attack again, the hypaspists would move out of the way to allow them through. If the horsemen were to retreat, the hypaspists would form a rearguard.

Unlike the foot companions, however, the hypaspists had roles off the open battlefield as well. When cities or fortresses are put under siege, it is the hypaspists who are described as being in action. They lead assaults, guard the Macedonian siege lines against sallies and are on stand by to meet any emergency. Likewise, whenever Philip or Alexander needed to send a small detachment off to secure some position or to undertake a mission it was the hypaspists which were sent. Clearly they were trusted to perform well when not under the immediate eyes of the king.

The hypaspists also feature as guards around the royal tent complex. They are mentioned as standing to attendance at formal banquets and other celebrations. At the very least they had a formal ceremonial role of some kind to carry out.

There were, in all, 6,000 hypaspists in the Macedonian army. These were organised into units of a thousand men, each perhaps subdivided into two groups of 500 men. Alexander took half of these men with him to Persia, leaving the rest with Antipater.

One thing about the hypaspists that is not clear from our sources relates to the unit called the Royal Hypaspists. This unit was clearly an elite within an elite, and it may have been they that undertook the formal ceremonial duties that the hypaspists are known to have carried out. They are mentioned only some years after the Granicus campaign, so it is not clear if they were in existence in 334BC or if they were formed later. Certainly they did not play any role in the campaign that was noticeably different from that of the regular hypaspists, so they can be discounted.

A body that was in existence in 334BC and that did take part in the Granicus campaign was the Bodyguard, the somatophylakia. This was a unit of about 200 men, all of them the sons of the leading nobility of Macedonia. They seem to have been armed in a similar fashion to the hypaspists, though their tasks were rather different. It is possible that there has been some confusion in the sources between the Bodyguard and the Royal Hypaspists. As we shall see in the next chapter the Bodyguard was not simply an elite group of noble soldiers, for it had duties that went way beyond that of merely fighting.

It is unfortunate that we know far less about the light infantry of the Macedonian army than about those who fought in phalanx formation. The ancient sources for the career of Alexander concentrate very much on the king and those soldiers that served with or close to him on the battlefield. Other sources tell us much about the mercenaries that served

A Thracian javelin thrower. This man is typical of the light infantry that Alexander recruited from the tribes around the northern borders of the Kingdom of Macedon. He carries a number of light javelins and has a small shield, probably made of leather stretched over wickerwork. He has no armour of any kind.

as light troops with the army, but of those light troops that belong to the Macedonian army we know relatively little.

We know that about 7,000 men recruited from among the wilder tribes on the northern fringes of Macedon marched out of Therme with Alexander, and that more joined the invasion force in the winter after the Granicus campaign was over. These men are said by Arrian to have been commanded by a man called 'Ptolemy of the Thracians'. This man is not known from any other source, and Arrian only mentions him once. His name is uncompromisingly Macedonian, not Thracian, and only some of the men under his command could be called Thracian. Presumably he was a Macedonian nobleman who had previously commanded Thracian troops and who was in 334BC put in command of all the tribal warriors serving as light troops.

His junior commanders were drawn from the noble and royal families of the tribes involved, so it is reasonable to assume that each tribal levy served as a distinct unit under its own commander. Prince Sitalkes of Odrysia, for instance, can be presumed to have commanded the Odrysians. We do not know who commanded the Triballians or Illyrians.

We know that the 500 men sent by the Agrianian tribe wore only a tunic and a cloak – having no armour and no shields. One source indicates that they discarded the tunic when going into battle and kept only the cloak. This was flung back over the shoulders when fighting actually began, leaving the men effectively naked. They were armed with three or more throwing javelins each, and a sword for close quarter work.

A thrown javelin of this period had an effective range of perhaps 50 metres. It was a light wooden weapon with a comparatively small iron head. It was able to pierce the linothorax and could knock a man out of a battle if it struck an unprotected arm or leg. These javelins could not, however, pierce helmets, greaves or other metal armour.

On the battlefield these javelin men were most likely thrown out ahead of the main phalanx. They would have showered the enemy formations with javelins in the hope of inflicting injuries and deaths so as to disorder the enemy ranks before the main fighting began. We also know that these men were used during sieges to support the assaulting hypaspists.

The infantry of the Macedonian army formed a formidable fighting force. The foot companions could crush anything in their path, while their flanks were guarded by the hypaspists. The light javelin men could be used to skirmish in battle or to take part in sieges. Effective and much feared though the Macedonian infantry was, they were not the main battle winning element of Alexander's army.

That was the cavalry.

CHAPTER THREE

The Macedonian Army: Cavalry

If the infantry formed the solid base of the Macedonian army, then the cavalry were the mobile striking force that were used to win battles. Again and again we read in the ancient sources that it was a charge by the cavalry that proved to be the crucial turning point in Alexander's battles.

In part, this emphasis on the cavalry might be due to the fact that Alexander was leading them and that the writers wanted to emphasis his personal contribution to victory. Nevertheless, the comparatively large numbers of horsemen in the Macedonian army and the ways in which they were handled were a key feature of the army and its success.

Unlike most of Greece, Macedonia had spreading plains and extensive upland pastures that were suitable for grazing horses and cattle. This ensured that the cavalry units in Alexander's army were well supplied with both horses and with men who could ride them.

Riding a horse back in the 4th century BC was a quite different matter than today. That ancient riders lacked stirrups is fairly well known, but it is not realised that at this early date they did not have saddles either. All that the men had to sit on were thick, woollen blankets held in position with a girth strap and, sometimes, another running around the horse's chest. The blankets may have been padded, but this is uncertain. Some men, presumably officers, are shown with an animal skin fixed over the blanket. A thick fur, such as that of a bear, might have been for comfort, though the leopard skins that feature so often on statues and carvings were probably more for show.

The bridles and reins that feature on carvings of this period may look fairly modern, but close inspection shows that they lack many of the detailed refinements that make a modern bridle such an effective means of controlling a horse. As a result the reins tended to be rather harsh on the animal's mouth. A Greek writer on horsemanship a few years before Alexander's time emphasised the need for using pressure exerted by the legs to control the horse as well as the reins.

These ancient horses also lacked metal horseshoes. This had little effect on how cavalry were used in battle, but had a massive impact on how horses were used on campaign. Without metal shoes, the hooves of a horse are very susceptible to damage. Horses evolved to live on open, grassy plains, and no matter how hard the ground might get in prolonged dry spells, it was never as hard as bare rock. Nor were the hooves expected to carry the weight of the horse, plus the weight of a rider. The result of this is that horses could not be ridden over rough ground for many hours a day without running the risk of damaging the hooves. On campaign a lame horse is a useless horse.

This meant that the cavalrymen actually marched alongside their horses for much of the time, far more than was to be normal in the cavalry units of more modern times. This slowed down the daily march rate that cavalry could achieve. Alexander needed his cavalry ready to fight, so care for the horses was paramount.

It was for this reason that each cavalryman had a slave or servant to act as a groom. This man had a horse, though whether he rode it or it was used as a pack animal is unclear in the sources. Nor is it very clear how the remounts were organised. We know that when he joined the Macedonian army a cavalryman was given a sum of money by the king with which to buy his main war horse. There was also a royal herd of horses that was drawn on to replace mounts killed in battle or that died on campaign. Whether men were issued with remounts to replace tired horses from this herd, or whether they were supposed already to have a second horse to hand themselves is not clear. In any case, the important point to note is that spare horses were usually available.

The type of horses used by the Macedonian army has been a subject of much debate over the years. Some sculptures and reliefs show horses that look rather like those of the modern day, though they appear rather more robust. Others show smaller horses that are not much bigger than ponies. Recent archaeological finds have gone some way to solving the riddle. Horse bones that have been recovered show that horses of this period were not much different in size from modern riding horses. They were, however, unmistakably heavier than is usual today. This may, in part, be due to the introduction of Arab bloodlines to nearly every breed of modern horse, or may reflect some centuries of selective breeding. Perhaps the reliefs that show pony sized horses reflect an artistic convention that shows the humans larger than in reality.

Whatever the horses were like, cavalrymen were still considerably faster and more mobile than infantry – especially if they had remounts to use so that they did not over exert any one particular animal. Throughout military history, cavalry have had the task of scouting and reconnaissance. The Macedonians had a type of cavalry specifically trained for this task: the prodromoi.

The word prodromoi is usually translated as 'scout', though some writers prefer to call these units 'lancers' in reference to their main weapon. This lance is referred to in ancient texts as a sarissa, the same name given to the 5.5 metre long pike used by the foot companion infantry that formed the core of the phalanx. If this really was the same weapon, rather than something similar adapted for cavalry use, it was a truly enormous object for a man to carry on horseback and wield with any real dexterity. The problems of using this long lance were compounded by the fact that without a saddle the men lacked a really firm seat on the horse.

Nevertheless, there is evidence that the prodromoi did use these weapons. The famous Alexander Mosaic from Pompeii, which was based on a now lost Greek painting, was completed while Alexander was still within living memory. It shows a horseman using a lance that is about 5 metres long. However a tomb contemporary to Alexander's reign shows what appears to be a prodromoi using a lance that was rather shorter, about 3.5 metres. This seems to be the weapon referred to in written sources as the xyston.

Whatever the size of the prodromoi lance, it was not the only weapon used by these men. They also carried two or three light javelins for throwing at the enemy. The prodromoi also carried a sword, though the precise type seems to have been a matter of personal preference as all sorts of swords are mentioned in relation to these horsemen. The swords were worn hanging from a belt that passed over the right shoulder so that the scabbard hung above the left hip.

The only armour used by the prodromoi were their helmets, but there is much dispute over what sorts of helmet they used on the Granicus campaign. We know that in the later campaigns of Philip's reign these men wore helmets of the Thracian style, very similar to those used by the pezhetairoi heavy infantry. Given that most of these men were recruited from the Thracian provinces annexed by Philip early in his reign this would make sense. However, by the time the army reached Babylon a few years after Granicus they were equipped with the boeotian helmet that was more usual for the Macedonian cavalry. Common sense would indicate that the prodromoi were re-equipped with their new helmets before the army set off from Therme, but this is by no means certain.

The boeotian helmet, as its name indicates, originated in the region of Boeotia that lay around the city of Thebes. It was made from bronze, with the finest examples being made from a single sheet of metal beaten laboriously into shape. The crown was in the shape of a half globe that fitted snugly over the head down to the temples. From the bottom edge of this flared out a brim. At the sides and rear of the helmet the brim fell down sharply, but not quite vertically, to provide protection to the neck. Over the forehead it pushed forwards at an angle down to the level of the eyebrows. At the sides there was a distinctive fold ending in a sharp spike that came down over the cheeks. Over the ears the brim flared out, perhaps to allow the wearer to hear commands more clearly.

This design of helmet was intended to give maximum breadth of vision while still providing a high degree of protection to the wearer. Given the fast-moving and very fluid nature of cavalry warfare at the time, the ability to see clearly around a wide range was essential.

The prodromoi wore a tunic that reached down to the knees and which had sleeves down to the wrist. They also had a long cloak that was worn fastened over one shoulder, usually the right so as to leave the weapon hand free. The colour of the cloak probably indicated the unit to which the man belonged, and in at least some instances the helmet was painted for a similar purpose.

The actual organisation of the prodromoi is not very clear. We know that there were four squadrons of prodromoi in the army that Alexander led to Asia, but their numbers seem to have fluctuated quite dramatically as reinforcements arrived and casualties were suffered. It is possible that the units were related to the tribes from which the men were drawn, rather than being a formalised unit of standardised size. In any case, there were 900 of these men with Alexander when he left Therme.

The main task of the prodromoi, as their name would suggest, was to scout ahead of the army. The importance of this in ancient warfare cannot be overemphasised. As a rule, ancient armies were very poor at scouting and reconnaissance. This was particularly the case in Greece, where the nature of warfare made formal clashes between armies on a level plain the rule rather than the exception. The accounts of ancient warfare are filled with battles where two armies blundered into each other, or conversely where armies stood and watched each other for weeks from fortified camps without any serious fighting taking place.

The style of warfare developed by Philip and perfected by Alexander was very different. They much preferred to choose the place and time of a battle, selecting a venue that gave themselves the maximum advantage over the enemy. For that it was essential to know where the enemy was, how strong his forces were and what he was doing. That was the job of the prodromoi.

Exactly how the prodromoi achieved their task is nowhere described in any great detail by the ancients. There are only a few passing references to these horsemen at work, but these can be used to put together a likely way of working. They seem to have operated in fairly small groups of about 30 or so men. They left early in the morning to ride ahead of the army and on its flanks. They seem to have stayed something over an hour's hard riding – say about 10km or so – from the main army. Obviously this distance would depend rather on the nature of the terrain being covered, so it should be thought of as an ideal rather than an absolute. The riders were also sent out to inspect features such as river crossings and mountain defiles. In such circumstances they may well have operated even further from the main force than was usual.

There is some indication that units of prodromoi may have stayed away from the main army camp for several nights in succession, though they were in touch with the army by means of gallopers passing back and forth. This may have been to maintain a screen of scouts some distance away from the army to watch for an enemy, or it may have been when the prodromoi were detached on some specific mission.

That the prodromoi had a reputation for being adept at looting and plundering would seem to indicate one mission on which they may have been routinely sent. Any army needs supplies and while Alexander usually managed to organise an effective logistics system, there were always times when this was not possible. The finding of green fodder for the horses and other animals was often a problem. The prodromoi may have been sent out to find pasture or cut hay which could be appropriated. Far from the watching eyes of senior commanders, the temptation to loot must have been considerable.

We know of one particular incident as it ended up with a captive woman being hauled before Alexander himself for judgement. During the campaign against Thebes a group of prodromoi had broken into the house of a noblewoman named Timocleia. They drank the cellar dry, looted the house of everything they could find and raped the women of the household. The senior prodromoi, coincidentally named Alexander, took it into his head that Timocleia must have some secret store of gold hidden away that his men had not found. He therefore made an excuse to return alone, put his sword to Timocleia's throat and demanded that she tell him where her treasure was.

Timocleia was clearly a woman of courage and intelligence. Despite everything that had happened, she was still able to think clearly. She told Alexander the prodromoi that her chest of jewels was hidden down the well in the courtyard of her house. When Alexander went to look, she pushed him down and then threw down a great boulder that killed the man instantly. The other prodromoi were outraged and dragged Timocleia off to face punishment.

Alexander heard of the event and went to hear the case himself. He decided that Alexander the prodromoi had overstepped the mark and got what he deserved. Timocleia was allowed to go free.

The incident is recorded by the ancient sources to show that Alexander enforced strict discipline among his men, which he undoubtedly did, but it is interesting in that it shows what Alexander considered was or was not acceptable behaviour for his prodromoi. In the context of the Theban campaign, Timocleia was an enemy civilian. As such her possessions were legitimate loot for Macedonian soldiers – and the fact that it was prodromoi who were first to reach her house and break in came as no surprise. It would seem that the rape of a noblewoman was not acceptable, however.

When fighting seemed imminent, the prodromoi were recalled to the main army to take their place in the line of battle. The usual position of the prodromoi in battle was on the right wing, close to the companion cavalry. They are sometimes stated as being on the left of the companion cavalry, sometimes to their right and on one occasion positioned far out on the right wing and separated from the rest of the army by quite a distance.

Their task seems to have been to move forward to probe the enemy for weaknesses. Presumably the prodromoi began by galloping forward, hurling a volley of javelins and then wheeling aside to ride back out of range. They may have delivered this javelin attack in a series of waves, each delivering its attack and then riding back to reform while the next wave went in. Such an attack was designed to disorder the enemy formation. Weaker or less determined men might begin to edge back, revealing to the watching Macedonians which enemy units were likely to crumble if subjected to a serious assault.

We know that the prodromoi also used their sarissas in battle. Perhaps they would close to combat once they had expended their javelins. Again they should be imagined as probing the enemy front rather than delivering a sustained and serious assault. They were looking to inflict casualties and disrupt the enemy rather than defeat him.

The main task of destruction was usually left to the companion cavalry, commanded by Alexander himself. It was the companion cavalry that most impressed contemporaries about the Macedonian army. There can be no doubt that they were a devastating weapon that won many battles for Philip and for Alexander, and they undoubtedly formed an elite within the army. It must be borne in mind, however, that their importance might have been overstated by the contemporary writers. They were writing the story of Alexander and, since Alexander led the companion cavalry, it would have been natural to write more about their exploits and to give their actions undue importance.

There were 15 squadrons, or ile, of companion cavalry in the army. Of these 14 were what might be termed regular companion cavalry, while one was the famed Royal Companions. The regular units were each 210 strong, the Royal Companions 300 strong, giving a total force of about 3,200 men. Alexander left seven units with Antipater and took eight with him – seven regular squadrons and the Royal Companions, some 1,800 men or so.

The companion cavalry were recruited from the richer families of Macedon, service in the force being counted a great honour. Each squadron was recruited from a different region of the kingdom, giving the unit a natural cohesion and group loyalty. Service in the Royal Companions seems to have been restricted to the sons of nobles or to men who were personally known to Alexander for one reason or another.

All the companion cavalry were equipped in similar fashion. They wore long-sleeved tunics of purple with short cloaks of yellow, edged with purple. These cloaks were of the distinctive Macedonian style. This garment was in the shape of a truncated cone cut so that when the short edge was fastened over the shoulder by a brooch, the long edge fell down to below the waist at both front and back. The right arm was left free by this style. When necessary, the cloak could easily be flung back to fall down the back alone, so exposing the left arm and freeing it for use.

For armour, the companion cavalry wore the boeotian helmet to protect their heads. For body armour they wore the linothorax, as did the foot companions, though some may have worn a bronze cuirass. Some of the carvings of companion cavalry that have survived show the helmet to be decorated with a wreath of leaves, apparently painted on to the metal. This seems to be a mark of rank, perhaps the colour of the wreath indicating the precise rank. The ilarch, the man who commanded a squadron or ile, had a long flowing horsehair plume cascading down from the crown to the back of his helmet.

For offensive weaponry the companion cavalry had both swords and lances. The swords used by the companion cavalry had straight blades about a metre long. They were designed to stab, not to slash as is more usual with cavalry swords. These swords were carried in a scabbard suspended from a shoulder belt so that they usually rested under the left arm.

The principal weapon was the lance, the xyston. This was about 3.5 metres long and ended with a leaf-shaped blade at either end. This seems to have been because the long, slender lance broke in action so often that a reserve head at the rear was needed. Given the length of this weapon it would have projected some two metres or so in front of the horse. This gave the horseman a good reach, exceeded at the time only by the pikes carried by the podromoi and the foot companions of the Macedonian army. Certainly it outreached the thrusting spears of the contemporary Greek hoplites.

This member of the Companion cavalry wears the Macedonian-style cloak that was issued to all men in the royal army. It would probably have been purple with a yellow border for this unit. He wears a boeotian style helmet with a horsehair crest dangling down the rear, which was a mark of rank reserved for senior officers. His xyston spear and short sword are typical weapons for Macedonian cavalry. He wears linothorax body armour and metal greaves on his shins. Note the lack of saddle or stirrups, neither of which had then been invented.

The way in which the xyston was used in action has been the subject of much debate. It was, just about, light enough to be held and wielded in one hand. It might, therefore, have been held overhead, or underarm. Reliefs and carvings from the time, or soon after, show the xyston in both positions. In either grip the xyston could be used to jab and thrust at the enemy. The height of a horseman would give him a natural advantage over an infantry-man, which would have been enhanced by the length of the xyston. In a contest of thrust and counter thrust a horseman using a xyston overhead or underarm would be able to overpower a man on foot. Even when the infantry were in a phalanx, the horsemen would be able to work their way forward, hustling and pushing onward as they jabbed with their lances.

The written sources, however, give a quite different view of how the companion cavalry were used. According to them, the companion cavalry were thrown into action at the gallop, crashing through enemy formations and brushing aside lines of defenders. What we know of companion formations and training would seem to support this much more dynamic view of the companion cavalry in action.

The fact that a regular squadron composed 210 men and the Royal Companions 300 men was dictated by the standard attack formation of these horsemen. They formed up in a wedge or triangular formation. The commanding officer was the front rider, with two men behind him, three behind them, four in the fourth rank and so on. This created a formation that had a very narrow front, but a great depth. It seems to have been designed to penetrate an enemy formation, then fan out to exploit the opening and so dislocate the enemy.

The shape of the formation contrasted with the contemporary pattern in other states which was to have a flat front. The only other people to adopt a wedge shape for their horsemen were the Thessalians, though they had a blunter shape with the commander being backed by three in the second rank, five in the third rank, seven in the fourth and so on.

With the narrow Macedonian wedge the leader could be followed with some ease by those who backed him whether he turned to left or right as he advanced. It was also easier for the men in the rear ranks to keep their station in the formation.

Much of the effectiveness of a cavalry charge comes from its impact on morale rather than its actual collision force. Unless they are very steady, well trained and confident in their abilities, infantry will tend to crumple when subjected to a cavalry charge. In many instances the infantry formation will begin to break up even before the cavalry arrive. This is perfectly understandable.

A man on a horse is a big, fast moving object of considerable weight and power. To see one coming towards you at the gallop can be

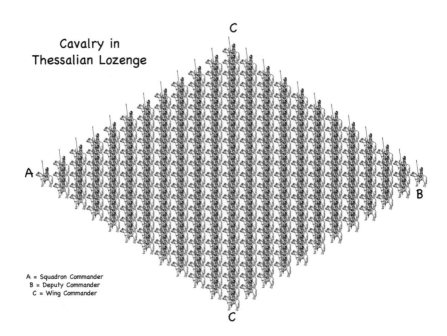

Cavalry in
Thessalian Lozenge

A = Squadron Commander
B = Deputy Commander
C = Wing Commander

Cavalry in Thessalian Lozenge

The horsemen of Thessaly could fight as either skirmishers with their throwing javelins or as heavy cavalry charging en mass. When performing the latter function they adopted the Lozenge formation that had been invented by the nobleman Jason of Pherae in about 375BC. Lacking either saddle or stirrups, the cavalry of this period could not charge home as could medieval knights or more recent cavalry. Instead, the cavalry would hope that the mere sight of such a dense and massive formation charging forward would cause any infantry in front of them to break and run. If that did not happen the lead horsemen would attack the infantry to their front. As the lead horsemen came to a halt, they would be pushed forward by those behind. The sheer momentum built up by the huge number of ranks was usually enough to shove infantry back. The shape of the formation enhanced this effect by pushing the infantry sideways as well as back. Eventually the infantry lines would part, allowing the horsemen to burst through and then fan out.

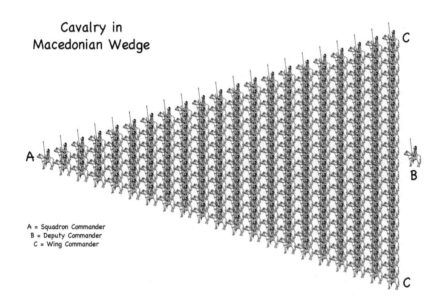

Cavalry in
Macedonian Wedge

A = Squadron Commander
B = Deputy Commander
C = Wing Commander

Cavalry in Macedonian Wedge

Philip of Macedon, Alexander's father, adapted the Thessalian Lozenge formation for his own heavy cavalry. Unlike the Thessalians the Macedonian Companion horsemen did not have any throwing javelins, but their thrusting spears were longer than was normal for horsemen. Philip made his Wedge longer and narrower than the Lozenge. This combined the maximum momentum with the narrowest frontage, thus increasing the force that these horsemen could deliver when charging. Alexander led his 300 strong Royal Squadron of Companions into the attack using this wedge formation at the crisis of the battle.

a terrifying sight. If it came to a collision between a man on foot and a charging horseman, there is no doubt that the man on foot would be knocked flying, probably sustaining serious injury, while the cavalryman would barely notice the impact. The shape of the companion cavalry wedge would leave no doubt in the minds of the infantry in front of them exactly where the point of impact was going to be. The men having the misfortune to be right in front of the lead horseman would naturally tend to edge back and sideways. As the horsemen got closer and the true awesome power of their advance became obvious, the thunder of hoofbeats grew to deafening proportions and war cries split the air, the average infantryman would turn tail and run.

Even if the opponents did not crumple and flee, the companion cavalry had a great advantage in their formation. The commanding officer, the lead rider, would hit the enemy at the gallop. His momentum would carry him some distance into the enemy formation, knocking down the front rank and pushing back those behind. Riding alone he would soon be stopped, but even as he was being slowed his comrades would reach the enemy. The two riders in the second rank would likewise ride down the first men they met, then push on.

The riders in each successive rank would crash into the developing melee. Those on the flanks would be hitting the front rank of the enemy formation, widening the area affected. Those at the centre, however, would be riding into the backs of their comrades who were already engaged. They would not be able to reach the enemy to kill or wound any of them, but their arrival would push forward the men to their front. This in turn would push back the enemy infantry so that a great backward bulge or bow developed in the enemy phalanx. As this bulge deepened, the depth of the defending phalanx would thin as it stretched and as men were cut down. Eventually the line would break.

The companion cavalry would then surge forward through the gap. As this happened the infantry men on either side of the gap would turn to run, widening the gap and allowing the companion cavalry wedge to push through, fan out and begin the pursuit.

There is, however, one problem with this dramatic scenario, and it has to do with how the companion cavalry sat their mounts. With neither a saddle nor stirrups to give him a secure seat, the rider was reliant on his ability to grip the horse's flanks with his knees and thighs. This may sound precarious, but in the case of an experienced and strong horseman is not as feeble as it appears. It is certainly possible to ride a horse at speed, jump fences and change direction with perfect security when riding bareback. Launching a charge is, however, another matter.

If horsemen using lances are to have a significant impact on defending infantry, they need to carry their lances couched under their arms. In this way the momentum of horse and rider is concentrated on the lance point, driving it with devastating force into whatever it hits. However the force of such an impact would be more than enough to knock any rider off a horse he was riding bareback. This quite obviously did not happen to Alexander and his companion cavalry. Some other scenario must be imagined.

Although the truth will probably never be known, it seems that the Macedonian companion cavalry delivered their charge in a fashion that was quite unique. The descriptions given of Alexander in battle with his companion cavalry make it clear that the charges frequently ended with a confused scrimmage. The companion cavalry are described as jabbing with their lances at the enemy, but also as using their swords, so they must have been knee to knee with the enemy.

Clearly we are looking at a charge that lacked the massive impact of those delivered by cavalry once both saddle and stirrup had been invented. It was, however, considerably more powerful and violent than anything that had been seen before. Perhaps the charge relied upon its morale power to cause enemy formations to waver or fragment before the impact, after which a melee with lance and sword would take place before the enemy fled. Or perhaps the impact of the charge took place with the companion cavalry relying on the sheer bulk of their horses to smash a way through the enemy formation, plying their weapons only once they had got in among their opponents. Whatever method they used, it was startlingly effective.

It is perhaps the great depth of the companion formation that gives the clue to what was really going on. If infantry stand firm, horses will not charge home. No horse can be induced to run into a solid object, and a line of men standing still can look as solid as a brick wall to a horse. It is this fact that has lain behind all successful infantry formations designed to halt a cavalry charge.

The famous squares adopted by the British infantry at Waterloo in 1815 and elsewhere consisted of infantry formed up into squares with each face made up of men three ranks deep. The front rank kneeled and presented their bayonets to the enemy, while the rear two ranks fired. Charging cavalry would shy away, flow around the sides of the square and pass by. The momentum of the cavalry charge would be dissipated, the cavalry formation broken up and thus made vulnerable to a counter charge by the British cavalry positioned some distance behind the infantry squares.

By the Napoleonic period formations adopted by charging cavalry were about four ranks deep. The reason for this was that while they advanced the horsemen would be subjected to cannon fire. The cannon balls were able to kill a man or horse, then plunge on to kill those behind. Positioning cavalry several ranks deep was simply suicidal. Moreover the falling men and horses of the lead ranks would trip those behind, or at least cause them to swerve. As a result any ranks more than four or five behind those in the lead would become hopelessly confused and scattered, rendering them effectively useless long before the formation reached the enemy.

However Alexander was operating in a world where there were no cannon and no weapons powerful enough to kill one man, then go on to kill those behind him. It was for this reason that the companion cavalry could adopt a formation 20 ranks deep. And it was that depth that may have been the key to their success. A lone horse faced by a line of infantry will shy away. Cavalry in four ranks will halt or move aside to avoid an impact, but a narrow column of horsemen 20 deep cannot do this. The sheer momentum built up by the formation means that those in the lead will be pushed forward by those behind. At the head of the cavalry wedge the lead horsemen will be shoved and pushed forward irresistibly into the infantry, whether the horses want to or not. It would be like a living battering ram of horses and men smashing their way forward.

If the charge by the companion cavalry was the most effective offensive tactic available to Alexander, and it was, the timing and positioning of that charge was crucial. Because Alexander won every battle that he fought, and because it was the assault by the companion cavalry that proved decisive, it is easy to misunderstand just how difficult his task actually was.

If the companion cavalry were launched too early, their charge might run into steady troops unaffected by previous skirmishing or fighting. No matter how determined or effective the cavalry charge might be, it could founder against a deep and well disciplined phalanx. Once it was brought to a halt and was disordered, a squadron of companion cavalry would be vulnerable to a countercharge by enemy cavalry. It was to guard against this eventuality that the hypaspists hurried forward with the cavalry, but they might not get into position in time or the companion squadron could fail to get back in time.

A premature charge by the companion cavalry might well founder and lead to disaster with high casualties among the horsemen. Given that it was the Macedonian king – Philip or Alexander – who led the charge this might mean the death of the king. With their commander in chief fallen, the Macedonian army would be lucky to extricate itself intact, never mind go on to win the battle.

Conversely if the companion cavalry charge was delivered too late the crucial moment might be missed. If the fighting by the infantry and lighter cavalry units was already clearly leading to a Macedonian victory, the opposing commander would begin to withdraw his army. If that retreating army could get back to defensive positions intact then the opportunity for a crushing victory would have been missed.

In ancient warfare it was the ability to begin and maintain a pursuit that could turn a battlefield advantage into an overwhelming victory. Far more men were killed when they were running away than in the battle itself. With their backs to the pursuing troops and very often having thrown away their weapons, fleeing soldiers are extremely vulnerable.

But it is not simply a matter of counting the bodies that makes for a military victory. It is the destruction of the enemy's ability to stop the attacker from achieving his aims that really counts. If the enemy army can be broken up, its units scattered and its cohesion destroyed then it will be effectively useless even if actual casualties are not particularly high. To achieve that it is necessary to chase, harry and pursue. The enemy supply system must be destroyed, which generally means capturing the baggage carts and pack animals. The enemy units must be pushed until they break, then given no chance to reform.

A truly effective pursuit of an enemy army might be completed within a few hours, or it may last days. To work, it must be continued ruthlessly.

But if the enemy army is given the chance to retreat in good order, with an effective rear guard holding off pursuit, then even the most dramatic battlefield win might turn out to be worthless in the long run. The charge of the companion cavalry had to be delivered at a time when the enemy army was still intact enough and in its positions so that a sudden breakthrough would disrupt it and leave it vulnerable to a destructive pursuit.

Alexander had to launch his battle-winning charge in that narrow window of opportunity after the enemy army had been weakened, but before it had begun an orderly withdrawal. That Alexander succeeded every time, and made it look not just easy but inevitable, is a testament to his military genius.

Crucial as battles are, no campaign is about battles alone. In the ancient world sieges of cities and fortresses were at least as important to the success of a campaign as any battles that might be fought – and the Granicus campaign was no different. Indeed, it was Alexander's exploits as a siege general that impressed his contemporaries as much as his skills in open battle.

He was helped by the fact that, under his father Philip, the Macedonians had developed an entirely new type of siege weapon. It was a highly prized secret that would prove to be devastating.

CHAPTER FOUR

The Macedonian Army: Support Services

Before Philip's time, the Greeks had been famously poor at siege warfare – be it on the defence or the attack. Some walls were built of stone, but many were of wood or mud brick. Most Greek cities had what was known as an acropolis, or high-town. This was an isolated, steep and craggy hill to which the population could retreat at times of danger with their belongings. The main defences of an acropolis were its slopes and sheer cliffs, sometimes made stronger by walls or fences. Given that most Greek armies were composed of part-time soldiers eager to get home again, an acropolis was usually enough to hold off attackers until they got fed up and left.

The invasion of Greece by the Persians in 480BC introduced the Greeks to some good siege techniques. The Persians brought with them three effective attack methods. The first of these was the battering ram. This was a large wooden beam tipped by a metal head, sometimes in the shape of a ram's head. This was suspended from wooden supports mounted on wheels. The whole contraption was topped by a roof covered with boiled hides to render it proof against arrows and javelins.

The battering ram was then pushed forward by teams of soldiers. Once up against the walls, the beam was set swinging back and forth with a steady rhythmic beat. With each swing the metal head struck against the walls with all the weight of the great wooden beam behind it. Against wood and mud brick the battering ram was devastatingly effective. Even when used against stone walls it would break through eventually. Once a hole was created, the soldiers of the besieging army could pour through.

Against stone walls a more effective technique was to undermine them. Tunnels braced by stout wooden props were dug that led to positions underneath the foundations of the walls. These tunnels were then filled with straw and twigs, and the wooden props smeared with fats and oils. The whole combustible mix was then set on fire. As the props burned through they weakened. When unable to support the weight of the walls above them, the props gave way and the tunnels caved in, bringing down the walls above. Again the attackers would then charge forward over the rubble to enter the fortress.

When tunnelling was not possible, perhaps because the walls were built on rock, the Persians resorted to building a mound. This involved piling up earth and stones, cross braced by a timber latticework, to produce a sloping ramp up to the tops of the walls. This would allow the attacks to gain the tops of the walls and get into the city.

During the invasion of 480BC, these techniques proved to be devastatingly effective and the Persians captured every city they attacked. It was not long, however, before countermeasures began to be developed. Mounds could be defeated by heightening the section of wall that was being approached. Rams could be set on fire by pouring burning pitch on to them, or dismounted by lowering grappling hooks to lift them up and overturn them. Tunnels could be defeated by digging counter tunnels through which defenders could attack the diggers.

In the years that followed new siege weapons were developed. Dionysius, the ruler of Syracuse in Sicily, went so far as to establish an official armaments factory that had a section dedicated to developing new siege weapons. One of the inventions this establishment produced was the siege tower. This was, effectively, a mobile mound. It consisted of a wooden tower mounted on wheels. Ladders inside the tower gave easy access from the ground to the top. At the top was a drawbridge that could be let down on to the enemy walls. All the attackers then needed to do was swarm up the ladders and dash over the drawbridge to enter the fortress. It had the advantage that it could be pushed into position before the defenders could heighten their walls, as they could do against a mound.

Dionysius' workshop also produced the gastraphetes, or winched bow. This consisted of an enormously powerful wooden bow mounted on a stand. The bow was too powerful for any human to draw. Instead it was equipped with a ratchet system operated by a winch so that the bow could be pulled back gradually by teams of workers. It fired an arrow much heavier than that used by conventional hand bows over a far greater distance, perhaps as much as 300 metres.

The great advance achieved by Philip was to use animal sinews instead of wood or metal as the means of propulsion for the gastraphetes. The method by which sinews were treated so that they remained supple and springy was a closely guarded secret of the Macedonian army, and it was not until after Alexander's death that details of the technique leaked out.

It was soon discovered that sinew had a great advantage over wood or metal. If the strands of sinew were twisted before they were put into the siege engine it meant that they were already under torsion. This meant that by pulling the mechanism back by the length of the arrow to be shot a far greater amount of energy was built up in the sinews than was possible in a wooden or metal bow that snapped back to rest when it was discharged. Effectively this meant that a bolt or stone could be shot with much greater force by the same sized mechanism. Macedonian siege weapons achieved much greater hitting power over a greater range than ever before.

These great siege engines weighed many tons and it was impracticable to haul them around the countryside with an army. Indeed, it was all but impossible to move them at all. Instead, Philip's engineers perfected the technique of reducing the key operating mechanism to a relatively few components. Each of these was small and light enough to mount on to a pack horse. These would then trail along behind the army.

When the siege engines were needed the pack horses would be unburdened and the assorted sections of metalwork and sinew laid out. The engineers would then fell trees and from them shape the timber pieces needed to complete the engines. It was a time consuming job that could take several days, even weeks if timber was scarce in the area, but it did mean that the Macedonian army had a fully effective siege train ready for use whenever it came up against a city that refused to surrender.

But the advances did not end there. Philip's engineers soon realised that it would be possible to produce highly effective weapons that were small enough to be carried with the army for use in the field. The actual design of these weapons at the time of Alexander is open to conjecture as they were highly secret. They do seem, however, to have been able to shoot a 10kg bolt over a distance of about 300 metres with a fair degree of accuracy.

This weapon was thus able to kill men and horses over a much greater range than any other weapon of the time. Alexander had an elementary form of field artillery – the first commander in history to possess such a weapon. These weapons were all the more effective as each one could be dismantled – wooden sections and all – and loaded on to pack horses. They could be reassembled within hours and ready for use. This was a real secret weapon if ever there was one.

The siege engines and field artillery, and the men to maintain and use them, were not the only support services in the Macedonian army. There was also a team of surveyors, tasked with keeping careful notes on the territory through which the army marched. This was not mere curiosity, but was designed to aid the army if it, or any detachment, ever needed to pass that way again. The quality of the roads or tracks was noted, along with their gradients and lengths. The location of flat areas of ground suitable for camps was recorded, and how many men each could accommodate. The surveyors also noted the presence, or otherwise, of fords and bridges over the rivers and how long it would take different units to traverse them.

Botanists and zoologists were also usual elements in the Macedonian army. Their task was to note down any edible or inedible plants that grew in the areas through which the army passed. Most were, of course, familiar to the Macedonians but the records kept showed how much fodder for the animals could be expected to be found along the routes at different times of year, and if there would be anything for the men to eat. Macedonian nobles were famously keen on hunting as a leisure activity, so the king and officers would want to know if there were any game animals close to a likely camping ground. There were also doctors, grooms, cooks, and a host of other servants of various kinds.

Wives and women were not encouraged to join the army, indeed we know of specific orders to leave them behind on particular campaigns. There were exceptions. Ptolemy, who later became the ruler of Egypt, has his Athenian mistress Thais with him throughout the Granicus campaign. There were probably other women involved.

Alexander made repeated efforts to cut the numbers of servants, women and hangers-on, not least to ease the problems of supplying the army with food. That he needed to dismiss these people on regular occasions shows that they kept creeping back.

When he set off to invade the Persian Empire, Alexander realised that he would be marching mostly through territory unfamiliar to the Macedonians, and indeed to the Greeks in general. He therefore increased the number of academics he took with him. There were not only botanists, zoologists and surveyors, but astronomers, mathematicians and architects as well. The latter, as we shall see, would play a major role in Alexander's efforts to gain support from the local population for his campaign.

Alexander went further, becoming the first commander in history to take along an official publicity and propaganda department with him on campaign. The leader of this section was clearly going to be an important person. While the army mustered at Therme, Alexander received recommendations from various quarters and interviewed applicants. In the end he appointed to the lucrative position the academic historian Callisthenes over the poets and bards that made up most of the applicants.

Callisthenes was, at the age of about 35, already famous for his work on the poems of Homer, using them to deduce dates for early Greek history and identifying the more obscure places mentioned. Himself a student of Homer, Alexander will have known of this work. Callisthenes also studied and produced works on other Greek writers, such as

Herodotus and Socrates. He could be a nitpicker over detail, and famously got into a bitter dispute with other historians over the fairly minor question of whether the dramatist Aeschylus wrote his works when sober or drunk.

He was recommended to Alexander by Aristotle, and maybe the king felt that he owed his old teacher at least this much. The fact that Callisthenes was Aristotle's nephew probably also helped. With not much to do before the invasion began, Callisthenes spent his first few weeks in the employment of Alexander producing a special copy of Homer's *Iliad*. The book was small enough to slip into a modest pouch and was specially bound to stand up to the rigours of campaign. Alexander kept it to the day of his death. According to later tradition he slept with it under his pillow every night.

Callisthenes boasted that 'Alexander's fame depends on me and my works'. It may have been an exaggeration, but there can be no doubt that the detailed and highly complimentary book produced by Callisthenes was the main source for many of the ancient books on Alexander. Unfortunately it has not survived.

Callisthenes was not the only writer. Alexander had the usual escort of scribes and accountants to deal with the day to day running of the army, and to keep in touch with Antipater in Greece so that Alexander could keep an eye on events at home while he was away. Alexander also took with him a number of poets so that proclamations and official letters would be elegantly phrased and impressively rhetorical. Even at this early stage, Alexander was clearly keen to create the best impression that he could both on his contemporaries and on posterity.

It is worth noting the presence in the Macedonian army, as with all others in the ancient world, of priests. The ancients took religion very seriously, and Alexander was no exception. He was avid in his search for signs of divine favour or anger. His visit to the oracle at Delphi before the invasion of Persia began was not necessary, but Alexander insisted on going in person to receive the advice of the god Apollo.

The ancients believed that the gods and goddesses were able to intervene on a day to day basis in the affairs of humans, and that they frequently did so. The proper rituals and rites had to be carried out in precisely the correct way on the correct day to keep the favour of the gods. It was thought that the deities placed great importance on this – far more so than on personal behaviour. Alexander took along a host of priests to ensure that the sacrifices were properly made and that no god was overlooked.

All these men, their equipment and staffs trailed along with the army in a compact baggage train. Alexander, like Philip before him, insisted that this baggage train be kept as small as possible and that it should be composed entirely of pack animals, not carts or carriages. The aim was, of course, to ensure that the army could move along poor roads or even cross country if necessary. This was part of the reason that the Macedonian army could move faster than any other contemporary force. Indeed, Alexander frequently accomplished marches that his enemies thought to be impossible.

When marching through hostile lands, the Macedonian army adopted a standard formation, though this had to be adapted to the terrain. The podromoi rode out some kilometres in front and to the flanks of the army. They may have ridden in the rear as well if a threat from that direction was thought likely. Their task was to scout for the enemy, but also to check out the route the army would take for any possible obstacles. If broken bridges, landslides or other obstructions were found, the podromai sent a message back to the main column.

The front units of the main column were made up of light infantry, accompanied by a group of engineers and several pack animals carrying shovels, picks and other tools. If the horsemen reported any problems, the light infantry and engineers would hurry forward to deal with it. While the cavalry and a detachment of the light infantry stood guard, the rest of the men would discard their weapons and pick up their tools. Under the supervision of the engineers they would clear the road for the main force behind them.

At the head of the main force marched the hypaspists. Behind them came the pezhetairoi with their sarissas dismantled and slung over their shoulders. The flanks of the pezhetairoi were guarded by more light infantry, apparently thrown out to form a loose screen several hundred metres to the sides of the road proper. If danger was expected from one particular flank, the bulk of the light infantry would fan out along that flank, leaving the other only lightly guarded. Behind the pezhetairoi came the cavalry and behind them more light infantry.

The position of the baggage train varied depending on the situation. As a rule they were placed on the side of the pezhetairoi furthest from the most likely line of attack. So if an attack were most likely from the rear, the baggage marched between the hypaspists and the pezhetairoi, but if from the front it was put between the pezhetairoi and the cavalry.

When the days march was over, the army would camp at a suitable site identified by the podromoi scouts. Although an army on the march, especially one moving through hostile territory, had to accept what was available, the Macedonians did tend to look for certain features. The presence of a nearby source of water was essential. Good grasslands where the cavalry horses and pack animals could be put to graze was ideal.

A typical camp scene from the time of the Granicus campaign. The style of tents is based on that shown on contemporary vases. In the Macedonian army each tent is thought to have been shared by two men. The shields, helmets and weapons are set out ready to be grabbed for instant use. (With thanks to the Hoplite Association)

If that could not be found, then somewhere for men to go cut fodder to carry back to camp would do. If possible the camp would be put where broken ground or a river protected one or more flanks. Bushes were cut to form a makeshift boundary to the camp. This was not much use against a determined assault, but did serve to keep wild animals out and the army's livestock in.

If they were intending to stay in one spot for longer than a single night, the army would entrench the camp. A ditch was dug around the perimeter, with the earth being thrown on the inside to form a parapet. On top of this would be erected a palisade of wooden stakes. These seem to have been cut from the vicinity of the camp rather than carried with the army.

Whether fortified or not, the camp was surrounded by sentries stationed some distance away. Closer to the camp were units of men who were allowed to rest, but who wore their armour and had their weapons readily to hand. This seems to have been a task for the pezhetairoi, a different lochos being on guard each night. The officers of the lochos had the task of moving from picket to picket, sentry to sentry to make sure that all was well and that the men were awake.

It can be appreciated that the Macedonian army, far from being a bunch of amateurs off to fight the enemy for a few days, was a highly organised and efficient force. To keep so many thousands of men and animals so well formed both at home and on the march took a considerable amount of organisational skill. For this the credit must go to Eumenes of Cardia. Under Philip, Eumenes had the post of secretary to the king, and Alexander kept him on in this post. It must be assumed that the secretary to the king was effectively the chief of staff for the army.

This Eumenes was a Greek, not a Macedonian. He had been given estates in Macedonia and was regarded as a Macedonian by Alexander. Some of the other Macedonian nobles seem to have resented the power given to Eumenes and we hear on occasion of their being reluctant to follow orders issued by Eumenes until Alexander stepped in personally. There is some indication that Eumenes may have been one of those highly skilled and efficient bureaucrats who can be testy and slightly superior in attitude to the rough soldiers with whom he had to deal. That, however, lay in the future. If there was any tension during the Granicus campaign there was no outward sign of it.

Eumenes had a permanent staff. Although we do not know how large this staff was, we know that it was composed mostly of able and educated men who because they were not nobles were not eligible for battlefield command. There were also a number of serving army officers who had been crippled by wounds or illness and so could not serve in the field.

The most important duty of the staff was to maintain accurate muster rolls. Alexander expected to know at a moment's notice how many men were fit for duty in any unit, how many were temporarily unfit and how many had died and needed replacing. It was on the basis of these muster rolls that Alexander allotted tasks and duties to the various units. Pay was also based on the muster rolls. Eumenes and his men were also responsible for issuing replacement horses, weapons and other equipment.

Some years after the Granicus campaign it is recorded that under Eumenes there were a number of secretaries, each assisted by a number of inspectors, who were responsible for the various branches of the army. The companion cavalry had one secretary, the hypaspists another and so on. It is reasonable to assume that the same system existed in 334.

It is not entirely clear if Eumenes and his staff were responsible for sourcing supplies and assistance from the territories through which the army moved. However, somebody had to liaise with local city councils, landowners and noblemen. It seems likely that Eumenes carried out this task.

Eumenes also kept an army diary. This recorded such administrative data as the muster rolls, pay issued, supplies gathered in and issued out. It also contained a copy of any orders issued and reports that came in. Eumenes inserted comments of his own which seem to have recorded where the army was at the end of each day and notes about the events of the day. It would seem that this was presented to Alexander on a regular basis, perhaps daily, for him to approve. Unlike the work produced by Callisthenes, the diary of Eumenes was not intended for publication.

In addition to Eumenes and his department, there were the body-guards. These were all young men drawn from the nobility of Macedonia. There were probably 200 of them when the Granicus campaign began, but their number subsequently fluctuated widely. Perhaps there was no fixed number. Alexander may have appointed men to the unit as and when he wanted to show favour to individuals or families.

This bodyguard certainly had the task of guarding the king, and it may have been divided into seven sections – one for each day of the week. Beyond that the bodyguards were used to carry messages, attend the king and his generals and undertake various ceremonial and other duties. There is some indication that the bodyguard formed a sort of unofficial training school for army officers. The men of the bodyguard would certainly have been close to the decision-making process at the highest level and under the eyes of the experienced senior officers. We know of several higher commanders who had previously served as bodyguards, but we do not know of any who had not. The bodyguards seem to have been equipped as hypaspists and, on a few occasions, are recorded as fighting alongside them in battle.

In charge of the bodyguards were seven Royal Bodyguards. These men came from the same group as did the commanders of the larger units in the army. Indeed, some unit commanders became Royal Bodyguards, and Royal Bodyguards became commanders. Individual senior officers could serve as either at the king's pleasure. The Royal Bodyguards had the duty of organising the bodyguard, but they were more important than that.

The Royal Bodyguards were in constant attendance on the king. In effect they were his war council. While the final decision in any circumstance lay with the king, he would ask for advice from his Royal Bodyguards. Indeed, the Royal Bodyguards felt that they had the right to give advice whether or not it was asked for. It is likely that the king chose these men for their technical knowledge or experience. He would seek to have one who knew about the cavalry, another who was an expert on siege warfare, a third who had visited the territory through which the army was moving and so forth. That at least is the theory. There must have always been a temptation for the king to appoint men who would agree with him rather than those who would give useful advice. Philip does not seem to have fallen into this trap, nor does Alexander – at least in his early years.

Waiting on the king and the Royal Bodyguards as servants were the royal pages. These were boys aged between about 10 and 15 who came from the noble families of Macedonia and the associated tribes that owed allegiance to the Macedonian kings. It seems that recruitment into the royal pages was obligatory rather than being either a choice or an honour.

There was probably an element of cold statecraft in this institution. Noblemen and the leaders of hilltribes were surely less likely to rebel or cause trouble if their sons were with the king. The Macedonian kings had, in the past, been ruthless with the families of those who caused them trouble. Imprisonment was the least that could be expected, execution was more likely.

On the other hand, the pages were given a sound education in philosophy, mathematics and other sciences. They were also taught all the skills needed in warfare, both on the practical fighting level and in the fields of command and organisation. They earned their keep, as it were, by working as the personal servants to the king and his high commanders. We know that they ran the king's bath, served his food at table and – at least in the days of the womanising Philip – escorted the concubine chosen for the night to the royal bedchamber. They wore a distinctive uniform which might have included a white cloak with a red border.

When they grew too old to be royal pages, the young men would be assessed by the king. They would then be allocated to the bodyguards – presumably if destined for command roles – or to the companion cavalry or the hypaspists.

Fitting somehow into this inner circle of pages, bodygaurds and secretaries were men known as the King's Friends. We do not know how many of these men there were, nor is it entirely clear if they were a distinct group or if the title was a rank. Perhaps the most senior of the pages or bodyguards were King's Friends.

Finally there was a select group of workmen who had the job of looking after the royal tent. This was an impressive structure made of wooden poles and linen or woollen cloth. It contained several rooms, including among others the royal bedchamber, the chamber of the Royal

Bodyguards – presumably a council chamber of some kind, the royal dining room, the outer chamber and the guardroom.

Efficient and well motivated it may have been, but the Macedonian army also needed discipline. Under Philip and Alexander this came in two forms: rewards and punishment. Promotion up the ranks to get higher pay was undoubtedly one system of reward for good service, but there were others. We know that some men who were not promoted were referred to as the best of their rank. Whether this was merely an honor or implied extra pay we are not certain. Alexander held periodic parades at which he paid out bonuses to some of his troops, presumably on the basis of brave or efficient service.

Punishments came in a wide range and, although these were usually imposed by the unit commander it seems that even the lowliest man had the right of appeal to the king. For minor offences a man might find himself given extra duties or forced to stand to attention in full equipment for hours on end. Flogging was usual for the more serious offences. Failure to parade in the correct gear resulted in a fine. If a missing piece of equipment could neither be produced nor a good reason for its loss given, the man had to pay for its replacement. Death was the punishment for mutiny, and only the king could order that punishment on any officer or man.

With its variety of troops, each with its allotted role in battle or on the march, its sophisticated command structure and administrative bureaucracy, the Macedonian army was a well constructed and highly effective instrument of war. But Alexander did not march out of Therme with the Macedonian army alone. Indeed, he was leaving over a third of his royal army with Antipater.

A large part of his army was made up of allies and mercenaries. The success of the invasion of Persia would depend on them every bit as much as on the Macedonian army.

CHAPTER FIVE

The Greek Allies

Those troops that marched with Alexander, but which were not drawn from the Kingdom of Macedon itself, are usually referred to loosely as allies. In fact they marched to war for a variety of reasons and motives. First there were those men drawn from states which, although not formally part of Macedon, were linked to and owed allegiance to the kings of Macedon. Secondly there were those troops drawn from the League of Corinth, those Greek states put together by Philip specifically for the invasion of Persia. Finally there were mercenaries, mostly hired from Greek states.

The rich, spreading plains of Thessaly had long enjoyed links to the Kingdom of Macedon that lay over the Olympos mountain range to their north. The area was made up of a patchwork of territories, estates and cities that all lay under the control of a few powerful noble families. Traditionally these families saw themselves, and the Thessalians that they ruled, as a distinct people within the Greek world, and most Greeks agreed. Philip had managed to get himself appointed to lead the Thessalian nobles, a position more usually held by a Thessalian, and Alexander was similarly elected after Philip's death.

Like the Macedonians, the Thessalians had enough grazing land to keep large numbers of horses, so it was cavalry that was the the most valuable contribution that the Thessalians made to Alexander's army. There were 1,800 of these horsemen gathering at Therme, probably divided into eight squadrons, or ile. These were probably based on the main regions of Thessaly, so that local men served together under the command of their local nobility.

The dress of the Thessalians is easier to reconstruct than their weaponry. Thessalian horsemen wore a broad-brimmed hat with a distinctive upturned front. They wore the famous Thessalian cloak, which consisted of a long strip of cloth about a metre wide. This was worn so that the long sides were horizontal, and the strip folded around the left side of the body, leaving the two short ends on the right side. It was held by a brooch at the right shoulder, then left to hang free. This gave a distinctive double pointed fold at front and rear that covered the body and upper legs, while the right arm was left free and the left arm covered by elegantly draped fabric. When the men galloped these cloaks billowed out behind them to form what Greek poets usually referred to as 'Thessalian wings'. On campaign the Thessalians also wore a knee-length tunic that could have long or short sleeves.

Less certain is whether or not the Thessalians were armoured. Some sources depict them wearing the linothorax, others do not. Similarly the presence of a helmet is not certain. It is likely that those men who rode with Alexander did wear both linothorax and the boeotian helmet, as did the companion cavalry. Just as one unit of the companion cavalry were led by Alexander, so one squadron of the Thessalians was led by Parmenio. As second in command to Alexander and, usually, commander of the left wing, Parmenio would have deserved nothing less.

As for weapons, Thessalian cavalry are usually depicted carrying two or three light throwing javelins. A favourite decoration on pottery in Thessaly was of horsemen throwing javelins at a target, and this seems to have been a favourite sport among the nobility. Such a skill would have suited the Thessalians to a light cavalry role. On the battlefield they could have galloped up to hurl their javelins into an enemy formation, then wheeled aside and riden off before the enemy could retaliate. Off the battlefield they could have scouted and foraged.

On the other hand the charge of the Thessalians in battle was said to have been irresistible. If delivered properly, no troops on earth could stand up to an assault by these horsemen. The key to this success was the distinctive rhomboid formation invented in around 375BC by Jason of Pherae, one of the larger cities in Thessaly. This formation had one man – the unit commander – in the front rank. Three men were in the second rank, five in the third, seven in the fourth and so on until the 11th rank, which had 23 riders abreast. The two outermost riders were officers. The formation then narrowed again at the same rate to end with a single rider, the second in command, in the 21st rank.

This formation gives a formal unit strength of 223, though as ever on campaign few units could field full strength in a battle due to injury, sickness and death. Eight such formations give a total of 1,784 men, which is close to the 1,800 Thessalians recorded as mustering at Therme. Presumably there were a few extra officers, trumpeters and the like to make up the total.

The Thessalian cavalry formation was blunter than the Macedonian wedge, but just as deep. It must be presumed that it operated in a similar way. It would have charged into the enemy, relying on the momentum and the pressure exerted by the many ranks behind the leaders to push them into the enemy formation and burst it apart.

What is not certain is what weapon the Thessalians used when charging in this fashion. The throwing javelin does not seem to be a very likely weapon. It would have been too short and light to have been much use against the standard thrusting spear of the infantry. It is most likely that these horsemen carried the xyston cavalry lance of the Companion cavalry, with a sword as a reserve weapon for use once a melee had formed.

On the field of battle, the Thessalians were invariably placed on the left wing. There they seem to have been intended to perform the same role as the Companion cavalry did on the right wing. Very often, however, the left wing was held back or refused. Its main role was to tie down the enemy facing them until Alexander had broken through on the right wing. Only then would they attack. Such a secondary role may not have been popular, but Alexander was the king and the glory of a victory rightly belonged to him.

Usually operating alongside the Thessalian cavalry were the 600 horsemen sent by the Greek states themselves. Cavalry did not often fight as such on Greek battlefields, where the clash between armoured infantry usually decided the day. When they did fight, the horsemen conventionally drew up either four or eight ranks deep and across as wide a front as they had men to fill. In other words they adopted a rectangular formation with the longest side facing the enemy. These cavalry formed three squadrons, with 200 men in each. This would mean that in battle they formed up either as blocks 50 men wide and four deep, or 25 wide and eight deep.

None of the Greek states could send enough horsemen to form a complete squadron, so each unit was made up of men from a number of different cities. The entire Pelopponese, for instance, combined to form one squadron while Malis and Phthiotis contributed a second and the Locrians and Phocians the third. The other states, such as Athens were presumably not asked to send horsemen.

When these Greek squadrons left Therme they were commanded by a man named Erigyos who was from Mitylene. This city was on Lesbos, an island just off the coast of Asia Minor. At some point in the campaign he was replaced by a Macedonian named Philip, son of Menelaos, who led the Greek cavalry at the Granicus. We do not know the reason for the change, but it was only temporary as Erigyos was back in command the following year. Perhaps he fell ill.

The Greek horsemen wore body armour and bronze helmets, and were armed with the xyston lance. This should have made them effective at delivering a charge on the battlefield, but the unit was not rated very

Cavalry in
Greek Deep Order

A = Squadron Commander
B = Deputy Commander

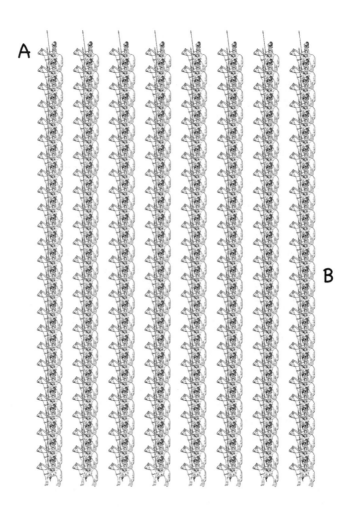

A

B

Cavalry in Greek Deep Order

The cavalry of the Greek larger city states formed units 200 strong. They were trained to form up 25 wide and 8 deep, as shown here. This gave a mass of horsemen about 60 metres wide and 30 metres deep. This formation was considered to be best suited to the horsemen from the city states, who were not as skilled at formation riding as those from Thessaly and Macedonia. These men tended to be the richer citizens and, as with most Greek soldiers, were a part time militia. The better formation riders would be in the front rank, those unable to devote much time to practising filled up the ranks behind. This formation lacked the punch of that used by the Thessalians or Macedonians, but did not call for such continual practice.

Cavalry in
Greek Shallow Order

A = Squadron Commander
B = Deputy Commander

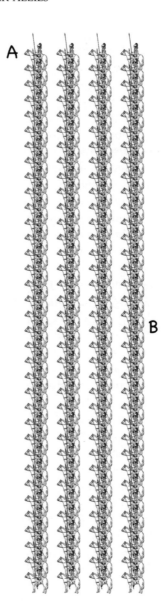

Greek Cavalry in Shallow Order

The Greek Cavalry sometimes adopted a formation only four ranks deep. This was often because the smaller city states could not muster 200 mounted men. However, even larger units would adopt this formation when they had to cover a wider frontage. At this period it seem to have been usual for the ranks to ride closer together than would be the case in more recent centuries. The reason for this seems to have been that there were no heavy weapons, such as cannon, that could hurl missiles able to strike more than one rank at a time.

highly and did not play much of a role in any of the battles where they were present. Since they were neither trained nor experienced in such a role it must be concluded that they were not terribly effective.

Rather better at their allotted task were the 900 light cavalry from Thrace and Paeonia. These men wore no armour and were armed with javelins, and at least some of them had the xyston lance. They lacked the training or armour to charge on the battlefield, and were almost certainly tribal levies raised from among the richer families. They were purely light cavalry and were used as such. On the march they were sent out scouting, and to forage for food and animal fodder. On the field of battle they were put next to one of the units of heavier horsemen. From there they would surge forward to hurl their javelins at the enemy to probe for weaknesses and disorder formations. Presumably they were also used to pursue the enemy once a battle had been won, though this is not mentioned.

Both the Thracians and Paeonians were, like the Thessalians, subject to the Kingdom of Macedon. The Paeonians were commanded by Ariston, son of the King of Paeonia, while the Odrysians were likewise led by a prince of their own royal family. There would therefore have been as many squadrons as there were tribes, with the squadrons being of irregular size depending on the men sent by that tribe. The whole group was put under the command of a Macedonian cavalry officer named Agathon, son of Tyrimmas.

Alexander was later to hire mercenary cavalry, but they do not seem to have been part of his original army and were not present in the Granicus campaign.

The states closely linked to Macedon by tribute and treaty provided thousands of light infantry. These came mostly from Thrace and were armed with either javelins or slings. When grouped together with similarly armed men from the wilder regions within Macedon that were grouped in the royal army, these men numbered 7,000. How many came from which source we do not know.

Alexander also took with him 5,000 mercenaries. Some of these were hoplites that would be used to garrison captured cities, guard lines of communication and other tasks, but most of them seem to have been specialist missile troops. These came in two forms: archers and slingers.

The traditional recruitment ground for mercenary archers was Crete. This island stayed resolutely neutral during most wars, but made a lot of money by sending mercenaries to fight on whichever side was willing to pay. The Cretans had a reputation for being excellent archers, but also for unreliability. They were effective enough at skirmishing, holding

An arrowhead found in Greece that dates to about the time of Alexander. The arrowhead is barely 15mm long and lightly constructed. The shaft was glued into a socket at the rear.

down civilians and other low risk operations, but had a nasty knack of making themselves scarce if things turned difficult. Nevertheless, Alexander hired many hundreds of them, so he must have been confident that he knew how to use them.

Just how effective these archers were is a matter of much conjecture. The bows were of the recurved style, and seem to have been made up of layered wood and horn. This should have produced a bow of great power, and certainly a few centuries later bows of this type were extremely effective. On the other hand all the arrowheads that have survived are small and light, as if they were to be shot from a low powered bow.

The accounts of archers in action at this period would seem to indicate that the bow could, indeed, provide only a relatively low velocity. Arrows are described as bouncing off even fairly light armour. On the other hand, the limbs of most soldiers and even the torsos of many were entirely

An arrowhead dating to just after the time of Alexander. The small size (about 20mm), light weight, triangular section and slightly barbed shape are typical of arrows used by the Cretan mercenaries who served in Alexander's army.

unarmoured, so there was plenty of damage that arrows could do to an army.

That archers were not terribly effective at this period can be deduced from the fact that javelin throwers and slingers were rated just as highly. We have already seen that Alexander recruited large numbers of javelin men from the tribes in and around Macedon, but he also took with him slingers. The sling could be more effective than the bow in the hands of a skilled practitioner.

Most slingers hurled stones that weighed up to 75 grams, though some used stones that were up to double that size – presumably at short range. Hurled at great speed, and often falling on to their victims at a high angle, sling stones could break arms or legs and smash skulls. Even when they struck helmets and armour, stones had the power to knock men over or stun them into unconsciousness.

A Greek slinger. This man is typical of the slingers that Alexander had in his army from a variety of sources. He is unarmoured, except for his small shield made of wood. He wears a typical Greek tunic and may have had a cloak for wearing in cold or wet weather. His sling is made of leather. He would have had a bag of stones or lead pellets slung from his waist. Further supplies of ammunition would have been carried with the army baggage.

More effective still were the lead weight shots that were generally used by mercenaries. These were cast in moulds that produced shot of an aerodynamically stable plum-shape with a sharp leading edge. They often had taunts such as 'take that' or 'got you' stamped on them. A skilled mercenary could hurl these missiles so that they flew through the air with their sharp edge leading the way.

When these hit armour they not only struck with stunning power, but were quite capable of penetrating light armour and of denting metal armour so badly as to render it unwearable. Against naked flesh they were horribly effective and produce nasty, jagged wounds that could prove as fatal through long term infection as through immediate blood loss.

In addition to these mercenaries, Alexander also took 7,000 hoplite heavy infantry sent by the states of the League of Corinth. These men were equipped in traditional hoplite fashion, with the shorter dory-style spear, large shield and helmet. Most of these men had body armour, either the linothorax or the more solid bronze muscled cuirass. A few had greaves, though these seem to have been unusual.

A few units, especially those from Athens and its close allies, may have been composed of lightly armed hoplites along the lines of those introduced by the Athenian commander Iphicrates some 60 years earlier. These men carried a spear about 3.5 metres long and a shield that, although smaller than the traditional hoplite shield, was still larger than that of the Macedonian pezhetairoi. These men had linothorax body armour, if any. They were a lighter form of hoplite able to advance more quickly over more broken ground than the more heavily equipped, traditional type of soldier.

In theory, each state was obliged by its membership of the League of Corinth to send a set number of its best men to join Alexander. These men marched to Therme in individual units, each commanded by an officer from their native city. However, several states had been coerced into League membership and would have been most unwilling to send its most effective fighting men to join a hazardous overseas expedition when there were plenty of enemies close at hand. Undoubtedly some states sent what were very far from being their best men, and there is some reason to believe that a few may have hired mercenaries to meet their obligations instead of sending their own citizens.

Once at Therme it would seem that they underwent some rudimentary training so that they could operate together as a single unit of heavy infantry. They were placed under the overall command of Parmenio, though given his other duties it is likely that they had their own unit

A Greek hoplite. This figure carries the shorter dory type of spear and the large shield of the typical hoplite. By this date most shields were decorated with a symbol of the owner's home city. His body armour is made up of over a dozen layers of linen glued together and reinforced with metal studs.

commander. This man would most likely have been a Macedonian, but none of the sources gives his name.

The importance of these men on the Granicus campaign was as much political as military – perhaps more so. Both Philip and Alexander ruled over the assorted Greek city states through indirect means. Each state was allowed to keep its own government, though this was very often headed by men handpicked by the Macedonian kings and garrisons of Macedonian troops were placed at strategic spots throughout Greece. This allowed the states the freedom to keep their own laws and to have some measure of self-government. There was no doubt, however, that the Macedonians were in command and no state could have contemplated taking action of which Philip or Alexander would have disapproved.

Having a large number of citizens with the Macedonian army would serve to deter any state from contemplating rebellion. This was particularly the case if those with Alexander were men who were accustomed to playing a lead role in the politics or administration of their home city. That would leave behind men unaccustomed to taking control and wary of offending their absent superiors.

But having the League of Corinth supply a part of the invasion army was not simply a matter of having hostages to enforce good behaviour. It also played a major positive role in the propaganda side of the war that Alexander was setting out to fight. Alexander proclaimed that the purpose of his invasion was twofold. First, he aimed to free the Greek states of Asia Minor that were then under Persian control. Second, he said that he was determined to gain revenge on Persia and the Persians for the damage and insults done to the Greeks during the two Persian invasions of 490 and 480BC, plus the series of wars fought since then.

The former ambition was unlikely to have been taken very seriously by the Greek cities in question if they thought that they would merely be exchanging rule by the Persian monarch for rule by the Macedonian monarch. By acting in the name of the League of Corinth, Alexander could pose as the champion of Greek freedoms. He could also claim to be merely the instrument of Greek revenge.

Even at the time few people took these claims terribly seriously. Alexander was known to be working for the good of himself and of the kingdom of Macedon. The League of Corinth was the mask that he put on to rule Greece and to justify his invasion of Persia.

From the military point of view, Alexander did not regard his Greek allied infantry very highly. He never put them in a position of importance on the battlefield, and preferred to keep them out of harms way altogether. Perhaps he doubted their loyalty and willingness to fight. Or he may

A Greek merchant ship from a vase painting. The sail was the only means of power, the oars at the stern being used for steering only. It was vessels of this type that accompanied Alexander's army to carry the food stores.

simply have thought their tactics and training so old fashioned and inferior to that of his own army that he did not believe that they could be very effective.

Of rather more use to Alexander were the ships contributed by the League of Corinth. This fleet does not often get a lot of attention from historians. Largely this is because Alexander disbanded it immediately after the Granicus campaign, and so it played no role in his later conquests and campaigns. It was, however, absolutely crucial to the Granicus campaign.

The ships of the ancient world were divided sharply between merchant ships and warships. The two types were of completely different design, motive power and purpose. Alexander took both with him, mustering them in the sheltered waters off Therme just as he gathered his army in the fields around the city.

Merchant ships were relatively stubby, round bottomed craft powered by the wind. The smaller ships were bout 12 metres long, 3.5 metres wide and drew a draft of around 3 metres. They could carry about 40 tons of cargo. Most merchant ships were larger, a typical example might have been 26 metres long and able to carry 250 tons of cargo. A few ships engaged in the corn trade might have been as much as 35 metres long, but these were rare.

We do not know how many merchant ships Alexander had with him when he left Therme. Given the amount of cargo that the ships had to carry, the total number was probably well over 150. It was a formidable fleet.

All merchant ships were powered by the wind. They had one or two masts, both of which carried a single square-set sail. The main mast of a two-masted ship was set just abaft the mid point, the smaller foremast was often sloping forward over the bows like a later bowsprit. This rig left the ships at the mercy of the winds to a large extent. They could make around 6 knots when the wind was astern, but could not sail at much of an angle to the winds and were unable to sail into the wind at all. Traditionally these craft put to sea only when a light, favourable wind was blowing, and would stay in harbour if rough weather threatened. They were manoeuvred in and out of harbour with oars, using up to 20 oarsmen hired from the port for the purpose. Once at sea, the oarsmen were sent back in a small boat and the ship would proceed on its way with its regular crew of 4 to 6 men.

Such craft were good enough for merchants who traversed sea lanes that they knew well and who were transporting goods such as pottery, wine or dried figs that would not take much harm from being held up for a week or two by contrary winds. For merchant ships carrying supplies for an army a delay of two weeks might prove to be fatal to the force waiting for food, ammunition or reinforcements.

A style of larger merchant ship equipped with oars and permanent rowers to move them against the wind or into small coves to be unloaded was produced to meet the needs of armies campaigning far from base. Unfortunately there is no evidence to prove or disprove that these ships had been developed by the time of Alexander's invasion. If they had been, Alexander would undoubtedly have used them. If they had not, he had to entrust himself and his army to the older style of sail-only ships.

If we are uncertain what types of merchant ships Alexander took with him, we do know the style of warship that he had. Greek warships of this period were oared galleys. They had a large square sail on a single mast, but this was used only for long distance cruising. Masts and sails were left ashore when going into battle as they served only to make the ship heavier and more difficult to manoeuvre.

The ships had one, two or three banks of oars to power them. Each oar was worked by a single man sitting on a bench inside the ship. Single banked ships, known as pentekonters from the fifty oars that they sported, were by this date considered unsuitable for battles. They were, however, cheap to build, fast to use and easy to maintain. Most fleets had a few for use carrying messages or senior personnel.

The main warship was the trireme. This was a galley with three banks of oars along each side. Each oar was powered by a single man, the lower

A bireme warship, taken from a Greek vase painting. The bireme had two banks of oars on each side. The ram at the prow and steering oars at the stern can be clearly seen. The sail would have been used only when the wind was astern, and was usually discarded before battle.

two ranks sitting on benches inside the ship and the third on an outrigger gallery hanging over the sides.These ships were about 36 metres long, 5.5 metres wide and drew a draft of less than a metre. They had 170 rowers, plus a few sailors to work the sails when they were used and a dozen or more soldiers.

Present in smaller numbers was the bireme, which sported two banks of oars. This was a revival of an older type that had long been outclassed by the trireme. Biremes were being developed as scouts and transport craft. They were equipped with more efficient sails than the triremes and with a following wind were the fastest ships afloat. Again the extent to which these craft were present in Alexander's fleet is unknown.

The main battle tactic of all these ships was to ram. A typical trireme had fitted to its prow a wooden beam that stuck forward about 2 metres and was tipped with a large bronze head about 75cm tall and a metre long. The usual design by this date was to have three prongs, one below the waterline, one on the waterline and one above it. This ram could punch a hole through the planking of a an enemy ship with comparative ease.

The main ambition of a ship's captain was to ram an enemy from the side with sufficient speed to inflict a large hole. He would then order his oarsmen to back water to free his ram so that he did not get stuck to the crippled enemy and so become vulnerable to attack himself. To achieve this, the captain needed to build up speed while approaching from the flank. This in turn called for both nimble steering and for disciplined and powerful rowing. Well trained rowing crews led by an experienced captain had a definite advantage over less experienced crews and captains in a world where speed and manoeuvre were paramount.

Alexander summoned 160 warships from the League of Corinth to join his invasion. The task of this fleet was, primarily, to protect the merchant ships carrying his supplies from attack by the Persian fleet. They were also expected to protect the merchant ships as they ferried the army over the Dardanelles into Asia.

Given that the Persian war fleet was around four times as large as that gathering in Therme, this was likely to be a difficult and hazardous task. But Alexander had a secret weapon on his side. Time.

CHAPTER SIX

Into Asia

With his army and fleet gathered, Alexander was almost ready to leave for Asia. First, however, there was the giving of gifts and awards that was traditional for a Macedonian king about to set off to war.

Such occasions were usually lavish both in terms of the ceremonial and the gifts given. Alexander, however, was in a rather embarrassing situation. His father had left him debts of about 500 talents. In part those had been paid off by the sack of Thebes, but Alexander was spending around 3,000 talents a year on his army at a time when the Kingdom of Macedon produced only around half that in taxes. The gold mines of Thrace produced another 1,000 talents, while tribute from subject tribes and kingdoms produced a few hundred more. It can be seen that the finances of the Kingdom of Macedon were shaky to say the least. By the spring of 334BC Alexander's known debts totalled about 200 talents.

It is difficult to be certain exactly how this translates into modern money. In terms of bullion, 200 talents of silver coin would today fetch around £600,000 or so. However, Alexander lived in a world that was basically agricultural and had an economy based on land, services and goods more than on money, which was then a fairly new invention. Certainly his contemporaries considered the debt to be enormous.

Alexander had just 70 talents in cash to take with him to pay the army, bribe Persian officials and pay expenses. This would not last him long on campaign. He could not, therefore, afford to hand out money to his commanders, nobles and officials. Instead he chose to hand out farms, estates and even entire villages from the royal estates. He went further, giving at least some of his nobles the tax revenues from ports and districts for the coming years. He was, in effect, pledging the future revenues of his kingdom. The scale of the gift giving may not have been unprecedented, but the types of gifts given were without parallel.

Perdiccas, one of Alexander's inner circle of Macedonian noblemen, was taken aback by what he was seeing. 'But your majesty,' he protested, 'what are you leaving for yourself?'

The obverse (top) and reverse (bottom) of an obol coin from the city of Histaia. Both sides carry a depiction of the sea goddess Histaia, that on the reverse shows her sitting on a warship. The depiction of patron deities on coins was the norm before Alexander put his portrait on those of Macedon.

Alexander replied simply 'My hopes'.

'Very well then,' said Perdiccas, 'those who serve with you will share those too.' He returned the gifts that Alexander had given him, and a few others followed suit.

Even so, Alexander had by this ceremony passed the point of no return. If he did not conquer in Asia and obtain new territories, new tax incomes and much loot then he and the Kingdom of Macedon would be bankrupt. This dire financial situation soon became known outside of Macedon, and news of Alexander's potential bankruptcy reached Asia Minor long before he did himself.

Some time in the first half of May, Alexander gave the order to set out. The date of this early start was forced upon Alexander by events far to the south in Egypt. Ideally, the army should have set off a month later. June was the start of the traditional campaigning season in Greece and Macedon. The month was chosen because the grain crops on which everyone depended for survival ripened in early June. Before the crop was in nobody had enough food to spare for a passing army. Notoriously the weeks just before the harvest were the hungriest in any agricultural society. Famine was a plague of the summer months, not the winter. Once the grain crops were ripe, they would take the farmers and their labourers a fortnight to gather in. By the middle of June it would be clear if there had been a good crop or not, and which areas had done well compared to others.

The importance of this was two fold. First it meant that the adult men would be free of agricultural duties once the crop was in. Since most Greek armies were made up of part-timers they could not realistically begin to campaign until the men were free to join the army. Secondly it indicated to the army commanders which areas would have enough spare grain to support a passing army as well as the resident population. Such knowledge would be essential when planning the coming campaign.

It is often said that armies 'lived off the land', but the phrase does take a bit of explanation. When marching through one's own territory, or that of allies, an army could not simply pillage and loot food. That food had to be bought and paid for, or the resident civilian population would soon turn hostile. That, in turn, meant that the locals had to have enough food to spare to sell. The most reliable time to achieve this was in the two or three months after the harvest was in. At that time the granaries were full – if there had been a good harvest – and farmers still had any surplus to hand and were looking for a quick and profitable sale.

The news that a friendly army was passing nearby was welcome to the farmers as it provided a handy and cash-rich market for surplus food. This was much more preferable than selling to the usual grain merchants who wanted the grain for export overseas. They did not usually pay a good price, and the amount they would take was unreliable. By the autumn the spare grain of a district would usually have been sold to merchants and so was no longer available to an army.

Even when marching through enemy territory, the timing of a campaign was crucial. News that an enemy army was approaching was the cue for all farmers to move their goods and their harvest into the nearest fortified city or fortress for safe keeping. Only in the first few days of a campaign, before news of the invasion had spread, would troops be able to loot grain from farmers who had not yet fled.

Usually an invading army would find the countryside stripped bare of grain, which was safely stored in fortified places. The commander then had to calculate how best to get the grain his men needed out of the strongholds where it lay. The usual route was to negotiate with the city or fortress commander. The invading army would promise to leave the city alone if a specified amount of grain and other supplies were handed over. Quite how much could be extracted depended on the defences of the city and the strength of the invading army. It was an inexact science and an unreliable method of supply.

Alexander, of course, was hoping that the Greek cities within the Persian Empire would welcome him as a liberator and so he would be able to buy food from them as if they were allies, rather than having to extort food as if they were enemies. What he did not know was how many cities would be constrained by having Persian garrisons, how much food they would have in store nor if they would actually welcome him at all.

Ideally, Alexander would have waited until the harvest was in before leaving Therme. He would then have marched through Macedon and Thrace at a time when the granaries were full and the local farmers eager to sell him their crops. This might have cost him money, but it would have meant that the 30 days supply of grain that we know he had prepared in Therme would have remained intact. He would have begun his invasion with a full month of supplies for his men and horses. Even if the local Greek cities did not throw their gates open, this would have given him the flexibility that he needed to fight a successful campaign on his own terms.

But Alexander was forced to move early because of the movements of the Persian fleet. With a strength of 400 galleys on permanent duty, plus many more held in reserve, the Persian fleet was much larger than Alexander's. It also had the advantage of being an homogeneous force that was accustomed to operating and fighting together as a unit. If the two fleets were to meet in open seas there would be no doubt of the outcome: a total Persian victory.

Given that Alexander was relying on a supply system based on merchant ships, he was vulnerable to the enemy fleet. He would be even more exposed when crossing the Dardanelles. If the Persian fleet arrived as the Macedonians were on board ship and being ferried across the sea, a massacre could be guaranteed to follow. Almost as bad would be if the Persian fleet arrived while Alexander was still in Europe. By cruising the seas they could keep him pinned down at Sestos until his food and money ran out. The war would be over before it began.

Alexander had to be over the Dardanelles before the Persian fleet arrived. The question was, when would that be?

The fleet of the Persian Empire was, in fact, not Persian at all. It was raised from the Phoenician cities such as Sidon and Tyre. The ships were Phoenician in design and construction. Their crews and captains were Phoenicians. Although the Persian monarch usually appointed a Persian as supreme commander, these men rarely had any real knowledge of or skill in maritime warfare. They were there to ensure the loyalty of the fleet, not to control it in action.

Egypt had long been a turbulent province of the Persian Empire. The native Egyptians had never really accepted Persian rule and caused frequent trouble. It might be a refusal to pay taxes, riots over religious rituals or even out and out rebellions, but the Persian monarchs could never be secure in their control of the wealthy and fertile kingdom of Egypt.

In 380BC all of Egypt had fallen under the control of Kheperkare, a native nobleman who declared himself to be pharaoh as Nectanebo, founder of the 30th Dynasty. His son, Teos not only solidified his control over Egypt, but then invaded Syria and Israel, both at this date satrapies within the Persian Empire. The invasion failed, but Egypt remained independent under Teos's grandson, Nectanebo II who came to the throne in 360BC.

In 350BC the Persian monarch Artaxerxes III finally found the time and resources to invade Egypt to put down the thirty-year old rebellion against Persian rule. The campaign ended in failure, but Artaxerxes returned in 343BC when he had secured an alliance with the nomads who always hovered around the frontiers of Egypt in search of plunder. In that first year he secured control of the Delta and part of the Nile Valley. It took another two years to subdue Nectanebo II completely.

In 338BC another Egyptian nobleman decided to try his luck. Khabash, provincial governor of Sais in the Delta, announced that he was founding a new Dynasty and was adopting the royal name of Senensetepenptah – a title honouring the mighty god Ptah. This might indicate that he based his uprising on Egyptian unease at the Persian's monotheistic Zoroastrian religion. Certainly Persian contempt for the Egyptian gods had caused trouble in the past, so it is natural to suspect that it was behind the unease that led to the rebellion of Khabash.

Support for Khabash spread rapidly. By the time the Nile floods came in 337BC he controlled all of the Nile Valley and at least most of the Delta. His name is engraved on the annual inscriptions at the Apis Temple at Saqqara, an honour given only to pharaohs. Khabash then promoted his son to be joint Pharaoh to secure the succession. It began to look as if a new independent dynasty was being established.

Darius was determined not to allow Egypt to split away from the Persian Empire. He knew that Philip was preparing a joint Macedonian-Greek invasion of Asia Minor and was rightly nervous about the loyalty of the Greek states under Persian rule in that area. What was needed, Darius thought, was a swift and brutal exhibition of Persian power and what happened to those who flouted it.

An expeditionary force was sent to deal with Khabash. Moving with both ships and men the Persians once again moved into Egypt. This force does not seem to have been commanded by Darius himself, nor to have had any elements of the Royal Army within it. It may have been drawn from the satrapies that bordered Egypt to the northeast. Certainly the fleet came from Phoenicia, so the army may have been drawn from Phoenicia, Syria and Israel as well.

This Persian expedition was successful. Khabash may have had religious backing, but he does not seem to have had much in the way of military backing. We know next to nothing about the course of this campaign, except that it was over by about January 334BC.

These various uprisings and campaigns in Egypt were important because they meant that most, if not all, of the Persian fleet was in Egypt in the spring of 334BC. Alexander will have known this. He will also have been aware of the strict limits that were placed on the movements of ancient warships.

Triremes, biremes and pentekonters were all light, handy and nimble in combat. That manoeuvrablity was achieved at a cost. The ships had virtually no hold and were quite unable to carry either food or water for their crews. Both had to be either acquired from a land base or carried on merchant ships that accompanied the war fleet. It was for this reason that warships tended to hug coastlines and why ancient battles were so often fought close to land.

The Persian fleet included something close to 50,000 men. The vast majority of these were oarsmen, but there were also marines, officers and other supernumeraries. The Persian fleet was, therefore, faced by the same problems as was Alexander. It could not move until its commanders were certain that the ports along its route would contain enough food to feed the vast numbers of men involved. That meant that the fleet could not pull out of the Egyptian delta until the harvest was in along the Palestinian coast. That harvest came a fortnight or so earlier than it did in Macedonia and Thrace.

If Alexander had left Therme when the harvest was in, he would have given the Persian fleet a two week start in the race for the Dardanelles. By leaving when he did, he gained a head start himself. Even so, it promised to be a race to get to the straits. If Alexander got there first he would get across in safety and his supply fleet would be securely anchored in harbour. But if the Persian fleet got there first, Alexander's hopes on which he had such great store when handing out gifts to his nobles in Therme would be dashed.

The army headed directly east along the southern shores of what are now lakes Koronia and Volvi, then Lake Cercinitis. The first halting place was Amphipolis, a three day march of around 90km – perfectly feasible for fresh men covering level ground on a good road.

The fleet, on the other hand, was faced by a rather more tricky operation. This was the most dangerous part of their route in terms of natural obstacles. Heading south out of the Thermaic Gulf, the ships had to round the three headlands of the Sithonian Peninsula. Of these by far the most dangerous was the most easterly, that of Mount Athos. The currents here combine with unpredictable winds to create sea conditions that can deteriorate rapidly and without warning.

In 490 the supply fleet for the Persian invasion had come to grief here. Ten years later Xerxes had dug a canal across the neck of the Athos Peninsula so that his ships could traverse the area in safety. There is no evidence that the canal had been maintained, so Alexander's fleet must have braved the tempestuous waters of Cape Athos. Clearly they got around safely as no problems are mentioned.

The fleet and army met again at Amphipolis. Stores were unloaded from the ships onto the pack animals and then both set off again. This section of the march was through the Thracian tribal areas that had been annexed by Philip. The army headed for Neapolis, then to Abdera, a further 115km from Amphipolis. It is not clear if the fleet put in at Neapolis, but it certainly came in to Abdera to unload more supplies. Once past Abdera the army was marching through the area of Thrace that was still independent of Macedon. Alexander had, however, ensured that the tribes were friendly so no problems were encountered.

The army then marched by way of Maroneia to Hebros, some 140km from Abdera, where it met the fleet, then on to Leuce Acte where the ships put in again. Finally the army made the short, but rugged march over what is now the Gallipoli Peninsula to the port city of Sestos, a final stretch of around 70km.

When he got there Alexander was able to gaze out across the Dardanelles and see, with considerable relief, that they were empty of Persian ships.

While his army trailed into Sestos and his fleet came up the Dardanelles, Alexander set off on the first of what would prove to be a whole series of neatly calculated and widely publicised propaganda moves. He rode with a small escort of horsemen down the Gallipoli peninsula to Elaeum. Just outside this small and otherwise insignificant town was located the tomb of the legendary hero Protesilaus. The name of Protesilaus is largely unknown, but in Alexander's day it was well known through the hero's role in the legendary siege of Troy.

Protesilaus was king of a part of Thessaly and uncle to the even greater hero Jason, who was later to go in search of the Golden Fleece. When the expedition to Troy was planned, Protesilaus brought 40 ships, complete with the crews and warriors to fill them. Given that these ships were probably pentekonters, or something similar, he will have been leading about 2,000 men. Before the expedition had set out the oracle at Delphi had predicted that the first Greek ashore on Asia would meet an early death, but win eternal fame. When the Greek fleet approached the Trojan shoreline, Protesilaus saw that he was leading the way and his ship was the first to run ashore. Being a hero of the old school, Protesilaus did not flinch. He leapt down into the surf and waded ashore. Within seconds he fell dead with a javelin in his chest that had been thrown by the Trojan hero Hector.

Reverently and with due ceremony, Alexander offered sacrifice on the tomb of Protesilaus. He then walked down to the harbour of Elaeum where he had built an altar dedicated to Zeus, Athene and Heracles. Having offered sacrifices there, Alexander boarded a warship, along with his entourage. Already on the ship was a bull, garlanded with flowers. When the ship reached the point halfway between Europe and Asia, Alexander sacrificed the bull to Poseidon, allowing the blood to flow into the seas. He then took a golden goblet of wine and poured that into the sea as a sacrifice to the Nerieds.

By the time the ship had reached the Asian shore, Alexander was in his full armour. The spot to land had been carefully chosen. It was the bay known as the Achaean Harbour, the same spot where the Greeks had landed when going to attack Troy. Like Protesilaus before him, Alexander jumped down from his ship and waded through the surf to reach the shore. Alexander then erected a second altar to Zeus, Athene and Heracles before making more sacrifices.

This curious little incident is often skated over by modern writers, but to the people of the time it was of huge importance and symbolism. By first visiting the tomb of Protesilaus, and then recreating his landing in Asia, Alexander was deliberately likening himself and his expedition to the great heroes of Homer's poems. Alexander was, we know, a great fan of Homer and sought consciously to emulate the men of whom the blind poet wrote. All Greeks were also familiar with the story of the Trojan War. They would have recognised at once the significance of Alexander's actions. Protesilaus had been the first man ashore into Asia of an army that went on to defeat and destroy the great Asian enemy of the Greeks.

Moreover, Protesilaus was a former ruler of Thessaly – probably from Phylace. Alexander was now the ruler of Thessaly and his army contained many men from that area of Greece. Those men would have particularly appreciated this gesture to their heroic forebear.

The dedication of the two altars to Zeus, Athene and Heracles also requires some explanation. Zeus was the greatest of the Greek gods and his influence over the affairs of humans was immense, so his favour was highly prized. Perhaps more practically, Zeus was probably the only deity who was worshiped equally by all the peoples of the Greek world. Given that he had with him men drawn from across Greece and beyond, it is likely that Alexander was seeking to emphasise the ties that bound them all together. The worship of Zeus was one such, and so needed to be made clear as the great invasion began.

Athene was the patron goddess of the city of Athens. By choosing this goddess, Alexander was partly showing his own admiration for Athenian culture and learning. He was also emphasising a link back to the dark days when Persia had invaded Greece in 490 and 480. On the former occasion, the Persian invasion had been defeated on the plains of Marathon by an army composed overwhelmingly of Athenians. The second Persian invasion had been resisted by the leadership of Athens and Sparta, though many smaller states had joined the war effort. The victory of the Athenian fleet at Salamis had undoubtedly been the turning point in that campaign, though it had been made possible only by the Spartans who delayed the Persians at Thermopylae and lost their lives doing it.

Alexander was, therefore, firmly attaching his invasion of the Persian Empire to that empire's invasion of the Greece so many years earlier. One of Alexander's declared aims in launching the invasion was to exact revenge on the Persians for the events of 490 and 480. Making these sacrifices to Athene was emphasising the point to the human world, while at the same time sending an equally clear message to the gods.

He was also, perhaps incidentally, delivering a snub to Sparta. As we have already seen, Sparta had refused to join the League of Corinth and sent none of her famous troops to take part in the invasion. By honouring Athene, Alexander was giving Athens precedence over Sparta.

The third of the deities to whom Alexander dedicated his two altars on either side of the Dardanelles was Heracles, or Hercules as he is more widely known today. Heracles was the supposed ancestor of the Macedonian royal family, so Alexander's choice might be interpreted as nothing more than family pride. More likely, Alexander was again playing on ancient legends to boost his present enterprise.

Today we know Heracles mostly as the personification of physical strength, but his chief role in Greek religion was as a protector of humanity against the passions and tempers of the gods. He was also held to have been the founder of the Olympic Games. These games had enormous importance among the Greeks. All wars were supposed to cease while the Olympic Games were in progress and anyone travelling to or from them was considered sacred. Like Zeus, Heracles had a widely spread cult and veneration of Heracles was a unifying factor among the Greeks.

During his many and varied adventures, Heracles had spent a good deal of time among the Greek cities of Asia Minor. He had rescued Ephesus from a gang of Cercopes, a form of malicious demons. He had rescued Hesione, daughter of the king of Ilium from a monstrous serpent. He had killed a gigantic snake that was eating livestock in the valley of the River Sagaris. He had also saved the lands around Miletus from the cruel tyrant Lityerses. This Lityerses was in the habit of abducting men to work in his fields and then, once the harvest was gathered in, of slitting their throats so that their blood would fertilise the fields for the next crop.

All these favours done to the peoples of Asia Minor will have been widely known to the Greeks who lived there in Alexander's day. By marking out Heracles as the recipient of sacrifices, Alexander was reminding them of these favours. He was, no doubt, seeking to liken himself to his semi-divine ancestor and to imply that he was coming to Asia to undertake similar acts and duties for the benefit of the Greeks who lived there. In particular the slaying by Heracles of the tyrant Lityerses would have been important. Along with revenge, Alexander was coming to Asia to free the Greek cities from Persian rule.

Having thus crossed to Asia in dramatic and symbolic style, Alexander rode south to fulfil more ritual and propaganda activities. A few kilometres to the south stood the town of Troy. Neither as a fan of Homer nor as the leader of a Greek invasion of Asia would Alexander have wanted to miss a visit to this great site. And Alexander was determined to milk the occasion for all it was worth.

By 334BC, Troy retained but a shadow of its former glory. The city that had been destroyed by Agamemnon and his fellow Greeks in Homer's works had been the chief city of the rich, fertile area known as Illium. The Trojan War of legend was believed in Alexander's day to have taken place around the year 1184BC, though it is now generally dated a century or two earlier when the power of Agamemnon's city of Mycenae was at its height. Since then Troy had been rebuilt since Illium was still a productive and wealthy agricultural district. Other cities had, however, taken over Troy's leading role in the area. When Alexander arrived, Troy was a small town, not much more than a village.

It did, however, retain its links to the past and there was plenty for the locals to show to tourists from Greece or from Greek cities. The latter day Trojans will have had some days warning that Alexander was on his way and clearly prepared the reception with care. They did not, however, get everything right.

Alexander's visit began well enough. Some distance north of Troy were the graves of Ajax, Achilles and Patroclus. At each he undertook a ceremony, the importance of which would have been appreciated by his contemporaries.

Achilles was the hero with whom Alexander most closely identified himself. In Homer, Achilles is the very epitome of the great warrior. He is equipped with magnificent arms and armour, by which he is recognised by friend and foe alike. His passions were as mighty as his skill with arms. He was famous both for his outbursts of generosity and for his anger and his infamous sulk which kept him in his tent for days on end. It was during this sulk that Achilles lent his armour to his friend Patroclus so that the Greeks would see their hero apparently joining the fight and so take heart in the battle. The ruse went horribly wrong when Patroclus was killed by Hector. This prompted Achilles to leave his tent and rejoin the battle. He killed Hector, but was himself killed storming the Scaean Gate of Troy as the city fell.

Alexander was already well known to idolise Achilles and to seek to emulate him in many ways. At Troy, he took this ambition very seriously.

When he arrived, Alexander was met by the elders of Troy. They offered to show him the lyre of Alexander, one of the sons of King Priam of Troy in Homer's *Iliad*. Presumably they thought that he would be interested in a link to his legendary namesake. But Alexander was playing the role of a Greek conqueror and he wanted links with Achilles. Alexander brushed the offer aside. 'For that lyre, I care little,' he said. 'I have come for the lyre of Achilles with which, as Homer says, he would sing of the prowess and glories of brave men.' Abashed, the Trojans withdrew.

Alexander had his own theatricals to hand. He summoned to his side an utterly obscure sailor from the fleet. This man had obviously been brought along to Troy for this moment alone as he is never mentioned again in any account of Alexander's life. The man's name was Menoitios, the name of the father of Patroclus. The sailor crowned Alexander with a golden crown to symbolise the homage of the ancient heroes to the new one.

Alexander then stripped naked and oiled his body. This was how athletes prepared for action in Alexander's day. Taking a sacred garland, Alexander then ran from the gates of Troy to the tomb of Achilles and laid the garland as a tribute to his hero. Meanwhile, Hephaistion likewise stripped and ran to put a garland on the tomb of Patroclus.

For all the importance of the relationship between Alexander and Hephaistion that the ancient sources emphasise again and again, this is the first time in Alexander's life that the two men are known to have been together. It is presumed that Hephaistion was educated by Aristotle alongside Alexander, but this is not certain. The relationship between the two young men was intense, but enigmatic. Ancient writers were not inclined to go into much detail, though gossip was never so reticent, and at this point in time it is difficult to be certain exactly what form the relationship took. But by allotting to Hephaistion the role of honouring Patroclus as he honoured Achilles, Alexander was making a very public statement about the strength of their friendship.

Alexander was now ready to enter Troy itself. He first visited the Temple of Zeus. Here he performed the usual ritual sacrifices. Then he prayed to the long dead King Priam of Troy, who had been killed by Neoptolemus, the son of Achilles, on this very spot. Alexander prayed that Priam would not be angry at the arrival in his old home of a new Greek army.

Alexander then made his way to the Temple of Athene. Having performed the usual sacrifices, Alexander took off his armour and laid it on the altar together with his weapons. In return the priests gave him a shield and sword that dated back to the days of the Homeric siege. These hallowed weapons would never leave his side, and would remain with him to his death. Here Alexander was deliberately copying Achilles. The long dead hero had been given sacred armour by the god Hephaestes, the blacksmith of the gods. Now Alexander had his sacred armour. The shield was particularly impressive and although the details of its design have not been recorded, it was instantly recognisable.

The altar of the Temple of Athene at Troy had been the scene of two previous events of great importance. In 380BC Xerxes, Emperor of Persia, had come here to sacrifice dozens of cattle to the goddess on his way to invade Greece and lay waste to Athens. As a Zoroastrian, Xerxes could not have been serious in trying to win the favour of the goddess, but he was seeking to show the Greeks that they were not alone in vying for the favours of the gods. Either way the sacrifice had failed, as did Xerxes's invasion of Greece. Perhaps Alexander wanted to blot out that memory and reclaim the alter for the Greeks.

Perhaps of more immediate interest to Alexander were the events that were believed to have taken place here during the sack of Troy. Cassandra was the beautiful daughter of King Priam. She had been spotted by the god Apollo who promised her the gift of prophecy if she would become his lover. Cassandra agreed, but as soon as she had got her gift she abandoned Apollo. The jilted god got his revenge by ensuring that although her predictions were true, nobody would ever believe her.

When the Greeks poured into Troy, having tricked their way in with the famous wooden horse, Cassandra fled for safety to the Temple of Athene. She put her arms around the cult statue of the goddess and claimed sanctuary. This was respected by the looting Greek warriors until Ajax arrived. Drunk with fury and hungry for revenge, Ajax tore Cassandra from the statue and raped her in the temple. Athene demanded recompense for this act of violent sacrilege, and so began one of the most bizarre and brutal religious rituals of the Greek world.

Ajax had come from the city of Locri in Thessaly, so it fell to the nobles of Locri to pay the price. Every year two young virgins from the nobility of Locri were selected. They were taken to the coast of Illium and put ashore. Alone and unarmed the frightened teenage girls then had to try to reach the Temple of Athene while the locals tried to catch and kill them. If either or both of the girls made it they had to shave their heads and serve as the Priestess of the Temple until another girl managed to survive the murderous rite. Either at the Temple of Athene or at the Tomb of Ajax, Alexander announced that the deadly ritual that had lasted almost a thousand years was at an end. The nobles of Locri were absolved from their punishment. In recompense, Alexander promised to completely rebuild the Temple of Athene. It is the ruins of that temple that stand on the site to this day.

Alexander had one more task to perform and, rather pointless as it may have seemed to those involved, it had enormous political impact. Alexander solemnly summoned the few people who lived in the small town to attend a meeting. The people of Troy may have wondered what this strange and powerful visitor from distant Macedon had in store for them. After all this was the king who boasted of emulating Achilles, the great hero of the campaign to destroy their city so many centuries earlier.

In fact Alexander announced that he was giving Troy a new constitution. That constitution was a democratic one in which all adult male citizens were to have an equal say in the government of the City of Troy. Once again, Alexander was playing politics on a grand stage knowing that his actions would be reported – after all he had a whole team of writers and poets to make sure of that.

The bemused citizens of Troy might have wondered what to make of their new rights, and even doubted whether they wanted them. But that was not the point. Alexander had intended his message for all the Greeks who lived in cities under the rule of the Persian Emperor. Alexander had already claimed that he was coming to set them free from Persian rule. Now, at the very first city that he had visited he had granted democracy to people who had never enjoyed it before. It was a powerful move, and one that was not missed by those who were intended to take notice.

Alexander then left Troy, sending his escort of Thessalian horsemen to ride around the tombs of Achilles, Ajax and Patroclus. The galloping riders called out the dead heroes to join the new Greek army in the new campaign against the Asiatic enemy. The gods had been appeased, the heroes had been called upon. Ritual and propaganda had been taken care of.

Everything had been prepared with care and precision. Now Alexander had to return to his army. The fighting was about to begin.

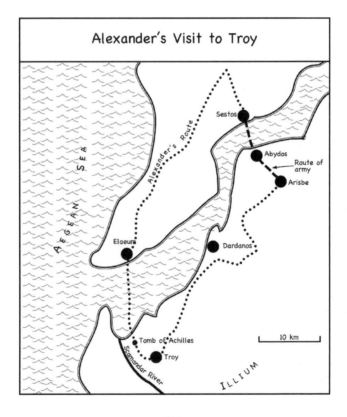

CHAPTER SEVEN

The Satraps Muster

The Persians knew that Alexander and his army were coming. Preparations on such a scale simply could not be hidden, even if Alexander had tried. In any case, the Macedonians had enough enemies in Greece to ensure that regular and accurate reports would be flowing across the Aegean Sea to the Persian Empire.

Exactly what Darius was doing about these reports is a matter of some confusion. The Persians did not write histories of their empire, so we are reduced to studying what other people wrote about them. Recently excavations have turned up a large number of documents from the Persian government archives from this period. Most of these are administrative documents that provide useful background, but little detail of events. In any case the Iran-Iraq area where most finds turn up is notoriously turbulent and archaeological work is usually difficult, sometimes dangerous and occasionally impossible.

To understand the reaction of the Persians to news of Alexander's coming campaign it is necessary first to have a brief look at the organisation of the Empire. In essence, the Persian Empire had not changed much over the previous two centuries. At its centre was the monarch, surrounded by a court of nobles and supported by a large and highly efficient bureaucracy. All the taxable wealth of the empire flooded into the royal court, which usually remained in Persia itself. The key communications links ran to and from the central area of Persia. It was, by this date, highly unusual for the monarch to leave the wealthy and productive central areas of the empire. When he did so it was a major event.

The empire was divided up into a number of satrapies, each governed by a satrap. The satraps were always noblemen of the highest rank, drawn from the leading families of Persia. These men were usually related to the emperor either by blood or by marriage. They were appointed by the monarch and remained in place for as long as the monarch wanted them to. A satrap might remain in place for decades, or be removed after a year or two. Whether these appointments and removals were a sign of the ruler's pleasure or if men were given specific tasks and moved on when they had completed their job we don't know. Certainly there does not seem to have been much unrest when a satrap was removed from office, so perhaps a satrapy was simply a rung on the career ladder of government officials.

On the other hand, there is no doubt that satraps had a large degree of freedom from central control. And this was especially the case in areas distant from Persia, such as Asia Minor. A satrap had the tasks of raising taxes, enforcing peace and dispensing justice in his satrapy. To fulfil these tasks he had his own court, his own bureaucracy and his own army. A proportion of the taxes, usually in the form of gold or silver bullion, had to be sent off to the central court. If the monarch decided that any particular task needed doing in an area, it was the responsibility of the satrap to get it done.

The key thing to bear in mind about the Persian Empire is that it was so vast. By the time Alexander invaded, it stretched from the Dardanelles to the Himalayas, from the Sudan to the far shores of the Caspian Sea. It was by far the largest state on earth, and the richest. It had more men and material than any Greek could imagine. The resources were inexhaustible. Darius knew that he could raise, train and despatch army after army to fight his enemies.

In the decades preceding Alexander's invasion the Persian Empire had shrunk somewhat. Thrace and the lower Danube had been abandoned a century or more before, while the lands east of the Himalayas had been allowed to drift into independence more recently. These losses were not particularly important. The lands in question were not very wealthy, and it probably cost the Persians more to hold on to them than they raised in taxes. Nevertheless the loss of these provinces might indicate an underlying decline in the empire.

Of rather more immediate concern was a series of murderous events within the Persian hierarchy itself. The exact course of events is confused, largely because Darius put about a version that, even at the time, was not accepted by everyone. He may have had a very good reason for covering up what had happened.

In 338BC the ruler Artaxerxes III died. He was succeeded by his eldest son, Ochus. This Ochus promptly died himself and was succeeded by his son, Arses. Arses was a young man and, although we don't know his precise age, he was old enough to have a wife and several children. The real power in Persia under Arses was the Egyptian eunuch Bagoas. This man had been promoted to be chief minister by Artaxerxes III, a position he retained during the brief rule of Ochus and into that of Arses. Although of humble, non-Persian origins, he had risen right to the top of the government of the Persian Empire.

In 336BC Arses died, along with his children. The descendants of Artaxerxes III were thus extinct, so the throne passed to a cousin named Darius, the third man of that name to rule the Persian Empire.

The new monarch immediately announced that the villain of the piece was the eunuch minister Bagoas. According to Darius, Bagoas had murdered Ochus in order to place the youthful and inexperienced Arses on the throne. As an older and experienced statesmen with a wide network of personal links, Bagoas had been able to treat Arses as a mere puppet, and Darius declared that Bagoas had been the real ruler of the empire.

The eunuch had turned against Arses, again according to Darius, when the young monarch had started to question his orders and overbearing manner. Bagoas had then poisoned Arses and his family. He had then turned to Darius, another young and relatively inexperienced prince, to again be a mere puppet through whom Bagoas could continue to rule. Darius claimed that he had uncovered the machinations of the evil eunuch just in time to stop himself from being disposed of in his turn.

Bagoas was dragged out and executed. More lurid details were then added to the story. The body of Ochus had been fed to cats to eat, while his leg bones were made into handles for the knives that Bagoas used at the dinner table. Darius produced the knives, which did have bone handles, as proof.

Exactly what had happened was not really clear. Perhaps Darius was telling the truth. But it must be said that an Egyptian eunuch who was already unpopular among the Persian nobles for throwing his weight around did make a very convenient scapegoat. It may be that Darius had murdered Arses to get the throne. Or he may simply have taken advantage of the sudden death of the monarch to grab power himself. We will never know.

What does seem certain, however, is that Darius was not from the inner circles of the royal family. He was descended from Darius II, who had died in 404BC. There were plenty of other princes closer to the throne than he was himself. There was almost certainly a coup of some kind. No doubt Darius played up the story of Bagoas – even if he did not invent it himself – in order to appeal to the Persian nobility whose support he needed.

These upheavals at the very heart of the empire cannot have failed to have had some sort of impact on the empire. Those men passed by when Darius took the throne might have been unhappy with the new monarch. Certainly many satraps and nobles in the provinces will have been related to Arses in some way. They might or might not have accepted Darius's version of events. They cannot have failed to be nervous about what orders might come out of the royal court. The murder or execution of rivals was not unknown in Persia.

One very immediate impact that these events had was that Darius kept the Royal Army with him in Persia. The elite of the Persian army was held back to secure Darius's grip on the throne and would not be available to confront Alexander when he first arrived in Asia.

Darius may have had another reason to keep most of his Royal Army at home. The Persians had been expecting the invasion to be led by Philip. The reputation of Philip had spread far and wide, even to the halls of the Persian monarch at the main imperial residence at Persepolis. Nobody doubted that Philip was a military genius. He had expanded Macedonian power, encroaching into lands that had once been Persian. He had remodelled the armed forces of Macedon to make them the finest in the Greek world. And he had conquered all the Greek states. He had won every battle he had fought, and won them convincingly.

The murder of Philip had been greeted with relief and jubilation by the enemies of Macedon. When it became clear that Alexander had secured his grip on power, Darius will undoubtedly have made inquiries about him. All that was known for certain about Alexander at this time was that he was a good horseman and courageous fighter who drank heavily and had a quick temper.

Macedon's enemies in the Greek states disparaged Alexander as 'the boy' and mocked his pretensions to homeric hero status. A famous series of jokes linked him not to Achilles – the great hero of Homer's works – but to Margites the buffoon. The wit of the jokes depends on a detailed knowledge of the works of Homer and other writers who dealt with the Trojan War, but the mockery of comparing Alexander to a man who could not count beyond ten and who lacked all the skills of war is clear enough.

Since the sources of information on which the Persians relied were those hostile to the Macedonians, it is likely that the picture they got of Alexander was of an untried and foolish teenager given to too much drink. With the benefit of hindsight, of course, we know that Alexander had great talents to match his faults, but Darius had only the reports that reached him.

The sudden fall of Thebes sent shock waves through the Greek world and the news will have quickly reached Darius in distant Persepolis. But even Alexander's most ardent supporters agreed that the city fell because of the quick thinking of Perdiccas and the dogged fighting ability of Philip's veterans. Alexander had had little to do with it. The event would have reinforced the view that the Macedonian army was magnificent, but that Alexander himself was nothing special.

But if Darius did not send the Royal Army to meet the invader, he did send a large amount of gold. It was with this help that the satraps of Asia Minor had to content themselves and lay their plans.

We do not know for certain what the original plans of the satraps were. The ancient writers tell us only what they did once Alexander arrived. It is not difficult to reconstruct those plans, however, by looking at the preparations that the satraps made and where they and their men were when Alexander crossed the Hellespont.

At this date, Asia Minor was divided into several satrapies: Hellespontine, Mysia, Lydia, Lycia, Pisidia, Cilicia, Cappadocia, Paphlagonia and Phrygia. Each of these was ruled by a Satrap, but the internal organisation of each was very different. The inland satrapies were governed more or less directly by the satraps, though the mountain tribes tended to be left to look after themselves so long as they paid tribute and caused no trouble. The coastal satrapies included many Greek cities and kingdoms. The precise way in which these were governed is a matter of dispute. Alexander and his supporters portrayed them as being ground under the heel of Persian brutality. Other sources make it clear that they enjoyed varying degrees of self-government. One thing is certain, the satraps did not trust them to remain loyal to Darius.

As well as the gold, Darius had sent to Asia Minor one other contribution to the war effort that was to prove to be of great use to the satraps: the mercenary Memnon of Rhodes.

This Memnon was a talented and highly regarded military leader. Certainly in 334BC he was reckoned to be far superior to the young Alexander who was marching against him. He had already served the Persian state for many years, and had taken a Persian wife named Barsine. This Barsine was a member of the royal family, later tradition made her a daughter of Darius himself. We know that in the final days of Artaxerxes III, Memnon had left Persian service and gone to Macedonia. No doubt he took the opportunity to study the Macedonian army and its tactical methods. It may be that Memnon left after he fell out with the old king, or perhaps with his chief minister Bagoas.

When he returned to Persia is unclear, but the fact that he was so highly regarded by Darius might indicate that he returned when that monarch gained the throne. It is possible, but no more than that, that Memnon might have had a hand in the coup that put Darius in power. That would certainly explain why a foreigner was married to the great king's daughter. It would also explain Memnon's position of power and influence, which seems to have been far greater than might be expected from a mere hired mercenary.

The author with a helmet of the style worn by Memnon of Rhodes, the mercenary commander on the Persian side during the Granicus campaign.

Memnon arrived in Asia Minor early in 335BC. It was he who fought Parmenio near Ephesus and chased the Greek mercenaries back north to take up winter quarters near the Hellespont. Memnon took it upon himself to mint coins with which to pay his men. Rather than use the coins of the satraps or nearby Greek cities, Memnon minted thousands of silver coins on which he stamped a map of the battlefield outside Ephesus.

As autumn closed in toward the end of 335, Memnon met with the satraps and drew up a plan to meet Alexander. When making their preparations, the satraps will have been as aware of the wider strategic issues as anyone else. They no doubt requested that the Persian fleet should come north to block the Dardanelles and stop Alexander from even entering the Persian Empire. They were not, however, in a position to order the fleet north. Darius had made it clear that the fleet's main focus had to be the defeat of the Egyptian revolt. If that task had not been completed, it was unlikely that the ships would come north.

The satraps had to lay their plans on the assumption that the fleet would remain tied up in Egypt and that Alexander would land in Asia Minor.

Like everyone else, they knew that the harvest was due to be reaped in early June. They expected Alexander to move out of Therme as the harvesting began so as to take advantage of the newly gathered crops during his march through Thrace. He would, therefore, arrive in Persian territory toward the end of the traditional harvest period ready to live off the land.

The Persians did not intend to give him the chance. Orders seem to have been issued that as grain was harvested it was to be gathered into cities and fortresses where it could be guarded securely. Livestock was also to be rounded up and driven to safety so that Alexander and his men would be unable to find meat on the hoof. No doubt the local peasants were also under orders to be ready to follow their crops and goods into strongholds. The nobles and wealthy families would need no prompting to move all their wealth and belongings to safekeeping as an enemy army approached.

Alexander and his Macedonians would, therefore, be faced with a land stripped clean of food. No matter how much food Alexander might bring with him on ships, the logistics of campaigning inland would severely limit his room for manoeuvre. Effectively he would be limited to campaigning close to the coast. And with all the good ports in fortified cities that had closed their gates to the Macedonians, the places where he could land food would be few and far between. Within a few weeks at most the Macedonians would be forced to withdraw or starve.

For the plan to work, however, the cities needed to be held firmly against Alexander. The events of the previous year when Parmenio had been campaigning along the western coast of Asia Minor had shown Memnon and the Satraps that some of those cities were not to be trusted. Nearly every Greek city in Asia Minor had a faction among its citizens that was supportive of the Macedonian invasion. In many cities that faction formed the majority. Even where it did not a city might be betrayed by even a small internal group when Alexander's army was camped outside.

It would be no good the satraps making even the most careful of arrangements to get food under lock and key, if the cities were to open their gates as soon as the Macedonians arrived. Each city had to be supplied with a garrison of tough troops whose loyalty to the Persian cause was beyond question.

That was where the cash sent by Darius came in. In the ancient world few military forces were as reliable as mercenaries who were being paid in cold, hard coins.

It must be borne in mind that throughout ancient times, becoming a mercenary was a perfectly acceptable, even respectable, career option for a young man. All free men were expected to know how to fight and to take their place in the army if called upon to do so. In the Greek world, citizens were expected to have immediately to hand weapons, arms and armour kept always in good condition and ready to use. All citizens underwent some form of military training before they legally became adults.

It was not at all unusual for these trained and armed young men to go off to serve as mercenaries for a few years. the temptation to do so was all the greater for sons who did not have the prospect of a farm or business to inherit. The money that could be earned by a few years as a mercenary could easily be enough to buy land to form a farm sufficiently productive enough to see the man settled for life.

Men from any area might choose to fight as mercenaries, but Greeks were especially prized as they came ready trained and ready equipped. The precise way in which the mercenary business was organised is not clear. In the ancient writings of this period we catch only glimpses of the trade.

Certainly respected and skilled commanders, such as Memnon of Rhodes, could hire themselves out as individuals. Some were used to command armies, others to train armies and some to do both. These famous leaders no doubt kept themselves informed of political events in the various states of the known world and remained in touch with kings, tyrants and city councils. They would apply for jobs, or be sent for, when the need arose.

Some of these leaders kept permanent forces of mercenaries in their employment. These men were tough, old regulars who formed a personal bodyguard for their leader in battle. At other times they might be viewed as being a team of trainers and drill instructors. A leader with a good body of supporters was highly valued. These small teams of full time mercenaries led by recognised chiefs were often hired by states to train the local militias. Theirs was a permanent way of life – a career with recognised ranks and opportunities for advancement.

The vast bulk of mercenaries, however, were rank and file soldiers who might have served for a few years only. They might then go home, or stay on to join the permanent mercenary cadres.

There seem to have been two ways in which such men might have joined the mercenary trade. The first was when recruiters travelled around villages and towns looking to hire men. One must imagine the permanent mercenaries tramping around remote areas looking for young men who owned their own gear and who could be induced to sign up.

Most governments were quite content to allow recruiters to move through their territory, so long as they did not come from an enemy. Most agricultural societies have more young men than they need, and more than there is land to support. Having these men go off to fight other people's wars was a convenient way to channel their aggressive instincts into activities that did not disrupt their home society. Indeed, the home country might well benefit from the cash earned.

There were also recognised mercenary markets, where young men would go when they wanted to become mercenaries or where experienced mercenaries would find a new employer when the old one did not need them any more. By the 340s the largest of these markets was to be found in the Spartan town of Taenarum. The city had a small port, a market place and plenty of open space in which mercenaries for hire could camp out.

It should be remembered that Sparta had not joined the League of Corinth, so the mercenary market of Taenarum would have remained open to Persian recruiters. These men were busy during the winter of 335–334BC. In 335 Memnon had begun his campaign against Parmenio with 5,000 mercenaries. By January 334, Memnon had no less than 20,000 Greek mercenaries under his command.

That Memnon was able to hire so many Greek mercenaries so easily speaks volumes for how the contemporary Greeks viewed Alexander's invasion. Alexander claimed to be acting for all Greeks when he sought revenge for the Persian invasions of 150 years before and in particular for those Greeks living under Persian rule. In reality, of course, the campaign was more about Macedonian power and enriching the Macedonian state than anything else. Many Greeks recognised this and were quite happy to join the Persians against the Macedonians.

Others resented Macedonian hegemony in Greece itself. They may have viewed service with the Persians as the best means of crushing Macedonian military might, and so paving the way for their own state to throw off Macedonian control. Still others were men who had been exiled on the orders of Philip or Alexander – or who had fled before they could be arrested.

In fact, we don't really know where Memnon recruited his Greek mercenaries. No doubt some of them came from the market at Taenarum, while others may have made their own way to Asia Minor. It is also likely that many men were recruited from the Greek states that lay under Persian rule in Asia Minor.

Wherever they came from, the vast majority of these men were armed and trained as hoplites, the traditional heavy infantry of Greece. Each man carried a large shield, the aspis. This was about a metre across and weighed around 6kg. The shield was constructed of thin layers of wood glued together so that their grains of one layer ran counter to that of the one beneath it. A thin sheet of beaten bronze

A heavy Greek hoplite of the type that served as mercenaries under Memnon of Rhodes in the Persian army. Under Macedonian influence this man is wearing greaves and body armour, both of which had fallen out of fashion on the Greek mainland around 400BC, but which were now being seen more often. He wears a one piece corinthian style helmet that gave extremely good protection, but hampered hearing. This was acceptable in a dense phalanx, but could stop a man hearing orders when fighting in a more open formation.

faced the shield to give it a smooth, slippery face off which arrows or javelins could glance. The rim of the shield was flat, but the central area was deeply concave. The rim braced the arched layers of wood that made up the centre, giving a tough rigidity to the shield that a flat design would not have.

By this date most hoplites had adopted similar types of helmet to those worn in the Macedonian army. The close-fitting helmet that came down to the chin leaving only the eyes and mouth uncovered is familiar today. It is generally referred to as the Corinthian style, but it was decidedly old fashioned by the 340s.

Body armour had fallen out of favour by this date. The key to success lay in preserving the tight formation of the phalanx as it manoeuvred over the battlefield. Heavy armour served to encumber the wearer while he was trying to stay in formation with his fellows. It was also rendered almost superfluous by the defensive properties of the large shield when used properly in a tightly formed phalanx. Under Macedonian influence, however, forms of body armour were beginning to reappear. At least some of Memnon's mercenaries will have worn either the linothorax or the muscled cuirass made of sheet bronze.

The key offensive weapon of the hoplite was the dory type of spear. This weapon was around 2.5 metres long. It had a shaft of ash, which combined lightness with strength, and a head of bronze, though iron was coming into favour about this date. The butt end had a spike that could be used to jab the spear into the ground so that it remained upright. In an emergency the spike could be used as a weapon. Most hoplites had a sword as a secondary weapon to use if the spear broke.

It was the phalanx that was the key to hoplite success on the battlefield. Traditionally the phalanx was formed up eight ranks deep. The most experienced men were in the front and rear ranks, with the others in between. Each man was allotted about 60cm of frontage, meaning that most would be standing should to shoulder with their neighbours. The shields were held in front, facing the enemy, so that each man's shield overlapped that of the man to his left. The spears were held overarm so that they were clear of the shields and could be jabbed down towards the heads, shoulders and chests of the enemy.

Keeping a phalanx in order as it advanced over broken ground called for a great degree of discipline and skill. Most armies preferred to advance in a number of small columns, forming up into phalanx only when they approached the enemy.

As the hoplites advanced toward the enemy, the men would sing. There were some songs that were ubiquitous across Greece – those in praise of Ares the god of war being most common – but others were unique to individual city states. The situation must have been similar to that at modern sports matches where the supporters of rival teams sing and chant to boost morale and intimidate the opponents.

When the phalanx was about 200 metres from the enemy it would halt briefly for the ranks to be dressed and straightened. Then the order to charge would be given. The phalanx would begin to advance at a brisk walk that soon became a jog and then finally a run. The impact of the two front lines of men colliding could be formidable. The crash of colliding shields was followed by screams of wounded men, then by the grinding noise of shields rubbing against each other.

As the second, third and other ranks of the phalanx joined the fray the struggle came to resemble a deadly scrum. The men in the front two or three ranks would be stabbing at each other with their spears. Those behind pushed their shields into the backs of those in front and heaved with all their might. The aim was to push and shove so hard that the two phalanxes, firmly locked together, would begin to move. Those on the side going back would be more inclined to trip or stumble, allowing those advancing to kill them and step into their place.

It was to bolster the chances of a phalanx holding that some commanders preferred to form up their men deeper than the traditional eight ranks. Among most city states on the Greek mainland, 12 ranks had become commonplace by the 350s. Some went even further and at one battle the Thebans were ranked 25 deep.

Eventually a backwards moving phalanx would begin to fragment and break up. The collapse usually began at the back, which is why the rear rank was made up of the more experienced men. Veterans are less likely to turn and flee than novices.

Once a phalanx gave way, the pursuit could begin. It is easier to kill men who are running away than those who are standing and fighting. The majority of casualties in any battle took place during the pursuit, and those that were defeated regularly lost three times as many men as the victors.

In fact, most hoplite battles did not get as far as this. Faced by greater numbers or more disciplined troops, many a phalanx faltered to a halt as it advanced. If a phalanx retreated in good order casualties would be low, but if it charged and then broke up they would be much heavier. Only men confident of victory could be induced to charge.

Some phalanxes broke up even before battle was joined. At the Battle of Amphipolis in 422 the Spartans faced an Athenian army. The Spartan phalanx advanced with its customary discipline and determination. They halted to dress their lines, then gave their usual wild war shout. At the sound, the Athenians fled.

Such were the men that Memnon had recruited to serve his Persian employer. But it must be said that the Persian plan did not envisage the hoplites facing the Macedonians in open battle. The primary role of the mercenary hoplites was to garrison cities and fortresses. They would man the walls, guard the gates and keep a close eye on the stored food. Memnon could rely on his hired mercenaries much better than on the militias of the cities.

But the armed forces waiting to meet Alexander were not composed exclusively of mercenary hoplites. There were also the local armies of the satrapies of Asia Minor. The men in these armies came as both cavalry and infantry, probably there were more of the latter. No accurate records have survived to tell us how many of these men were available to the Persian satraps.

It seems reasonable to assume that these part-time militias could turn out in large numbers for short periods, especially for action within the boundaries of their home territory. When campaigning further afield, it would be reasonable to assume that a smaller number of men were sent. Perhaps the young and unmarried were asked to go outside their own satrapy.

The tribesmen of Mysia traditionally fought as javelin-armed light infantry. They seem to have carried three or four javelins each. The men had a small, round wooden shield and a simple conical helmet as defensive armour. They would probably do best when fighting a fluid, skirmishing type of battle and excelled at ambushes, raids and other guerrilla-style tactics.

The Mysians seem to have been habitually brigaded with the men raised from Lydia. The Lydians were not Greek, although several Greek cities lay along the Lydian coast. The culture of the Lydians and neighbouring Greek cities had, to some extent, fused. The Greeks had, for instance, adopted the Lydian invention of coins with enthusiasm. The Lydians, for their part, had adopted the Greek style of warfare. Their armies were equipped as hoplites and fought in phalanx.

The fact that the Lydians and Mysians were so often put together would indicate that they operated a joint tactical system when in battle. Presumably the Mysians used their javelins to skirmish with the enemy army, seeking to probe for weak spots and disrupt the formation. The Lydian phalanx would then charge the weakened enemy and seek to break through and begin the pursuit.

The Lycians were famous bowman. They seem to have been equipped with a lightweight bow which, like that used by the Cretans serving with Alexander, shot a short arrow with a small head. It must be assumed that these arrows were not very effective against armour, but given

A man from the militia raised in Mysia. He is typical of the militia infantry that would have been raised from the satrapies of Asia Minor and which fought at the Granicus. He has a simple helmet, perhaps of boiled leather, and a wooden shield. This man has two spears, though others carried three or four. These are intermediate weight weapons that could have been thrown or used for thrusting. Some men preferred to have a single heavier thrusting spear and two or more light javelins for throwing. Weaponry and equipment was very much down to personal choice and cost, but this figure is not untypical.

Alexander tames the horse Bucephalas. The story of how the teenage prince tamed the wild horse that nobody else could ride was one of the most widely reported events of his youth.

A young Alexander and his companions listen to a reading of the works of Homer. Alexander first heard the heroic stories of Homer when he was a boy and remained devoted to them throughout his life.

Alexander at the sack of Thebes. Having ordered that all citizens of the city should be sold as slaves, except those known to have opposed the rebellion against Macedonian rule, Alexander intervened to spare the descendants of the poet Pindar, whose works he admired.

Thais, the Athenian courtesan, tempts Alexander to set fire to the palace of the Persian Emperors during a drunken banquet. The burning of Persepolis was regretted by Alexander when he sobered up, but by then it was too late. Thais was the mistress of Ptolemy, one of Alexander's close friends and later the Pharaoh of Egypt.

A panel from the 'Alexander Sarcophagus'. The carving shows Alexander on a lion hunt with his closest companions and gives a good idea of the everyday dress of the Macedonians.

The figure of Alexander from the 'Alexander Sarcophagus'. The portrait was probably carved only a few years after Alexander's death. Although the sarcophagus shows Alexander on two of its four panels, it is thought to have been made for Abdalonymus, the nobleman appointed to rule the city of Sidon by Alexander. Abdalonymus appears on the two smaller carved panels.

Alexander sends the trophies of victory to Athens from the battlefield of Granicus on the day after the battle. The trophies included several sets of Persian armour, a traditional symbol of victory in ancient Greece.

A contemporary bust of Alexander the Great. The straight nose and flowing, wavy hair are features of all his portraits, as is the leftward tilt of the head.

The Propylaea entrance to the Acropolis of Athens as it appeared in Alexander's time. Alexander admired the culture of Athens, but remained wary of her power.

The Athenian Acropolis as it was in Alexander's day. The Acropolis was originally the fortified citadel, but by this date had become the centre of the religious and ceremonial life of the city.

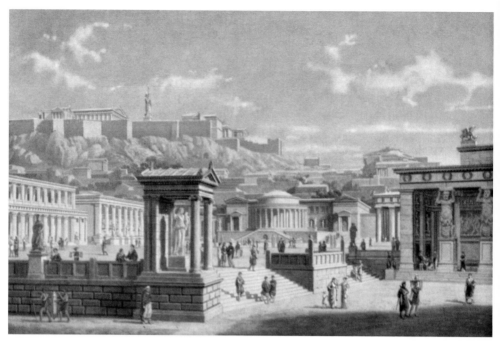

The Athenian Agora, or marketplace, as it was a few years after Alexander's time. The Agora was the focus of Athenian business and financial affairs.

The facade of the Temple of Athena on the Athenian Acropolis. This temple was the focus for Athenian civic pride, so when Alexander sent the spoils of the Granicus to this temple he was making a powerful political statement.

The interior of the Temple of Athena was dominated by a massive statue of the goddess. The statue was made entirely of ivory, for the deity's skin, and gold, for her clothes.

The ruins of the Temple of Apollo at Corinth. It was here that Alexander called the meeting of the Greek League to approve his leadership of the joint expedition to invade Persia.

The Treasury of the Athenians at Delphi, a small temple reconstructed from the fallen stones in the 19th century. This is the most complete building on the site today.

The ruins of the oracular temple at Delphi. It was here that Alexander had his famous confrontation with the chief priestess that ended with him being declared to be 'The Invincible'.

The temple and religious complex at Delphi as it appeared about the time of Alexander's visit. This was the most important religious site in Greece at the time.

The Athenian orator Demosthenes makes one of his famous anti-Macedonian speeches on the Pnyx, the meeting place of the Athenian Council. After the destruction of Thebes, Athens turned against Demosthenes.

The great goddess Artemis as usually shown by Greek sculptors (right) and in the form of her cult statue at Ephesus (left). It is thought that the Ephesians' fertility goddess may have originally been a different deity from the Greek hunter goddess.

A Victorian reconstruction of the great Temple of Artemis at Ephesus as it was rebuilt after Alexander's visit.

A statue of the god Dionysus. This Greek god of wine and revelry was believed to have embarked on a lengthy tour of Asia in prehistoric times. Alexander's journeys were often likened to those of this god.

A Roman statue of the Greek hero Herakles, called Hercules by the Romans. Alexander believed himself to be descended from Herakles by way of his father and, therefore, from the great god Zeus who fathered Herakles on a mortal woman.

The great god Zeus was considered to be the father and ruler of most other deities in the Greek pantheon. He was believed to live on Mount Olympos from where he dispensed good and evil to mankind.

The goddess Athena, patron deity of Athens. The goddess was a virgin warrior goddess who protected heroes and, as here, mourned their death.

The Mausoleum of Halicarnassos was counted one of the Seven Wonders of the World. It was only about 25 years old when Alexander laid siege to the city. The huge size of the tomb and its magnificent sculptures impressed all who saw them.

A carving from Persepolis depicts a Persian monarch attended by servants carrying a parasol to shade him from the fierce sun.

The interior courtyard at Persepolis as imagined by a Victorian artist. The wealth of luxury at the palace amazed the Macedonians.

A Persian monarch supervises a feast, as depicted on a doorway at Persepolis. State entertainments and social functions fullfilled an important role in the Persian monarchy.

The 'Door of Darius' at Persepolis which carries a carving of that monarch. Each Persian monarch added to the complex of buildings at Persepolis.

The Gate of Xerxes, one of the main entrances to Persepolis. The massive stone carvings of winged bulls with the heads of gods were copied directly from earlier Assyrian gateways.

A view of the Gate of Xerxes at Persepolis. After the palace was destroyed by a fire begun by Alexander the site was abandoned.

The mighty stone carvings that flank the Gate of Xerxes at Persepolis. The sheer scale of the Persian monarch's royal palace dwarfed that of Alexander at Pella in Macedonia.

A reconstruction of the Gate of Xerxes as it was when first built. This was designed to be the main ceremonial entrance to Persepolis.

The main ceremonial centre of Persepolis as it was when Alexander arrived. Although shown here surrounded by empty space it in fact lay at the centre of an extensive complex of kitchens, storerooms and servant accommodation.

The royal palace of Persepolis as it appeared after excavation in the late 19th century.

The walls of the Great Staircase at Persepolis are carved with representations of the Persian monarch's subject peoples bringing tribute to the palace.

The Great Staircase of Persepolis as it was after excavation in the 19th century. The structure has since been partially restored.

The entrance to the mighty Hypostyle Hall of Persepolis. It was here that Alexander began the fire that destroyed the palace. Scorch marks can still be seen on the stonework near the foot of this doorway.

The exterior of the Hypostyle Hall of Persepolis as imagined by a Victorian artist. Most of what is shown here is based on the excavations of the site, though much of the detail is taken from other sites and written descriptions.

The ruins of the hypostyle hall as they appeared after the 19th century excavations. The standing pillars are all reconstructions.

The formal entrance to the Hypostyle Hall at Persepolis. The stones still bear the marks of the fire begun by Alexander that destroyed this magnificent building – possibly the largest roofed structure in the world at the time.

A largely imaginary reconstruction of the roof of the Hypostyle Hall of Persepolis. We know that the roof was constructed of cedar wood, painted in bright colours and hung with fabric, but the details shown here are drawn mostly from other structures.

Persian spearmen as carved into the walls of Persepolis. The flowing robes shown here were typical of the Persians, but were reserved for ceremonial occasions. The soldiers wore more practical tunics and trousers on campaign.

Soldiers of the Persian royal guard as depicted on glazed tiles found at Persepolis. These figures date from about a century before Alexander's time. The bows and arrows seem to have been abandoned by the time the Persians faced the Macedonians.

A Persian monarch kills a lion in a carving from Persepolis. Persian rulers were often depicted in this sort of stylised pose.

A reconstruction of the palace facade at Persepolis drawn by a Victorian artist. This view is based on the 19th century excavations and a fair amount of imagination.

Bandits wait to waylay a rider on the Persian Royal Road. The construction of this road and its various extensions was one of the most impressive feats of the Persian Empire. It was used by Alexander as a route for much of the later stages of his invasion of the Persian Empire.

The sale of slaves after the siege of Thebes. At least 3,000 citizens of Thebes, plus their wives and children were all sold into slavery at Alexander's command. It was a harsh and ruthless decision that served to cow all of Greece for the rest of Alexander's lifetime and ensure that no other rebellions took place.

Thessalian cavalry practice throwing javelins at a target while riding at full gallop. The skill of the Thessalian horsemen was widely admired and was much used by Alexander in his campaigns.

Thessalian cavalry as depicted on a Greek vase. The broad-brimmed hats and loose cloaks with the right arm left free were distinctive features of the Thessalians.

Alexander the Great, as depicted on a silver drachma coin issued early in his reign. Alexander is shown here wearing the lion's head helmet that was traditionally worn by the demi-god Herakles (Hercules). The Macedonian royal family claimed to be descended from Herakles. Never before had a mortal been portrayed on a coin. This move by Alexander was a bold departure from tradition.

The reverse of the silver drachma of Alexander the Great. This shows the god Zeus seated on his throne and holding an eagle and a sceptre. This is a conventional representation of the greatest god of the Greek pantheon.

The famous Gorgon's Head sculpture located at the Temple of Apollo at Didyma. Alexander visited this shrine after the Battle of the Granicus and subsequently adopted this sculpture as a symbol. He later had it painted or embossed on to his armour.

The interior of the Temple of Apollo at Didyma. Now roofless, this would have been a chamber kept in semi-darkness when Alexander visited. It was here that a miracle occurred that was interpreted as confirming the approval of Apollo for Alexander's invasion of the Persian Empire.

The colonnaded main street of Ephesus. The city's council chamber, where Alexander announced his instructions to the city, stood behind the row of columns to the right of this photo.

The tumbled ruins of the fabulous Temple of Artemis at Ephesus. The temple lay in ruins when Alexander visited as it had burned down on the day he was born and had not yet been rebuilt. Alexander donated money to the reconstruction, which resulted in the temple becoming one of the Seven Wonders of the Ancient World.

A modern re-enactor in hoplite equipment. This man wears a linothorax with scale armour sewn on to the main body section and shoulder straps. His helmet is of the bronze corinthian design. The size of his shield and spear are clear. This equipment is typical for the hoplites who fought on both sides during the Granicus campaign. (With thanks to the Hoplite Association)

A body of hoplites advance with shields held rim to rim and spears in the overarm position. In battle a phalanx would be made up of eight ranks of men, one close behind the other. (with thanks to the Hoplite Association)

The author at Didyma. Alexander the Great came to this famous sanctuary of Apollo after winning the Battle of the Granicus.

the small proportion of the body usually covered by armour at this time they were still very useful.

The Phrygians seem to have provided a higher proportion of cavalry than the other regions. They came with javelins and shields, and most of them seem to have carried swords as well.

The men from the Hellespontine and Paphlogonian areas were also armed primarily with javelins, though they had a heavy thrusting spear similar to that of the hoplite. Their shields were comparatively small, about 60cm across, so they would have formed a less impressively defensive phalanx than the hoplites. It is thought that they would open a battle with a shower of javelins, then charge forward with their thrusting spears in an attempt to smash a path through the enemy formation before it could recover from the damage caused by the javelins.

With the possible exception of the joint Mysian-Lydian units, the local troops that could be raised from the satrapies of Asia Minor would clearly be no match for the professional and carefully balanced Macedonian army in an open fight. They were too lightly armed and equipped to stand up to the dense phalanx and long sarissas of the invaders. Where they would excel would be at ambush and raids.

The local militias would be operating on their home ground where they would be familiar with the roads, paths, fords and passes. They could harass the invaders, coming out to strike when they had an advantage, then melt away into the hills or swamps when they did not.

At some point over the winter, the local satraps and Memnon received a welcome reinforcement from Darius. Mithridates, a son in law of Darius, arrived with a contingent of the Royal Army. Unlike the local levies, these men were hardened professionals with the equipment and training needed to take on Alexander's men with a reasonable chance of success. Unfortunately it is quite unclear how many men arrived with Mithridates.

Mithridates had with him at least one squadron – perhaps a thousand men – of the royal cavalry. These men were more heavily armoured than any horsemen in Alexander's army. They wore bronze helmets that had cheek flaps reaching down to lace up under the chin, so giving secure protection to the sides of the head. A deep brim jutting forward from the front and rear of the helmet gave protection to the face and back of the neck.

The royal horsemen also wore body armour. This seems to have been made up of a sleeveless linen jacket to which were sewn overlapping bronze scales. The left forearm was protected by leather or scale armour. The legs were covered by more scale armour in the form of wide flaps that reached from the hips to the ankles. The horse was also armoured.

This heavy Persian cavalryman is of a type that would have served only in the royal army. He carries two heavy throwing javelins plus a sword for hand to hand fighting. He wears a sleeveless tunic covered with metal scale armour, which also encases his legs. The horse has a metal plate on the front of its head and a scale armour apron protecting its chest. The helmet has a flared brim and hinged cheek pieces. Heavy cavalry serving in satrapal guard units would have been similar, but would have had less armour.

The front of the head was protected by a bronze plate, kept in place around the ears and muzzle. The horse's chest was covered by a sheet of scale armour held in place by leather straps that ran up and round the horse's neck.

As offensive weapons, these armoured horsemen carried two or three throwing javelins, and a long, slashing sword. It must be presumed that they would begin an action by launching a series of sweeping, wheeling attacks past and around the enemy during which they would hurl their javelins. When the enemy was sufficiently disordered, the horsemen would draw their swords to launch a battering-ram style charge with cold steel. We know that these men could launch an attack in a pointed formation. While we don't know the precise layout of this attack formation it seems to have been similar to that used by the Thessalians.

Mithridates also had with him a force of Bactrian light cavalry, perhaps around 2,000 men. These men lacked the armour of their comrades, but carried the same offensive weaponry of javelins and swords. They are assumed to have fought in a similar fashion, though their charges would have been less effective.

We do not know if Mithridates brought any of the professional infantry of the royal army, but it is reasonable to assume that he did. These men carried dished, round shields not unlike those of the Greek hoplites. They also each had a heavy, thrusting spear about three metres long. They lacked body armour or helmets of any kind. These men were trained to form up in a phalanx, though it may have been slightly looser than that of the Greeks. Their aim was to advance in support of the cavalry, then to charge forward to tackle any enemy formations that had not already given way.

Although it is nowhere stated, it seems that Mithridates and his men were intended to carry out the second part of Memnon's plan for the coming campaign. Assuming that the Persian fleet did arrive at some point, Memnon planned to send a sizeable force across the Aegean to Greece. He was well aware that many Greek states resented Macedonian control and were on the look out for an opportunity to throw off Alexander's rule. Memnon was probably in touch with many of Alexander's more implacable opponents. Once Mithridates and his men arrived in Greece, these states could be expected to rise in open rebellion against Macedon. While Alexander was in the Persian Empire champion-ing freedom for the Greek cities there, Mithridates would be in Greece doing exactly the same thing.

There is nothing fantastic or unbelievable about this overseas plan of Memnon. Persian armies had been transported across the sea before, and the Persian fleet was more than equal to the task. Moreover we know

This Persian light cavalryman is typical of the local militias that fought at the Granicus. He carries two throwing javelins and a sword for close combat. Neither he nor his horse has any form of armour, though some men may have worn helmets and a few had linothorax body armour.

that Demosthenes in Athens had received a consignment of Persian gold the year before to sustain his anti-Macedonian activities. No doubt more money was ready to be sent across the Aegean.

When the spring came in 334BC, Memnon put the plan that had been agreed with the satraps into operation. The mercenary hoplites were already in position as garrisons of the various cities and fotressess. They could be relied upon to keep the gates shut against Alexander, and to supervise the harvest so that every last sack of grain was brought inside the defensive walls.

The local militias were under orders to muster for war when the harvesting was over. They were not to offer a formal battle, but to harass and raid the invading army whenever they got the chance.

Mithridates and his men, probably grouped together with some mercenary hoplites, were to serve with Memnon himself. If Alexander got over the Dardanelles before the Persian fleet arrived from Egypt, Memnon probably intended to keep this high quality, heavily equipped force tightly under his own control so that he could use it to strike at Alexander whenever the opportunity arose. Once the fleet was off the Asian coast, Memnon would make a decision as to whether or not to send Mithridates to Greece. He later said that he was in favour of doing so.

It was undoubtedly a good plan that made the most of the resources available to Memnon and sought to minimise the advantages held by Alexander. But it depended entirely on getting the harvest in before Alexander arrived.

Towards the end of May, just as the harvesting was beginning, the thunderstroke fell. Memnon learned that Alexander was already on the march, was out of Macedonia and well on his way through Thrace. He would be in Asia before the harvest was in.

For neither the first nor the last time, Alexander would ruin his enemy's plans by marching faster than expected.

Hurriedly Memnon sent out messages to the satraps with the terrible news. Memnon was at the town of Zeleia with his mobile striking force. It was a good choice for an initial position to see what Alexander would do. Memnon knew that Callas and his men were encamped near Troy, so it was fairly obvious that Alexander would cross into Asia at the Hellespont, not far to the northeast at Byzantium – now Istanbul.

Immediately inland from the Hellespont was the vast mountain mass of Mount Ida and its adjacent massif. Alexander would have a choice of only two routes. He could march east along the coast toward Cyzicus, the wealthy island city that had already declared for him, or he could turn south toward the majority of the Greek cities that he claimed to be on his way to free from Persian rule.

Memnon must have calculated that Alexander would head for Cyzicus as his first move. By camping at Zeleia, Memnon was in a position to block Alexander's advance. He was also close to what is now the River Gonen, we do not know its ancient name. This river falls down from the Mount Ida massif, carving a valley as it does so. This valley offers a good route up over a rocky shoulder of Mout Ida and down to the coast at what is now the Edremit Gulf.

Getting an entire army over this rugged route would take a long time, if it were possible at all given the cumbersome size that was traditional to the Persians. Memnon and a small mounted force, however, could have made the journey in three days, much quicker than Alexnder could march his army around the longer coastal route. That would put Memnon on the spot to take command of local levies and organise the defences of rich cities such as Astyra or Pergamum. With luck he could block Alexander's advance at the spot near Assus, now Kucukkuyu, where the mountains come right down to the coast and the route between the two is only a few yards wide. By the mere fact that he had chosen Zeleia as the place to wait for news of Alexander's movements, Memnon showed his military skill.

It was at Zeleia that he met those satraps that arrived in time. These included Spithridates, satrap of Lydia, and Arsites, satrap of Phrygia. Also present were Arsamenes, Rheomithras, Petines and Niphates. All four of these men were satraps who came with their elite mounted units, though we do not know of which satrapies each was the ruler.

There followed a hurried discussion as to what should be done. It is a shame that our sources for the Persian side of things are so weak. The only version of what happened seems to come from the Greek mercenary who was used by Cleitarchus as a source. He was not present, being in the garrison at Halicarnassos, but he spoke to somebody who had been, perhaps even to Memnon himself.

According to this account, Memnon wanted to stick with a variation of the original plan. The crops would by this date be what was known as 'milk-ripe'. This means that the grains were ripe enough to harvest, store and use but had not yet become fully ripe. Milk-ripe crops do not give yields as heavy as those allowed to ripen fully. Memnon suggested that the harvesting should go ahead as fast as possible in those areas that the Macedonians had not yet reached.

However, he wanted to use his mobile striking force to lay waste the lands in front of the Macedonian army. Wherever Alexander went, Memnon wanted to greet him with fields where the crops had been burned in the fields. Once harvest time was over, Memnon would revert to his original plan. It was bold and decisive, but it had enormous costs.

Depending on how quickly the Macedonians moved and where they chose to go, vast stretches of farmland would be destroyed. Huge quantities of grain would be burned before it could be harvested. That promised to be expensive not only in terms of the value of the crop in monetary terms, but might easily lead to mass starvation in the areas affected. Nobody knew how long the war was likely to last. If entire satrapies lost their whole crop, as might well happen, who knew when conditions would permit cargo ships to transport grain to the starving populations.

It is hardly surprising that the satraps objected to Memnon's plan. Even if concern for the civilian populations of their satrapies were not enough, all the satraps owned extensive estates in their lands themselves. They were being asked to bankrupt themselves and their peoples as well as run the very real risk of starvation. The satraps refused to agree. Perhaps Mithridates backed them, fearful of the his father-in-law's reaction to the loss of tax revenues that would inevitably follow Memnon's plan.

Instead, the satraps suggested a different plan. Over the years there has been a huge amount of speculation about what the satraps intended to do and why. The ancient sources are not particularly informative, no doubt because none of them draw directly, or even indirectly on the Persian commanders who were present.

Arrian states that, after Memnon had suggested his plan, 'Arsites, however, is said to have replied to this proposal that he would not consent to the destruction of a single house belonging to any of his men. The other commanders supported him. No doubt they had their suspicions of Memnon, and guessed that he was afraid of losing the position he held from Darius if the fighting started too soon.'

The first part of Arrian's explanation is clear enough: The Persian satraps did not fancy destroying their own lands, wealth and food. This is fair enough in the circumstances, but the second part of Arrian's explanation is a bit more obscure. Up to this point Arrian has not actually stated what Memnon's official position was – only that he commanded the Greek mercenaries serving on the Persian side. Memnon was later to be appointed to command all Persian forces and resources in Asia Minor, but that was an emergency decree issued by Darius after the Battle of the Granicus. Other sources are not much clearer on the subject. As a son in law of Darius, Memnon was clearly an important man so it must be assumed that he had an important and official role of some kind that Arrian thinks he would not want to put at risk.

Quite why Memnon stood to lose his position, whatever it was, if 'the fighting started too soon' is equally obscure. That Darius would be angry if Memnon failed is common sense, but that he should be displeased if Memnon fought too early does not really make sense. Perhaps there was some reason favouring delay of which we are unaware. There may have been reinforcements on the way. Or the plan of refusing food to Alexander may have been previously agreed with Darius. Or there may have been some religious objection. We simply do not know. It is possible that Arrian did not know either, and just as likely that he misunderstood his sources.

Diodorus, relying on the anonymous Greek mercenary in Persian service, speaking through Cleitarchus, says that 'Memnon failed to win over the other commanders, since his advice seemed beneath the dignity of the Persians'. In other words, the Persians were rash to the point of foolishness. They wanted a fight and were keen to cross swords with the impudent Alexander as quickly as possible.

As we have already seen, Alexander at this point in his career was not rated very highly as either a commander or a king. He was too young and inexperienced to have established much of a reputation, and what was known of him was not very flattering. It is possible that the Persian satraps looked on him with contempt and thought that they could defeat him easily.

On the other hand, the Macedonian army was very highly regarded and was recognised as being, for its size, the best in the known world. Parmenio had been campaigning in Asia the previous year with some success, so the satraps will have had first hand experience of Greek soldiers and would have known that they were not easy to defeat. Many commentators have chosen to accept the explanation given by Diodorus. They have written off the Persian campaign plan as being little more than a bald-headed and exceptionally rash attempt to attack Alexander at the first opportunity. Such a plan is, rightly, dismissed as being foolish and doomed to failure. The satraps are frequently considered to have been little more than a bunch of idiots.

But just because the Persian plan turned out to be a failure does not mean that it was an inherently foolish or ridiculous plan. After all, the actual actions of the satraps argues that their plan was not to attack Alexander at all.

If the Persians wanted simply to force a battle, they went a strange way about it. They could have marched straight toward Arisbe and hurled themselves on the Macedonian army. The land around Arisbe is open country where the terrain would favour the cavalry of which the satraps were most proud and confident. It would also meet the aim that Arrian ascribes to the satraps, that of preventing a single house or farm from being destroyed.

But the Persians did not do this. Again the anonymous mercenary is the most likely source for the movements of the Persians. As rendered by Diodorus this reads 'Summoning forces from every quarter and heavily outnumbering the Macedonians, they advanced in the direction of the Hellespontine. They then pitched camp by the River Granicus, using the bed of the river as a line of defence.'

This is quite clearly no rash and hurried advance by over confident commanders intent on crushing an inferior opponent at the first opportunity. They had selected a strong defensive position, then sat down to await the arrival of the enemy. Obviously, they had something else in mind.

From the actual actions of the Persians, as opposed to what Arrian and other pro-Alexander writers said they intended, it is possible to reconstruct what they intended to do. The satraps wanted to summon as many of the local militia as they could to take up strongly defensive positions, as the mercenary of Cleitarchus says, blocking Alexander's route inland. Thus they would seek to hem Alexander in to as small an area as possible during the critical harvest period. Once that was over, they could revert to the original plan, as the harvest would be in and no food would be left outside the walls of the cities.

Of course the local levies could not be expected to hold even the strongest position against anything more than a Macedonian reconnaissance in force. If the main Macedonian army was to be stopped, it had to be met by Memnon's striking force of professional soldiers.

The key to this plan was to find out where Alexander was heading. The satraps would then use their local knowledge to locate a good defensive position along Alexander's route of march and hurry to occupy it before Alexander got there. With his way forward blocked, Alexander would turn aside to head for another objective. The Persians would then seek to outmarch him to occupy a fresh blocking position.

All this is supposition as none of the ancient sources knew what the Persians intended to do. However, it does make sense of what the Persians actually did. It ties in with what we know of the Persian plan that had been rendered useless by Alexander's early arrival. Above all it makes sense from the Persian point of view as far as they knew it in the early summer of 334BC. It may not make much sense to commentators writing with hindsight, but then that was not available to the satraps.

Unfortunately we do not know the precise timing of the Persian movements in relation to those of Alexander. Diodorus, having described Alexander's trip to Troy, moves on to the Persian conference at Zeleia saying only 'meanwhile', which could mean almost anything. Arrian is not much clearer saying that 'on receiving the report that Alexander had crossed into Asia, they met'. Plutarch and others do not mention the meeting at all, but recount events only from the Macedonian viewpoint.

It is possible, however, to reconstruct a likely schedule of events. Memnon will probably have heard that Alexander had left Therme only a few days after the event, and certainly long before Alexander got anywhere near the Dardanelles. Realising that Alexander was on the move early and likely to arrive before the Persian fleet could block the Dardanelles, Memnon would have sent out messengers to summon the satraps to Zeleia. We know that only six satraps arrived in time to take part in the conference that followed.

The efficiency of the Persian courier system was famous. There were frequent stops along the main routes where riders could change horses to maintain a high speed. In emergencies, and this was nothing if not an emergency, the message bag would be passed on from rider to rider so that there were no delays for meals or rests. Under these circumstances a message could travel at the then unheard of speed of about 250km a day. Memnon's message must have reached all the satraps within two or three days of being sent.

The satraps then had to get their personal bodyguard ready to march, perhaps a day was taken doing this. They then had to make their way to Zeleia, at a much slower speed than the couriers could manage but certainly moving faster than was normal for an army. That six of the nine known satraps arrived would indicate that they had had a week or ten days to get to Zeleia after receiving Memnon's message.

This might indicate that the fateful conference took place about the time that Alexander was marching through Leuce Acte, and certainly before he got his army into Asia. It must be assumed that before they left their home satrapies, each satrap had given orders for the local levies to be called out ready to march as soon as orders were sent back to them. The nearer forces may have been given orders to head for Zeleia as soon as possible. At any rate such orders were sent out as soon as the satraps and Memnon had had their conference.

News came that Alexander was at Troy, but that his invasion force was resting at Arisbe. The question the satraps had to answer was simple. Where would Alexander go next?

CHAPTER EIGHT

The March to the Granicus

While the Satraps met with Memnon to discuss their options and Alexander was visiting Troy, the task of getting the main army across the Hellespont and into Asia was entrusted to Parmenio, Philip's old second in command. Parmenio was now Alexander's deputy and it was he who had been campaigning in Asia Minor.

Parmenio had returned to Macedon late the previous autumn, probably around October. There he had helped Alexander get the invasion force organised and played a role in planning the invasion. He had left his army in Asia Minor with orders to go into winter quarters and to do nothing to antagonise the Persians nor to provoke them into action before Alexander arrived.

It is not entirely certain what orders Parmenio had been given by Philip when he was sent to Asia some time in 336BC, nor how well he had fulfiled them. He had with him some 10,000 men. Only about a thousand cavalry were Macedonians, the rest were Thracians and hired mercenary Greek infantry. Nevertheless it was a substantial force and Philip must have expected Parmenio to achieve something with it. Philip used to joke that there were many generals in the world, but that he had only ever met one real general: Parmenio. Having sent his best commander to Asia Minor, Philip must have had a definite goal in mind.

At the very least, Parmenio should have been conducting a detailed and extensive reconnaissance in force. When the main army arrived to campaign in earnest there would need to be detailed notes on roads, camping grounds, watering places, grazing grounds and potential sources of food. Parmenio would also have been expected to amass as much information as possible about the towns and cities in the area. He would need to know their wealth, their population sizes and the strengths of their fortifications. Crucially, Parmenio must have been expected to make contact with the citizens of those cities with a view to discovering their attitude to the Macedonian invader who was coming with promises of liberty and freedom from Persian rule.

Parmenio would also have been given the task of assessing the military resources of the Persian Empire in Asia Minor. Philip will have known that the financial resources of the enemy were vast. The Persians would not encounter any problems paying their men, buying weapons or hiring mercenaries. But how much money Darius was prepared to spend in Asia Minor was open to question. Macedonian hegemony in Greece was not untroubled, nor was it entirely secure – as the rebellion of Thebes was to show. Darius may have preferred to wait until a Macedonian invasion actually began before spending much money. On the other hand he might have decided to spend money at that earlier time in order to deter the Macedonian invasion from happening at all.

What is entirely unknown is to what extent Parmenio and his men were expected to test the Persian defences in action. Nor is it clear if this advance guard was entrusted with the task of persuading the Greek cities of Asia Minor to rise up against the Persians before the main invasion force arrived.

Just as it is unclear what Parmenio was expected to do, it is equally obscure what he actually did. We know that at one point he got as far south as Ephesus and was in talks with the city council. He fought an action near this city against Memnon which did not produce a clear result, though the Macedonian force fell back soon after. Perhaps it was a victory for Memnon.

Diodorus also tells us that Parmenio captured the city of Grynium, but failed to take Pitane. These were both cities facing on to the Bay of Eleaea, now the Sea of Marmara. We don't know when these two sieges took place, but Diodorus does tell us that after Parmenio left, Memnon moved to attack the force he had left behind. By this date, probably sometime in November, the Macedonians were commanded by Callas. This Callas, or Calas, was a son of Harpalus. Harpalus was a leading Macedonian noble-man and while his role at this time is unclear he would later become one of Alexander's most trusted financial officers. Memnon inflicted a severe defeat on Callas, who then retreated to a fortified base at Rhoeteium, a small promontory on the Dardanelles coast of the Trojan Plain. How many men he had lost in the battle with Memnon is not clear.

What is known for certain is that by the time Alexander arrived, Callas and his surviving forces were ready for action and met him at Arisbe. We also know that at this point none of the Greek cities in the Persian Empire were openly for Alexander. Whatever promises they had made to Parmenio, these were obviously conditional on the Macedonian army actually arriving.

There was one exception, and it was an important one. The small city of Cyzicus was not a formal part of the Persian Empire, and never had been. It stood on an island off the coast to the east of Troy and had some of the toughest and most impressive fortifications of any city in the area. Cyzicus had been won over the previous year, either by Parmenio or by messages sent direct from Philip.

The reason why this was important was that Cyzicus was the banking centre for Asia Minor. The coinage of the city was recognised and accepted by all traders, merchants and markets in the region. Even more important, the mercenaries who served in the Persian army trusted Cyzicus coins, but not those minted in Persia. Memnon made repeated attempts to capture Cyzicus, or to persuade the city authorities to relent, but without avail. The city was to remain a thorn in the side of the Persians throughout the Granicus Campaign.

Alexander, meanwhile, had problems of his own.

When he arrived at Arisbe, Alexander had no idea of where the Persian army was, nor what Memnon had in store for him. From Parmenio's experiences the previous year, Alexander would have known that Memnon was a skilled commander who could be relied upon to fight with ability. Alexander would also have appreciated that Memnon knew that the invading army was on its way and would have laid careful and well considered plans. What those were Alexander did not know.

What Alexander did know was that he himself was short of money and that his army was short of food. It is likely that he had hoped to be received with open arms by the local Greek cities. These would have been a source of both food and money, but it is clear that this did not happen. The cities in question were garrisoned by Memnon's well paid mercenaries and showed no signs of opening their gates.

The crops in the fields were just about ripe enough to harvest. One option was to use his troops to harvest the grain in the immediate vicinity of Arisbe. This could then be used to feed his army. After all, the vast majority of the soldiers came from rural areas and would have had experience of harvesting, winnowing and threshing the grain. The plan had its attractions, but was fraught with danger.

Harvesting crops was a labour intensive operation in the days before mechanised reaping machines. Large numbers of men would need to be spread out over the fields to cut the standing grain. Spread out in this way, Alexander's army would be an easy target for a Persian attack. Alexander will have known that the Persians were strong in cavalry, particularly light cavalry. They would have been ideally placed to swoop down, massacre a harvesting detachment and gallop off before the Macedonians could send a force to intervene. Alexander would have been laying his men open to a bloodbath.

The only solution seemed to be to find out if the Persian army was nearby or not. If it was, it might be brought to battle on terms favourable to the Macedonians and so disposed of. If not, it could be ignored for the present. Either would put Alexander in a strong position regarding the local food supply. If there were no Persian troops nearby he could use his men to harvest the fields himself. Alternatively, he could put pressure on the local towns to open their gates or, failing that, to supply him with at least some food for his men.

Arisbe lay in the satrapy of Hellespontine. The capital city of that satrapy was at Dascylium to the east. Alexander seems to have reasoned that the forces of the local satrap would be gathering there if they were in the satrapy at all. He therefore set out for that city in the hopes of either finding no Persian troops, or defeating those he did find. Alexander now had a strict time limit. The army had only ten days of grain left out of its initial stores. If Alexander did not find a reliable source of food within little over a week, he and his army would be in serious trouble.

It was at this point in the campaign that the Macedonian supply system first came under real pressure. Thus far, the army had marched in a series of three or four day hops from one friendly seaport to the next. This had enabled the army to march light and fast, the bulk of the food and perhaps the rest of the baggage being carried on the ships. It seems that Alexander was hoping to repeat the trick on his march out of Arisbe by using the Greek port city of Lampsakos, now Lamsaki, as his next staging post.

At this time Alexander's main problems related to his food supply system, and this in turn was linked to the logistics system of the Macedonian army. The logistical back up and food supply system was almost certainly in the hands of Eumenes. This talented bureaucrat was certainly in charge of replacing broken weapons or dead horses, and it would seem that handling the central food supplies was also his preserve.

Philip had some years earlier banned the Macedonian army from using carts to transport food or equipment of any kind. Everything had to be carried by the men or on pack animals. The reasons for this were three fold.

First, carts could operate only on good roads. At the time of Alexander the only roads to have paved surfaces were those within towns and cities or the limited number of sacred roads that linked temples, shrines and cult centres. Processions moved along such roads and needed flat, secure paving to take the weight of the large carts that carried cult statues. Good as such roads were, they did not tend to go where armies would want to march.

The vast majority of roads were little more than strips of ground that were cleared of boulders, bushes and other obstructions. In wet weather they quickly deteriorated to quagmires interrupted by deep puddles. In dry weather they turned to dust that flew up in clouds of choking powder that got into noses, mouths and eyes. So irritating and penetrating could this dust be that 'traveller's eye' was a recognised complaint. In any case, such roads as there were existed only in the lowlands. Mountains were crossed by paths and tracks that no cart could traverse.

If the army had depended on carts for transport it would have been tied to lowland roads. That would be bad enough in territory that had been thoroughly scouted and efficiently mapped. But no army can rely on fighting only over such lands. By abandoning carts, the Macedonian army was freed to march over rough ground and high passes that were impassable to more traditional military forces.

A second problem with carts was their speed. The usual draught animal in ancient Greece was the ox. Oxen can plod along at only around 3.5 kilometres per hour. Moreover an ox can work for only five hours per day if it is to keep up a sustained effort. The resulting average daily speed of 17 kilometres was very slow. A fit man can easily sustain daily speeds of 30 kilometres or more. Relying on carts drawn by oxen would slow the army down considerably.

Even if horse-drawn carts were used, which could keep up with a man's daily marching rate, there was a third problem. Until some anonymous genius of the early medieval period invented the horsecollar made from straw-stuffed leather and braced by metal fittings, the only horse collar available was the throat and girth harness. This has the unfortunate effect of exerting pressure on the horse's windpipe. The harder the horse pulls, the more it is choked by the weight it is pulling. This put a strict limit on the amount of weight that a horse could pull. Bizarre as it may seem, this meant that a horse could actually carry on its back more than it could pull.

Carts retained their uses, of course. If a single object of great weight needed to be moved there was no alternative to the cart. If the weight was too great for one horse to carry, it had to be put on a cart and dragged forward by four or more horses. For Alexander's army, however, this was not the case. Everything that the army needed could be packed into loads suitable for a single horse, mule or donkey to carry on its back.

An average horse can carry about 520kg or so on an extended march lasting several days. Sacks of grain, bundles of weapons and cooking pots could obviously be put together into the correct sized packs. The problem came with larger objects. The best known of these carried by the Macedonian army were its highly effective catapults and other artillery. The very largest artillery, used for pounding city walls, was not carried by the army in its entirety as this would have been far too heavy, and the individual timber components simply too big and unwieldy. Instead only the key metal and sinew parts were carried, the wooden pieces being felled, cut and shaped when needed. The lighter field artillery was, however, transported on pack animals. Each of the lighter catapults could be dismantled and loaded on to two pack horses and then reassembled in a matter of hours to be ready for instant use.

But it was not simply a matter of loading equipment and food on to pack animals and setting off. The task of Eumenes was far more complicated than that. We do not know exactly how the different units organised their transport, but the system for the pezhetairoi at least is clear.

Each file of 16 men had a servant and a pack animal to carry their immediate equipment. We know that each man had to carry his own armour and weapons, but he was not expected to carry anything else. Tents, cooking pots, mugs, handmills and other equipment was left to the servant and horse. We don't know how much all this gear weighed in the Macedonian army, but in the later Roman army – another ancient force famed for its logistics when marching – it came to about 200kg.

That left around 320kg of spare carrying capacity. On campaign, this would have been allocated for the food needed by the file unit. The carrying capacity of the horse and rate at which the food it carried was consumed would put a limit on how long the army could operate without replenishing the stores from ships, cities or other sources.

Average marching conditions can be assumed to consist of good weather, reasonably level tracks and a daily march rate of about 27km or so. Under such conditions the absolute minimum that a man would need when carrying the sorts of loads that a pezhetairoi had was about 1.5kg of grain. Ideally this should be supplemented by another 500g or so of dried fruit, dried fish, hard cheese or other foods to supply the nutrients lacking in grain. A fit man could do without these additional foods for a few days without suffering ill effects, but for no more than a week if his ability to march and fight were not to be impaired.

The horse, meanwhile, would need at least 4.5 kg of grain plus another 5kg or so of hay, chaff or straw. This could be reduced if the horse was allowed time to graze, but grazing would cut the daily march rate.

For a group of 16 pezhetairoi, one servant and one horse, the daily requirement for food on the march adds up to a total of 43.5kg, which could be reduced to 35kg for short periods of a few days only. The 320 kg that could be carried on the horse would be consumed within seven days.

It is generally considered that an army on the march needs to stop to rest one day in six. The day of rest is needed to allow the horses, mules and other pack animals the time to graze on fresh grass and recover their strength. The men, meanwhile, need a day to grind grain into flour and then bake it into biscuits – if ample supplies of fat are available – or into bread if not. Thus the seven days ration that a pack horse could carry for its unit of pezhetairoi actually means only six days of marching.

At a daily march rate of 27km that gives a maximum range for Alexander's infantry of about 160km before they ran out of food. If they were to march to an objective and then return to base, that distance should be halved to 80km. In the context of the invasion of an empire, that is not very far.

All this calculation is assuming that the army was marching through country where there was plenty of water available at frequent watering holes. A marching soldier needs a minimum of 3 litres of water a day in reasonable weather, more in hot weather. A horse needs about 30 litres per day. If that heavy weight had to be carried in addition to food, the range of the army would be severely curtailed.

We are quite ignorant of the transport system of the cavalry units, but it must be assumed that they were roughly similar to those of the infantry.

It was not just the soldiers that had to be fed. As we have already seen, there were large numbers of non-combatants in Alexander's army. It is thought that there were, in all, around 10,000 cooks, doctors, servants, horse grooms, bureaucrats, trumpeters, courtesans and so forth. To carry enough supplies to allow these people to keep up with the army on a seven day march would need just over 1,000 pack animals. Given that the assorted hangers on all had equipment of their own that also needed transporting, that number should be pushed up to about 1,300.

Given the total numbers of soldiers, support staff, pack animals, cavalry horses and so forth, the Macedonian army would have consumed a total of about 135,000 kg of food each and every day. Sourcing such a quantity of food in hostile territory would be a formidable task in itself, never mind then transporting it.

Such was the task that Alexander set Eumenes as the army prepared to set off from Arisbe.

The army marched northeast along the coast. The fleet was moving off the coast alongside them, though the captains must by now have been growing increasingly nervous about the whereabouts of the Persian war fleet.

At some point in this early stage of the journey, Alexander came across a temple to the goddess Athene, officiated over by a priest with the fortuitous name of Alexander. There has been some confusion over where this shrine or temple was located. However, Diodorus, who is the only source for the events that followed, quite clearly says that Alexander visited the shrine after he had rejoined his main army. It must have been been close to Arisbe on the army's route of march to the northeast.

Wherever the shrine was, the first thing that Alexander noticed as he approached was a statue fallen off its pedestal with its face in the dust. Alexander the priest told the king that the statue was that of Ariobarzanes, a former satrap of Phrygia. This was, in fact, the satrap who had ruled the area from 388 to 361BC. He rebelled against the rule of the Persian emperor Artaxerxes II, but was overcome and executed.

It is likely that his statue was overturned by imperial order at the time he was executed. Alexander the priest, however, claimed to Alexander the king that the fall of the statue was an omen of good luck to the Macedonians. The priest went further. He assured the king that the goddess Athene had spoken to him. The goddess, the priest said, had assured him that Alexander the king would win a great battle in Phrygia and would, with his own hands, kill an enemy general. Athene, the priest concluded, was on the side of the Macedonians.

The visit to the temple was a godsend, or rather a goddess send, to Alexander. He was just embarking on the most dangerous stage of his invasion of Asia Minor. He had orchestrated some impressive rituals around the Dardanelles and again at Troy, but there had been no sign from the Gods that they had noticed. But now the great goddess Athene had spontaneously announced that she was on Alexander's side and that he was going to win a battle.

There is a great temptation to be cynical about events such as this. It has been speculated that the whole thing had been stage managed in advance. Parmenio had campaigned through this territory the previous year. It is likely that he would have come across this temple and its priest. And that same Parmenio had been camped at Arisbe for a day, possibly two, while Alexander visited Troy. It is very possible that Parmenio would have had a quiet word with the priest, perhaps making a handy donation to the temple's funds, and instructed him to behave like this when Alexander passed by. Or Alexander may have been told that he was going to pass the temple and had sent a messenger on ahead to make arrangements. Or it may be that Alexander the priest simply saw a good opportunity when he saw one and decided to try to cash in on the passing army and its king.

Thinking that is to ignore two factors. First the Persian monarch, as a Zoroastrian, did not believe in Athene and would not have hesitated to punish her priest for such disloyalty to the Persian state. Alexander the priest would have been behaving rashly, even foolishly, if he were simply trying to get a donation.

Second, the people of the time really did believe in deities such as Athene. Just because we, today, do not believe that these deities ever existed, does not mean that the ancients did not. They genuinely believed that by studying the way birds flew, or if they listened to the rustling of the leaves of trees that grew in sacred ground then they would be able to listen to the gods. The indications seem to be that this Alexander the priest really did have a dream or experience that he interpreted and genuinely believed to be a message from the goddess Athene. No doubt Alexander made much of the event and broadcast it through his army to raise morale, but that does not mean that the encounter itself was fabricated.

The small town of Percote was reached the evening after the encounter with the priest of Athene. It had a tiny harbour. The army arrived at the end of the first day's march. The city had only the weakest of fortifications, so Alexander had little difficulty in persuading the citizens to open their gates to him. The fleet would, no doubt, have taken the opportunity of offloading some supplies to be distributed to the army.

The next day the army marched on to the much larger and richer city of Lampsakos – famous throughout the Greek world for the fine quality of its rich, red wines that were exported in huge quantities. Alexander and his army began arriving outside the city walls in the later afternoon of their second day on the march. They met with an immediate rebuff. The city had strong walls and the gates were firmly closed. Alexander sent forward messengers to ask that the gates be opened, no doubt backed by the threat that if they were not the army would attack the city. The citizens of Lampsakos refused.

The refusal was a blow to Alexander. This was the first Greek city of any real size that he had reached since crossing into the Persian Empire. He had proclaimed his intentions of restoring liberty to the Greek cities, and had ostentatiously granted Troy a democratic constitution. And yet the Greeks refused to open their gates. The citizens of Lampsakos later explained that they had been threatened with bloody revenge by Darius if they should welcome Alexander. This, they said, had so frightened them that they simply could not bring themselves to open their gates – even though they had desperately wanted to do so. The explanation was no doubt true, and it gave Alexander a very strong message. No city was going to welcome him unless it looked as if he was going to win the war. The citizens simply had too much to lose if they supported him, and then had to face the wrath of Darius.

Strong and impressive as the fortifications of Lampsakos were, they were in reality no match for the siege techniques of the Macedonians.

Certainly if Alexander had the components of his siege engines unpacked, fitted to timber cut on site and then put into action, Lampsakos would not have stood a chance. Even if only the field artillery were used, the city defences would probably have crumbled within a couple of weeks. But time was the one thing Alexander did not have. His food was running out. The citizens of Lampsakos may not have known the precise condition of the Macedonian army, but they could have guessed that Alexander would not want to spend days, or weeks, sitting before a relatively unimportant city like Lampsakos. Alexander's threat to attack was a bluff, and the city called it successfully.

Some have suggested that Lampsakos may have bought off Alexander either with food or with money – the Macedonians were falling short of both by this time. This is possible, but unlikely. Alexander was not going to hang around in front of a city when he had only six or seven days worth of food left. If a town did not open its gates at once, he had to move on.

Alexander camped that night on the banks of the River Practius, little more than a stream that flowed down from the heights of the Mount Ida massif into the Dardanelles just east of Lampsakos. Next day the army recommenced its march. The army passed the village of Colonae, probably modern Adatepe. Next the army came to Hermotus, the site of which has been lost. These two places were not fortified, and may have been abandoned by their inhabitants. At any rate they were ignored by the Macedonians as they passed by. There was obviously nothing there that they needed.

The army then turned away from the coast and headed inland. Ahead of them was the rugged, rocky headland of Pegai. The only coastal route snaked its tortuous way around the inhospitable terrain. It was a long and arduous route that offered no harbours at which the army could replenish its stores from the fleet, nor any towns worth the bother of approaching.

The better route on the way to the satrapal capital of Dascylium was to cut inland to avoid the rugged peninsula and then emerge into the wide plain beyond. This is what Alexander did. It was while engaged on this march that he received the very good news that the city of Priapos was opening its gates to the Macedonians. The defection of Priapos was a welcome and important move. Now known as Karabiga, Priapos was and is a medium sized port and reasonably prosperous city. On a practical front it gave Alexander a port into which his fleet could move, both to unload whatever food was left and to find shelter from the Persian fleet – whenever it turned up. Politically the acquisition of the city was vital. It showed the army that they were welcome in the area and that other cities could be expected to come over to them in due course.

Priapos was a Greek city and was sacred to the fertility god of the same name. The god was mostly concerned with the fecundity of flocks of sheep and goats, though he was also linked to bee-keeping and fishing. At Priapos, where the god had probably originated before being introduced to the wider Greek world, donkeys were sacrificed to him in an elaborate ritual. For once, Alexander was uninterested in divine favours or ritual.

The town was not on his route of march and a minor deity such as Priapos had little to offer the army. Alexander therefore sent a detachment commanded by Panegorus, son of Lycagorus, to occupy the city. This man is described by Arrian as one of Alexander's Guards. He is otherwise not mentioned by any ancient source. Presumably he was a competent, but fairly junior officer who could be trusted to undertake a mission away from the main army, but not so important as to be missed. It must be assumed that the unit he led was fairly modest in size and was probably made up of hoplites, troops suitable for manning defences. Alexander would not have sent many good men. He needed all his fighting men with him.

Throughout the main march, the Macedonian army was covering about 25km per day or so. This indicates that they were not slowing down to harvest crops standing in the fields. They were living off the stored grain that they had carried with them all the way from Therme. That grain was now running out fast. As Priapos surrendered, Alexander cannot have had more than three or four days of food left.

What happened next is unclear. Arrian believed that Alexander was coming down from the hills east of Hermotus into a wide plain. He was probably somewhere near the modern town of Baliklicesme. Thus far the army had been marching in the usual order for moving through hostile territory. The main army, including the baggage train, was in a straggling column while parties of light horsemen rode out ahead and on the flanks.

Now Alexander altered his formation. This was probably as the army began a day's march, having camped overnight on the hills before venturing out on to the open plains. He now formed his army up in a formation from which it could deploy rapidly into a battle order. The infantry was massed into two large columns. These were probably formed up as they would have been in battle, but with the men marching in column rather than line. To form into a battle line they would have wheeled to one side so that they were marching parallel to the enemy. By then making a quarter turn to face the enemy they would fall instantly into a phalanx ready to commence action.

The bulk of the cavalry were likewise divided into two tight columns. One column rode alongside, but outside one infantry column and the second in a similar position flanking the other infantry column. It must be presumed that the right hand cavalry column consisted of the cavalry of the right wing, while that on the left comprised the left wing cavalry. If the enemy were spotted, the two cavalry formations would swing out to take up their stations on the flanks of the army while the infantry plodded into their positions.

Arrian reports that the baggage 'had orders to follow on behind'. The wording is vague, but it would seem that the baggage was some distance behind the main army. Presumably Alexander expected to find the enemy to his front, and wanted to keep all his administrative staff, supplies of spare weapons, food and so forth well out of harm's way. Presumably the baggage had a guard of some kind, perhaps the allied hoplites.

Riding ahead of the army were the podromoi light cavalry under the command of an officer named Hegelochus. Included in this force were 500 light infantry, perhaps the highly trained javelin men sent by the Agrianian tribe. These men were reckoned the best light infantry in the army, so it would be natural to send them forward to support the scouting cavalry. Sometime in the afternoon, Hegelochus came spurring back to the main army. He reported that a huge Persian army was drawn up in a defensive position behind the River Granicus that lay some kilometres ahead.

It is unfortunate that none of the ancient sources gives any geographical details that would allow us to pin down exactly which of the various rivers that lay along Alexander's path was the Granicus. It must be presumed that in their day everybody likely to read the accounts of Alexander's exploits would have known where the Granicus was – just as today most readers of this book would know where the Nile is to be found. But none of the rivers in this area is today called the Granicus or anything like it.

Given the clues that ancients do include, it would seem that what is now called the Gonen was too far to the east. The last firm geographical fix that any ancient writers provide is the surrender of Priapos, now Karabiga. The messengers bringing this news to Alexander arrived the day before Hegelochus found the Persians. It is unlikely that envoys carrying such news would risk riding far through lands patrolled by Persian cavalry scouts. Nor would the city want to surrender until Alexander was close by, in case he and his army changed direction and left them at the mercy of Memnon.

The most likely place for the envoys from Priapos to meet Alexander would have been where the road from Arisbe to Dascylium forks. One branch ran along the rugged coast, the other cut inland. Whichever route Alexander chose, the envoys would have been certain of meeting him here. That road junction lies near the modern village of Celikguru. The Macedonian army stopped at least one more night on the march before it adopted the new marching formation. The Persians were sighted on the first day of this new formation. Given the marching rate, this would put the Granicus somewhere between 25 and 50 km east of Celikguru.

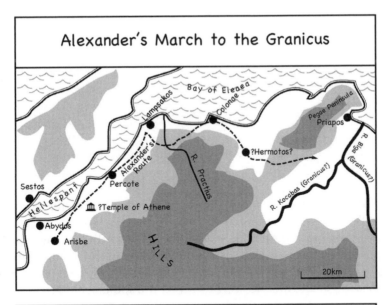

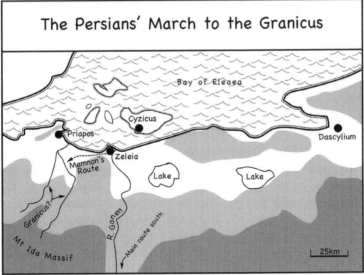

Most modern commentators choose the River Biga, but the Kocabas is just as likely. Both rivers match the descriptions given in the various accounts, and both are in about the right place.

If historians cannot agree about which river should be identified as the Granicus, that is as nothing compared to the disagreements that have arisen as to what happened once Alexander got there.

CHAPTER NINE

The Granicus, Day One

As soon as Hegelochus and his men came galloping in with the news that a Persian army had been located, Alexander would have ridden forward to see for himself. He would have taken with him his guard to protect him against a sudden assault by the Persians. He would also have taken with him the seven Bodyguards, or as many of them as could be found in the time. These senior generals and leading noblemen made up the command council or senior staff of the Macedonian army. Alexander, as king, was obliged to listen to their advice, though the decision was his alone.

These were all experienced and skilled military men. The most respected of them all was Parmenio. Aged 66 years of age by this date, Parmenio had spent his entire adult life in the saddle. He had begun his military career under King Amyntas II of Macedon in around 380BC. As a young man he saw Macedon overrun by wild Illyrian tribesmen and, for a time, went into exile along with Amyntas. The king found support among the Thessalians, returning at the head of a large army of Thessalian horsemen. The Macedonians rose to support him and the Illyrians were expelled.

Parmenio worked his way up through the command ranks of the Macedonian army under Amyntas and saw much campaigning against the Illyrians and Epirots. It was during the reign of Amyntas that the hill tribes of Upper Macedonia were brought under more direct rule by the Kings of Macedon. Until then the kings had ruled the lowlands directly, and exercised only a vague sort of control over the hill tribes. How much fighting was involved in this we don't know, but Parmenio would have been involved in what there was. In later life Amyntas narrowly survived an attempt at a palace coup organised by his wife. Executions followed, but Parmenio must have chosen the winning side, as he survived.

When Amyntas died, Parmenio was a fairly senior, but not top ranking commander. The new king Perdiccas, did not survive long as he was killed invading Illyria. Perdiccas left an infant son, Amyntas, with his own adult brother Philip as regent. Philip wasted little time getting the army on his side and then ousted Amyntas. It must be presumed that Parmenio had played some role in the coup as he was immediately favoured and promoted by Philip.

When Philip in turn died, Parmenio had been in distant Asia with the advance guard of 10,000 men sent to prepare the way for the invasion of the Persian Empire. His second in command was the nobleman Attalus, great uncle of the young prince who was Alexander's half brother and main rival for the throne. When men arrived from Alexander with orders to execute Attalus, Parmenio let them do their work despite the fact that his daughter was the wife of Attalus.

Parmenio had thus survived three major rounds of executions among the Macedonian nobility, each linked to a different attempt to put a new king on the throne. He must have been as wily a politician as he was a successful general. His relationship to Alexander is not entirely clear. He was certainly a supporter of the young king and one of the inner circle of Bodyguards. Parmenio's son, Philotas, was a boyhood friend of Alexander's. Although the two youngsters had never been particularly close, Alexander had appointed Philotas to command the companion cavalry as the expedition to Asia set out from Therme.

Perhaps it is best to see Parmenio as a much respected advisor, but not a man who was very close to Alexander on a personal level. There are some hints that in times of crisis the veterans of Philip's army were inclined to look toward Parmenio, not Alexander. This would have been perfectly understandable for men risking their lives on campaign, but must have rankled with Alexander who was, after all, both king and commander in chief. This tension between the young king and his older, more experienced second in command would later become more pro-nounced. It did, however, exist at this time and must have served as the background to the dispute that now followed.

As they sat their horses some distance from the west bank of the Granicus surveying the position taken up by Memnon, it was immediately clear to Alexander and his Bodyguards that they had been outmanoeuvred on the strategic level. The road that Memnon and the Persians blocked led on to Cyzicus as well as to Dascylium. Cyzicus was the only large, wealthy city in Asia that had so far declared openly for the Macedonians. There was, no doubt, food and money waiting in Cyzicus for Alexander. Now he could not get to it.

Behind the Macedonians the only really sizeable city that they had reached, Lampsakos, had refused them entry. Percote, Colonae and Hermotos were little more than villages. The defection of Priapos from Persian control to the Macedonian cause had been welcome, but more as a political gesture than for any material support that such a small city could offer to Alexander. If Alexander turned back now he would be retracing his steps across largely hostile territory that must have already been stripped of anything useful that an army on the march had the time to locate and purloin.

It would have taken Alexander several days to get back to Arisbe and then head southwest past Troy to try the other route open to him, that around the coast to Pergamum. Even if he had been inclined to risk the blow to morale that this move would have entailed, Alexander knew that the choice was not really open to him.

Food must by now have been getting critically short. Even allowing for some food to have been foraged on the march and for some to have been sold to the army by Percote, Colonae, Hermotos and Priapos, the Macedonians could not have had more than two or three days worth of food left.

Alexander had no choice. He had to get over the Granicus to reach Cyzicus.

But looking at the situation to their front, this must have seemed a daunting prospect. The Granicus was no mere trickle of water, but a real river now running in spate as the late spring warmth melted the snows of the Mount Ida massif to the south. In places the river was too deep for a man to wade across. The river bottom was firm in some places, but elsewhere was too boggy for cavalry or was scattered with large boulders that would break up any infantry formation that tried to cross. If that were not enough, the far banks were steep and high. In places they were some five or six metres tall, and as sheer as a cliff. Elsewhere they were lower and less precipitous, but they were slippy with mud.

These were daunting obstacles in themselves, but Memnon had made them worse. He and his army had been camped here for several days. They had had plenty of time to clear the banks of any bushes or trees that might provide cover to the advancing Macedonians. They may even have constructed rough fieldworks to make the river an even more formidable barrier, though it must be admitted that the ancient authors do not mention this.

The anonymous mercenary on the Persian side speaking through Cleitarchus and quoted by Diodorus may or may not have been present on the Granicus. If he wasn't he certainly had the opportunity to talk to plenty of men who had been, including perhaps Memnon himself when the two men were together in Halicarnossos later that year. According to this source 'the Persians, resting on high ground, made no move, intending to fall upon the foe as he crossed the river for they supposed they could easily carry the day when the Macedonian phalanx was divided'.

This was a plan that made the best use of the terrain and cleverly exploited the strengths of the Persian army while negating the main strength of the Macedonians. The exact size and composition of the Persian army at the Granicus has been the cause of much debate. According to Diodorus, quoting the anonymous mercenary, 'in all the cavalry amounted to more than 10,000. The Persian foot soldiers were not fewer than 100,000'. Arrian says that the Persians had '20,000 cavalry and nearly the same number of mercenaries fighting on foot'. Plutarch merely says the Persian army was 'large', though he later claims that 20,000 infantry and 2,500 cavalry were killed or captured.

At first sight the figures seem to be contradictory, so the safest thing that might be said is that Memnon had a very large force that was, probably, substantially larger than that of Alexander. However, it is possible to go rather further than this by analysing what the writers have said in a bit more depth, and by considering the strategic position in which Memnon found himself and the preparations he had made.

Taking the estimates from the Greek side first it is easy to see that the figures given by Plutarch and Arrian can be readily reconciled. Arrian says that there were 20,000 cavalry, Plutarch claims that 2,500 of them were killed or captured. A casualty rate of around 12% is not unreasonable for an army at this date, so the estimates of Plutarch and Arrian seem to be compatible with each other.

For the infantry on the Persian side, Arrian says that there were almost 20,000 mercenaries, but makes no mention of any local levies or troops drawn from the central Persian army. Plutarch says that 20,000 infantry were killed, but does not say if they were mercenaries, local levies or royal troops. If Arrian should be understood to mean that the mercenaries were the only infantry present, this would give a casualty rate of 100%. This would be extremely unusual for the time. Even though all writers make it clear that Alexander chose to make a very harsh example of the Greek mercenaries fighting on the Persian side at the Granicus, such extermination would still be quite remarkable.

Perhaps the best way to interpret the figures as they stand is that Memnon had with him 20,000 Greek mercenaries, plus an unknown but large number of other troops. Of this unknown total, some 20,000 were killed. This is, however, unlikely to be the truth.

Memnon and his agents had been busy over the previous winter hiring mercenaries from wherever they could find them, using the gold and silver sent by Darius. It is generally thought that about 20,000 mercenaries had been recruited from the Greek world. We know that most of these men were, in fact, posted to form garrisons in the various cities and fortresses of Asia Minor. Memnon had kept only a minority – perhaps between 2,000 and 4,000 with him as part of his mobile striking force. Even if he had summoned the garrisons to join him once the satraps had decided to face Alexander in battle, the timescale available means that only a few hundred would have had time to reach the Granicus.

It seems likely that those writers drawing on Macedonian sources knew that a substantial number of Greek mercenaries had fought for Memnon at the Granicus. They also knew that Memnon had recruited about 20,000 such mercenaries. Finally they knew that virtually all the mercenaries who fought at the Granicus were killed or captured. Putting these three figures together it can be seen how they arrived at the figures that they did: 20,000 mercenaries fighting at the Granicus, all of whom were killed or captured.

The previous year, Memnon had kept a field army of 5,000 hoplite mercenaries with him on his various marches and battles against Parmenio. It would be reasonable to assume that he would have had a similar number with him as part of his mobile striking force for the campaign of 334BC.

Turning to the figures given by Diodorus, these total 10,000 cavalry and 100,000 infantry. However, Diodorus actually gives a detailed list of cavalry formations as follows. On the left wing were cavalry units, of unknown number, commanded by Memnon and by Arsamenes. On their immediate right was another unit of undisclosed size commanded by Arsites and raised in Paphlagonia. To the right of that unit was one of Hyrcanian horsemen commanded by Spithrobates.

The right wing was made up of a thousand Medes and two thousand others from the Persian royal army. The Medes were commanded by Mithridates and the others by Rheomithras. The right wing also consisted of 'Bactrians of a like number', presumably between 2,000 and 3,000. The Bactrians came from the far northeast of the empire and, like the Medes, must have been part of the royal army brought by Mithridates. It is likely that this right wing consisted entirely of the cavalry of the royal army.

The centre was composed of 'other national contingents, numerous and picked for their valour'. It is after this statement that Diodorus makes his estimate of 10,000 cavalry.

It can be seen at once that the figure given by Diodorus, as we have them, don't add up. The right wing cavalry alone total 6,000 men. The left wing, like that on the right, was composed of three units. It must have been numbered about the same. That gives a total of 10,000 to 12,000 for the two wings. It was customary for the centre formation of an army to be of at least the same size as either wing, and usually significantly larger. The fact that it is described as being made up of several units which are 'numerous' would seem to indicate that this was the case here. The centre must, therefore, have been at least 6,000 strong and possibly much larger.

Looking again at the words used by Diodorus and remembering that he is paraphrasing what Cleitarchus wrote down, which in turn had come from a verbal account by the anonymous mercenary, it is possible to see what might have happened. The total of 10,000 could easily have applied to assorted units in the centre, rather than to the entire cavalry force.

If this is how the passage should be read, it would give a total of 5,000 to 6,000 on each wing, plus 10,000 in the centre. The total would then be between 20,000 and 22,000, which is more or less what the writers drawing on Macedonian sources estimated.

Regarding the infantry, Diodorus is not very helpful. The estimate of 100,000 men is a suspiciously round number that is used by other ancient writers to mean simply a vast number of indeterminate size. Diodorus does not break down the total into units or types of soldier at all. However, when speaking of the conference between the satraps and Memnon at Zeleia, Diodorus had said 'they decided to fight and summoning forces from every quarter and heavily outnumbering the Macedonians they advanced in the direction of Hellespontine. They pitched camp by the river Granicus.'

In other words, the satraps had sent orders back to their home satrapies summoning their troops to come to the banks of the Granicus. It is most likely that the satraps had brought with them their personal guard and satrapal core of professional troops. The list of cavalry units shows that these had arrived from Paphlagonia and from whichever satrapy was under Arsamenes – assuming he commanded the men from his own area which would be logical. The closest satrapy after Paphlagonia that is known to have supplied cavalry levies was Phrygia. Presumably Arsamenes was the satrap of Phrygia and these cavalry came from that area. Spithrobates commanded the Hyrcanians, so presumably his own Lydians had not arrived.

No other formed units are identified by name, the central mass being described as being formed up of various contingents drawn from different nationalities. We have a clue as to exactly what had happened when Diodorus tells us that the men in this central mass were 'picked for their valour'. These may have been the personal guards brought along by the satraps.

In other words, the full area militia cavalry units of Phrygia and Paphlagonia had arrived, but not from any of the other satrapies. It must be presumed that these men had been originally intended to fight in their own areas, and so had not yet had time to arrive. Only the elite guard units from the other satrapies had arrived.

If that was the position for the cavalry, it was very likely the same for the infantry. So in addition to the Greek mercenaries there would have been the guard units for the six satraps who had arrived, plus the wider militia from Paphlagonia and Phrygia. Documents from the time of the Granicus campaign are lacking, but from some years earlier we know that both Paphlagonia and Phrygia were expected to contribute 30,000 men to the Persian army. It would be unlikely that this figure had changed very much by 334BC.

The infantry would be slower to mobilise and gather together than the cavalry so it is unlikely that all 60,000 militia had arrived in Memnon's camp by the time Alexander arrived. However, most of them would have done, and there is always the possibility that the advance troops from other satrapies had begun to come in. There is no real reason to doubt Diodorus when he writes that they heavily outnumbered the Macedonians.

The best estimate of the army that Memnon had gathered on the eastern bank of the Granicus is, therefore, as follows:

Cavalry:

Paphlagonians	2,000
Phrygians	2,000
Hyrcanians	2,000
Medes	1,000
Bactrians	3,000
Other royal cavalry	2,000
Satrapal guards and assorted local units	10,000
TOTAL:	22,000

Infantry:

Greek Mercenaries	c.5,000
Satrapal guards	c.5,000
Phrygians	c.20,000
Paphlagonians	c.25,000
Other local units	c.5,000
TOTAL:	c.60,000

This can only be a rough estimate, but it would not be too far from the truth. A total force of 80,000 is large for an army of those days, but not unprecedented. It was certainly within the administrative capabilities of the Persian empire to raise, arm and supply such a force. Even when dealing with local satrapal organisational ability, an army of this size was perfectly feasible.

To face them, Alexander had the army with which he had left Therme, plus the advance fore that had overwintered in its fortified base near Troy. Our sources for the Macedonians are much more complete than those for the Persians, so the size and composition of Alexander's army can be given with rather more confidence.

Cavalry:

Companion	1,800
Thessalian	1,800
Allied Greeks	600
Thracian & Paeonian	900
Podromoi	1,000
TOTAL:	6,100

Infantry:

Pezhetairoi	9,000
Hypaspists	3,000
Allied Greeks	7,000
Other Greeks	5,000
Hill tribes men	7,000
Cretan archers	500
Agrianian javelinmen	500
TOTAL:	32,000

These totals represent the maximum force that Alexander had with him in Asia. There will have been some losses to disease or accidents on the march, plus the men sent to occupy Priapos. It is unlikely that these amounted to more than a few hundred. The 5,000 'other Greeks' are generally thought to represent the mercenaries who overwintered near Troy with Callas.

As they sat on their horses gazing across the Granicus, Alexander, Parmenio and the other senior officers would have known precisely how many men they had. They would also have been able to view the Persian army, and so would have been in a much better position to assess it than we are today. They could also view the river and the natural obstacle that it presented. Again, they would have had a much clearer view of this than we can hope to have. We are not even certain which river was involved, never mind where along its length the confrontation took place.

Of the debate that followed this scouting of the enemy position we have two versions, one from Plutarch and one from Arrian. According to Plutarch:

> Most of the Macedonian officers were afraid of the depth of the river, and of the roughness and unevenness of the farther bank, up which they would have to climb while fighting. Some, too, thought they ought to observe carefully the customary practice in regard to the month – in the month of Daesius the kings of Macedon were not wont to take the field with an army.

He goes on to say that 'Parmenio objected to them risking the passage on the grounds that it was too late in the day'.

Arrian has Parmenio voicing the objections and quotes him as saying:

> To attempt to cross in the present circumstances would, I think, be a grave risk. We cannot manage the crossing in line on a broad front, because in many places the river is obviously deep, the banks very high and, here and there, almost sheer. We should have to cross, therefore in column, and in loose order at that with the result that their massed cavalry will be upon us just as we are struggling out of the water and at the greatest possible disadvantage. A failure at the outset would be a serious thing now, and highly detrimental to our success in the long run.

So Arrian has Parmenio voice a more detailed version of the practical difficulties that Plutarch says troubled the majority of the senior officers.

Alexander had an answer to both the practical and the religious objections. His religious solution was the neatest and most obviously successful. He proclaimed that instead of the month Daesius, he was celebrating a repeat of the previous month: Artemisius. This was a clever way around a customary practice that was inconvenient to Alexander, and may have been influenced by the fact that Cyzicus was sacred to the goddess Artemis.

The ancient Greeks, and Macedonians, took their religion very seriously. They would often do things for religious reasons that to us seem bizarre. In 490BC the Spartan army had famously delayed marching to help the Athenians fight the Battle of Marathon because their soldiers were celebrating a week long religious festival. To modern eyes, the decision to delay sending an army to fight against an invader may seem close to suicidal. To ancient minds it made perfect sense. If the army had abandoned the festival and marched, the gods would have been offended.

The angry deities would then make sure that the army met defeat in battle. To the way ancient Spartans thought it was far more dangerous to march than to stay at home.

Despite this, it would seem that the old tradition cannot have been taken very seriously by anyone present at the Granicus. The Macedonian army was already on the march by the time the month of Daesius had begun and we know that Philip had himself campaigned in that month more than once. It seems more likely that, on seeing the strength of the Persian position, one of the officers had recalled the old custom and voiced it. Perhaps he wanted an excuse for delay, or thought it would be wise to appease the gods with sacrifices.

Of rather more concern were the practical difficulties raised by Parmenio and the others. The objections that they raised were very real. Indeed, Parmenio was most perceptive when he said that the Persian cavalry was likely to attack as the Macedonians were struggling out of the water. The anonymous mercenary reported that this was exactly what Memnon had in mind.

Parmenio's objection that it was too late in the day to begin a battle is interesting. We know that the army had been marching for at least 20km by the time it reached the Granicus. It had, moreover, been marching in a form of extended battle order that would have slowed it down. There can be no doubt that it was the afternoon by the time Alexander and his Bodyguards began their discussion on the banks of the Granicus, and it would take the army another hour or two to catch up.

Fighting a battle takes time. The army has to be formed up, the troops led into battle and the fighting take place. Moreover, the strategic situation into which Alexander had led his men meant that he had to win a convincing victory. If all he achieved was to push the Persians back from the Granicus, in the long term he would not have won very much at all. He would have been able to march through to Cyzicus without further trouble. There he would have been able to pick up fresh supplies of money and food.

However, the overall strategic situation would not have changed for the better. If anything it would have got worse. Memnon would have his army still intact, and could be expected to have a larger army very soon as his reinforcements came in. This would force Alexander to keep his men in a compact body, so they would be unable to spread out to harvest crops in the fields. The continued presence of a large Persian army in the area would also dissuade the Greek cities from defecting to Alexander. Like Lamposakos they would keep their gates closed and their food stores securely under lock and key. All Alexander would have achieved would have been to put off the day that starvation forced his retreat by a week or two.

What Alexander needed to achieve, as Parmenio seems to have realised, is a complete and overwhelming victory. Given the sizes of the armies facing each other over the Granicus, that could not be achieved in the two to three hours of daylight left to them that day. Not only would a battle need to be fought and won, but the Macedonian cavalry would have to drive the Persian units from the field, capture their baggage, destroy their supply system and smash any attempt to regroup. That alone could take the best part of a day to achieve.

Parmenio was right, late afternoon was no time to start crossing a defended river.

One aspect of the dispute which none of the surviving sources alludes to directly also has some bearing on events. The ancient writers may not have referred to this matter directly because they assumed that their readers would already know and so would not need telling again. The fact was that the Macedonian army had perfected a method for forcing their way across a defended river crossing.

This tactic was always successful and did not vary, except on two occasions. First the field artillery would be unpacked and assembled. This would then be brought forward to the Macedonian bank of the river, escorted by archers and slingers. Together these men and engines deluged the far bank with missiles of every kind. This hail of missiles, particularly the heavy bolts and stones shot by the field artillery, would disorder the enemy on the far bank, inflicting casualties and breaking their formations. A tightly knit unit of infantry, probably the hypaspists, then waded over the river to establish a bridgehead into which the rest of the army could cross. The army would then form up and attack.

The only two battles around river crossings in which this pattern was not repeated were the crossing of the Danube in 335BC and at the Granicus the following year. At the Danube a ford over the river was defended by the army of the Getae tribe. The river was too wide for slingers and archers to get their missiles across. Alexander therefore resorted to subterfuge. He got his hypaspists to stuff their waterproof leather tent covers with straw so that they would act as floats. Alexander then found a spot a few kilometres away from the ford where vegetation on the far bank offered cover from enemy scouts. As dawn approached, he led his men over the river. Each man swam, balancing his gear on the tent-cover floats.

Once on the far side, Alexander formed up the hypaspists in a defensive phalanx while other men crossed behind them. Only when more infantry and some cavalry were across did Alexander lead them forward. This advance force was led along the river bank to fall upon the flank of the enemy army that was still watching the ford to its front. The sudden eruption of Alexander's flanking force on their side of the mighty Danube caused the Getae army to flee with barely a fight.

As second in command of the army, Parmenio had a great number of duties. One of these was to look after the baggage train. This was not the food supply system, which was the responsibility of Eumenes, but the mass of men who transported the royal tent, the royal servants and – crucially – the artillery. If forcing a passage across a defended river necessitated having the field artillery in position, then it was Parmenio's job to get it there. And here was Parmenio arguing that the assault should be left to the next day.

In every account that we have of the Battle of the Granicus, the field artillery is conspicuous by its absence. So, interestingly, are the hoplites of the allied Greek states. The conclusion is inescapable that they were not at the Granicus because they were somewhere else, but where?

We know that on coming down from the hills and on to the plain of the River Granicus, Alexander had ordered his army to adopt a marching formation that approximated to that of its battle order. At the same time, Arrian tells us, 'all the transport had orders to follow in the rear'. Now, it is very unlikely that the transport would have been given orders to do anything if it were still with the main army. Alexander could simply have ridden over and told them himself. The way that Arrian puts this indicates that the transport and baggage was in such a position that Alexander could not simply tell them what to do. In other words they were detached from Alexander and the main army.

The most logical conclusion is that the baggage and transport had been left behind in a place of comparative safety when the army began its advance across the plain in battle formation. The obvious place was somewhere in the range of hills that the army had crossed after leaving Colonae. Alexander must have found a hill with steep sides or surrounded by ravines and crags that was large enough to shelter the transport train.

But the sort of valuable kit and equipment that was included in the baggage train could not simply be left lying about in hostile territory in the care of a bunch of horsegrooms and bureaucrats. Even if a part of the Persian army did not turn up, the easy pickings of an army baggage train would be an enormous temptation to local toughs.

The baggage train had to be guarded. That is almost certainly where the allied Greek hoplites were. Neither Alexander nor his generals rated the hoplites very highly on the field of battle. The Macedonians had defeated too many armies of hoplites over the years for Alexander to count the Greek allies among his elite forces. They had been brought along partly for political reasons, but also to spare the Macedonians from having to undertake routine, back up tasks – such as guarding the baggage train.

Detaching the baggage train in this way as the army was moving out on to flat land would have made sense. The Persians were known to be strong in horsemen, particularly light cavalry, who could make sweeping raids into the Macedonian column. Having several thousand horses and men that needed guarding would have been a worry that Alexander could well do without. So he had left them all behind in a place of safety.

But it did leave him in an awkward position. He was faced with a defended river crossing, while the field artillery needed to force the ford was stuck a full day's march behind him. The field artillery should have been separated out from the rest of the transport and brought along with the army. It would have been a sensible precaution to take in this situation, but Alexander had not taken it.

It was undoubtedly an awkward moment for Alexander. It was probably made all the worse by the knowing glances passing between the senior officers who were all too experienced in such matters to have made such an error, understandable though it was. Old Parmenio's comments must have rankled particularly. All the more because Alexander knew that the elderly second in command was right.

No wonder Alexander lost his temper.

According to Plutarch Alexander 'declared that the Hellespont would blush for shame if, after having crossed that strait, he should be afraid of the Granicus. He plunged into the stream with 13 troops of horsemen. And since he was charging against hostile missiles and precipitous positions covered with infantry and cavalry, and through a stream that swept men off their feet and surged about them, he seemed to be acting like a frenzied and foolish commander rather than a wise one.'

Arrian portrays Alexander as responding with rather more tact and care, though the result was the same:

Alexander had his answer. 'Yes, Parmenio,' he said, 'but I should be ashamed of myself if a little trickle of water like this – a very derogatory way of referring to the Granicus – were too much for us to cross without further preparation, when I had no difficulty whatever in crossing the Hellespont. Such hesitancy would be unworthy of the fighting fame of our people and of my own promptitude in the face of danger. Without doubt it would give the Persians added confidence. Nothing has yet happened to them to cause them alarm, and they would begin to think they were as good soldiers as we are.'

Arrian then gives a detailed description of the various units in the Macedonian army, some of which would have been arriving by this time, and who commanded them before picking up the train of events again.

> Then Alexander leapt upon his horse and called upon his guard to follow and to behave like men ... The leading files were met as they gained the river bank by volleys of missiles from the Persians who kept up a continuous shower into the river both from their commanding position on the banks above and from the comparatively flat strip right down by the water's edge. A hand to hand struggle developed, the Greek mounted troops trying to force their way out of the water, the Persians doing their utmost to prevent them. Persian javelins flew thick and fast. The long Macedonian spears thrust and stabbed. In this first onslaught Alexander's men, heavily outnumbered, suffered severely. Their foothold was insecure and down there in the water they had to contend with an enemy in a strong position on the bank above them – not to mention the fact that they met there the fine flower of the Persian horse, with Memnon and his sons braving the fortune of battle in its midst.

The scene is easy to picture and to imagine. Alexander, young headstrong and knowing himself to be highly talented, felt himself to be held back by the old greybeards he had inherited from his father. The situation was all the more galling as he knew that he was in the wrong. It was, perhaps, natural for him to try to prove his elders wrong by seeking to lead his own personal guard in an assault over the river. Perhaps he trusted to speed and elan to win him a way across the rushing waters. If so, he failed.

However, there are problems about the whole episode, and it is around these that the majority of the disputes and disagreements regarding the Battle of Granicus revolve. According to both Arrian and Plutarch, drawing on accounts written by Alexander's friends, this impetuous and disastrous assault was followed immediately by the rest of the battle.

They would have us believe that the bloody repulse of Alexander and his personal guard acted as the inspiration for the rest of the army to get itself underway, cross the river and defeat the entire Persian army. It simply does not make sense, and for a number of reasons.

First it would have taken a considerable amount of time for the army to get itself from its marching formation into a position suitable for crossing a defended river. According to Plutarch, Alexander stormed out of the meeting and attacked at once. It would have taken only minutes for his assault to be thrown back. Even if Arrian is correct and Alexander prepared for his attack a bit more carefully, issuing orders to the rest of his army to follow him, the account does not ring true. Alexander was riding straight into the trap, suffering heavy casualties and then suddenly turning the tide for no readily apparent reason. There was simply not enough time, as the story stands, for the army to get organised and follow Alexander. Even if it did, it seems rather unlikely that they could have overcome the defensive position of Memnon and his men.

In any case, it is clear from all the accounts of the battle that we have that it lasted for some considerable time, and was followed by a lengthy pursuit. Yet it was, all are agreed, early evening by the time this began. The accounts written by Alexander's friends simply do not make sense as they stand.

The most likely explanation for this is that the chief sources used by Plutarch and Arrian have glossed over this mistake by Alexander. They made the events of the following day run on directly from Alexander's abortive assault so that his failure was followed by and, by implication, was responsible for the eventual victory.

We know that Arrian chiefly used Ptolemy son of Lagus and Aristoboulos. Both these men were with Alexander at the Granicus. Ptolemy was a personal friend, Aristoboulos was one of the official geographers on the expedition. Both owed their positions directly to Alexander. They would have had a strong incentive to make Alexander look good. By the time that they were writing, Alexander had been declared a god, conquered the world and died a hero. Nobody wanted to be reminded of his youthful mistakes.

For a rather different account of the battle we have the anonymous mercenary whose account, albeit at third hand, is preserved in Diodorus. That account of the events of this evening are simple. 'When Alexander learned of the concentration of the Persian forces, he advanced rapidly. He then encamped opposite the Persians so that the Granicus flowed between the encampments.'

The mercenary would, of course, not have been privy to the events at the meeting of Alexander and his senior officers. He probably did not even know that it had taken place. He would have known only what could be seen from the Persian side of Granicus. What was seen was the Macedonian army advancing from the west, then turning aside to pitch camp.

Diodorus makes no mention at all of Alexander's disastrous and abortive attack. This may be because the men on the Persian side did not realise that it was Alexander himself who was making it. In such a situation, with two large and hostile armies camped close together and separated only by a river, skirmishes and probing attacks were to be expected. Perhaps the Persians took the rash attack by Alexander to be no more than one such minor assault and so paid it little attention.

Those on the Macedonian side, knowing who had led the attack, viewed the matter much more seriously and recorded it as a more major event.

Whatever the truth, it seems most likely that the day ended with both armies in camp. Scouts and sentries would have been posted before the sun went down on a tense and expectant scene. It would prove to be an eventful night.

CHAPTER TEN

The Granicus, Night

The soft twilight of an early summer evening saw the two armies camped on opposite sides of the Granicus River. None of the surviving sources give a very clear account of what happened during those hours of darkness. However, it is fairly easy to reconstruct what passed by looking at what happened the following morning and working back, using comparisons with what happened in similar circumstances on other occasions, to reconstruct the missing events.

The Persian satraps would have been pleased with the events of the first day on the Granicus. The Macedonians had advanced along the road to Cyzicus, as Memnon had correctly predicted they would do. Arriving at the Granicus, they had launched a probing attack with cavalry to test the strength of the Persian defences. That had been thrown back with what seemed to be relatively heavy losses. Now the Macedonians had withdrawn to camp.

So far as the Satraps were concerned, their plan was going exactly to expectations. Alexander had been drawn forward to find his way blocked at a defensive position of the Persians' choosing. The strength of that position had been shown by the repulse of the cavalry attack that had taken place in late afternoon. The satraps must have been certain that things were going their way. They will have looked forward confidently to the following day when Alexander might renew his assault. No doubt, the satraps thought, any new attack would be driven back decisively.

When dusk fell, the Persian troops would have trailed back to their camp, which seems to have been located fairly close to the river. Persian camps were famously comfortable affairs – it was bad enough being on campaign without being forced to rough it. Certainly the satraps and officers would have had comfortable tents and pavilions with servants, fine foods and entertainments. With a battle due on the morrow, it is unlikely that any of the satraps or senior officers indulged themselves too much. For the soldiers of the royal army there would have been food, tents and servants as well, though not of such high quality.

The bulk of the local militia would not have been so well served. They had to make do with whatever they had brought with them. This might have amounted to not much more than a sack of bread and hard cheese, with a thick blanket for cover. But the night seems to have been a dry and warm one – none of the sources speak of any inclement weather. Diodorus, with his interest in the conditions for the ordinary soldier, would have been bound to mention any rain or cold. No doubt the men were comfortable enough, though they had no luxuries.

Persian military camps were notoriously poorly organised. Each group of men put themselves down where they liked with no real regard for order or discipline. The officers were not always with their men, nor were entire units always camping together. Much more notice was taken of how far it was to water, or if a wall offered shelter from a strong wind. The result was that Persian camps were often a disorganised mass of tents, bivouacs and cooking fires. The men themselves were often more comfortable than those in more disciplined camps.

In fact, as marching camps went, the Persians seem to have developed a habit of being able to produce order out of apparent chaos. It seems that because everyone involved knew that there was no real order, they were accustomed to fitting in around everyone else. Perhaps there was some sort of unofficial order of precedence that saw the satrapian guards choose their camping ground before the cavalry militia, who had precedence over the infantry militia. We don't really know, but the arrangements obviously worked. There are no instances anywhere or at any time of a Persian army getting itself confused while in camp.

The Persian army had been on the banks of the Granicus for at least a day, possibly three or four. They had had plenty of time to adopt whatever system they had and to get accustomed to the layout of their camp. Events next morning were to show that they were able to mobilise and march out for battle with efficiency and speed.

One aspect of Persian camping that the Greeks ridiculed at some length was the complete lack of entrenching and formal defensive measures. It must be said that compared to the later Roman army, or indeed to modern practise, the Greeks themselves were fairly poor in this respect. The Persians seem to have been even weaker. They dug no ditches around their marching camps, nor erected palisades of wooden stakes.

Much of what we know about Persian military camps comes from the writings of the Athenian Xenophon, who served as a mercenary in Persia some 70 years before Alexander's time. According to Xenophon, the Persians did not post sentries around their camps, nor did they keep any unit of men awake and armed to face any surprise attack. The cavalry hobbled their horses before going to sleep, but made no effort to coral them or to protect them against a sneak enemy attack.

According to Xenophon, the only effort the Persians made in the way of defending their camps was to make the layout as jumbled and confused as possible. There were no neat lanes between the tents, as was the case in Greek camps, nor was there a broad lane leading to the commander's tent from the camp entrance – since Persian camps lacked a surrounding entrenchment it must be presumed that they had no formal entrance either. The guy ropes of tents formed a web, there were spears stuck upright in the ground and sleeping men might be tripped over anywhere.

This higgledly layout meant that no attacking force could charge through the camp, dealing out death and destruction as it did so. If any force tried a surprise attack they would quickly get entangled in tents, sleeping blankets and the like. It may sound a fairly passive and unsophisticated way of going about things, but it clearly worked for the Persians.

On this occasion, of course, the Persians were not alone. They had Memnon and his 5,000 mercenaries with them. These men were more accustomed to adopting a formal camp layout with at least some efforts at temporary fortifications around it. They may have grown lax in Persian service, but with thousands of Macedonians only a short distance away it is likely that they made some attempt at adopting a more Greek style of camp.

Of rather more importance for what was to follow, Memnon did not share the satraps belief that all was well. He had not wanted to get this close to the Macedonians, nor to Alexander and Parmenio. He had lived in Macedon for several months, perhaps as long as a couple of years. He had seen the Macedonian army up close and knew what it was capable of. He had almost certainly met Parmenio, as well as other senior Macedonian commanders. If he did not know Alexander, the boy had probably been off being educated when Memnon was in Macedonia, Memnon had known his father Philip.

Memnon was not prepared simply to sit back and wait for the Macedonians to march, once more, into the trap laid for them. He thought that the Macedonians would try something. He did not know what, but he was taking no chances. After all, Memnon had not wanted to risk a battle against the Macedonians in the open field at all. He had wanted to trust in the defences of the cities to wear down the enemy, exhaust their supplies and thin their ranks. If he was intending to use his mobile striking force at all, it was either to land in Greece or to chase Alexander out of Asia when he was already beaten.

Memnon sent out scouts and patrols to watch what the Macedonians were up to. We do not know how many men he sent out, nor who they were, but it is easy to guess. Memnon had with him thousands of Greek mercenaries. These included some of his own small group of permanent men as well as a much larger number of rank and file. No doubt he had detailed some of his permanent force to guard the more important cities, but he would have had most of them with him. We know that at least a few hundred of Memnon's mercenaries were cavalry. It would have made most sense for him to send these men out to watch the Macedonians. Events would prove that whoever the scouts were, they were mounted.

As dusk settled down, Memnon would have sent riders forward to watch the Macedonian camp. They would most likely have sat their horses atop the steep banks of the Granicus, from which they could see the enemy clearly. Later on, perhaps as a result of reports these men sent back, Memnon seems to have become nervous. He sent other riders out to north and to south to patrol the river banks.

Over on the Macedonian side of the river, rather more was happening. Returning from his abortive foray, Alexander had given orders for his army to camp. The writers who were drawing on Macedonian sources skip over the events of the night completely. They jump straight from Alexander's rash attack to the main crossing of the army. Again, however, it is fairly clear what happened.

The army camped some distance back from the river – perhaps as much as a mile. Mounted scouts – presumably men from the prodromoi – were sent forwards to patrol the river banks and keep Memnon's scouts at a safe distance. Alexander then had to decide how to proceed. His original plan of forcing a crossing had failed and he was a good enough commander, even at this early stage in his career, to realise that things were not going to get any better the next day. Equally, Alexander knew that to retreat would be disastrous. The Macedonians simply had to get over that river.

It can be imagined that the last thing Alexander wanted to do, however, was to adopt the plan put forward by Parmenio. If we have reconstructed the earlier discussions correctly, Parmenio had wanted to send back to the baggage for the field artillery and then force a river crossing in the usual fashion. Parmenio was, after all, an experienced commander who had seen this tactic work successfully before.

Alexander had other ideas. He decided to use his own tactical innovation that had worked so well the previous year when crossing the Danube. This tactic had two strong advantages to Alexander. First he had done it before and knew it worked. Second it was his idea – Parmenio had been campaigning in Asia Minor when Alexander had been crossing the Danube.

The crossing of the Danube had been in the face of a large, but undisciplined army of tribal levies. The army on the far side of the Granicus was a different proposition, being both more professional and led by professional officers, but that did not mean that the tactic would not work again.

Alexander will have sent out mounted scouts to north and south looking for a crossing place. Like the crossing point at the Danube, this place had to offer both an easy crossing and be invisible to the enemy. Alexander will have guessed that Memnon would send out scouts, even if the satraps did not, so he would have told his prodromoi that they had to get at least four or five kilometres away from the camp before they began searching for a crossing point.

Given that the Granicus was deep only in places, the scouts were looking for somewhere that had gentle, sloping banks extending for some considerable distance. The river along this stretch also needed to have a firm bottom to give secure footing for the men. Ideally the army should be able to cross on a broad frontage so that it could get across quickly. If the crossing point was too narrow it would take too long to the get the army across.

One of the prodromoi found a suitable spot fairly early on in the night. Given the time of year and the latitude of the Granicus, there would have been only about nine hours of darkness. Alexander could not risk sending out his scouts until it was dark enough for them not to be seen leaving the Macedonian camp by Memnon's patrols on the far side of the Granicus. Even if a suitable crossing point was found quickly, it would have taken the prodromoi an hour or so to find the place and return to camp.

Alexander then had to get his army out of camp and over the new crossing point without their being seen. The first task was to get the army out of its camp without Memnon's men knowing that they had left. Assuming that Alexander had been planning a night move when he gave the order to camp, he would have put the camp far enough away from the Granicus so that the sounds of men on the march would not carry to the far bank. But it is not sounds alone that could alert an enemy.

We know that some years after Alexander's death another Macedonian army found itself being pursued by a much larger force and needed to move out of its camp at night without being detected. On that occasion the main force was mustered to march two hours after dark fell. Silence was strictly enforced as the men left camp and moved off. Meanwhile strong mounted patrols were out, fending off the enemy scouts and vigorously driving them well back.

More cavalry were left in the camp. They kept their horses at the rear of the camp, out of sight of the enemy. These men had orders to keep the camping fires well banked up until after midnight. They also had to walk around continuously crossing and recrossing in front of the camp fires. This gave the impression of there being a much larger number of men present. At midnight most fires were abandoned and allowed to die down naturally as if the men they served had gone to bed. Only a small group of fires to one side was kept going with fresh supplies of wood. An hour before dawn the camp was finally abandoned and the men rode off to join the main army, which by then had got almost 15km away.

Dawn broke to show the camp standing as it had been the night before. All tents were in their lines, all cooking fires slowly dying down. Even the commander's conference tent was standing. But the men and all their weapons had gone.

It must be presumed that on the night beside the Granicus, Alexander did a similar thing. He will have had his men ready to move, setting out as soon as the prodromoi came in with news that a crossing place had been found. Meanwhile, his scouts would have been patrolling aggressively along the river banks. They could be imagined splashing into the river water to give the impression of testing the alertness of Memnon's scouts or looking for a stretch of river with a firm bottom. Back at camp a small number of men would be busy keeping the fires fed with fresh wood and walking about to give the impression that the army was still there.

Performing a night march is a notoriously difficult operation fraught with difficulty. Military history is filled with accounts of armies losing their way, getting disorganised or blundering off the road. Alexander seems to have achieved this night march, as he did that prior to crossing the Danube, with skill and success. As it was a fine night, it may have been cloudless. Even the faint light shed by the stars can be enough to stop men walking into ditches or tripping over stones.

Although this is not certain, it seems that the Macedonian army reached the new crossing point over the Granicus some hours before dawn. Alexander let his men rest for the remainder of the night.

As the cold, chill light of dawn crept up over the horizon the Macedonian army was on the move again. Although the field artillery was absent, the Cretan archers and Agrianian javelin men were present.

They were probably set to line the river, ready to discharge their missiles if any enemy troops appeared on the far bank. None did.

Alexander pushed his cavalry over first. It would have made sense to get the best units across first. These were the Thessalian cavalry, led by the same Callas who had taken over from Parmenio the previous autumn, and the companion cavalry under the command of Philotas, son of Parmenio. This Philotas was about the same age as Alexander. Years earlier, when Alexander quarrelled with Philip, Philotas had taken his side against the king and his own father. This act must have endeared him to Alexander and convinced the young king that Philotas could be trusted with the companion cavalry. He had been appointed to command the unit before leaving Therme and, as the king traditionally led these elite troops in battle, it was a responsible position of great honour for such a young man.

Alexander was hoping that he could get his entire army across the river before the Persians awoke to the threat. He would not, therefore, have sent these horsemen riding far beyond the landing place. They would have been kept closely in hand, but ready to attack if any enemy units turned up.

Next over would have been the light Thracian horse commanded by Agathon. Not much is known of this cavalry officer. His name would indicate that he was more likely to have been Greek than Macedonian, and even less likely to have been Thracian. Of course, he might have had a Greek mother, in which case he may have been born the son of a Macedonian or Thracian noble, but that is only speculation. The job of these light, unarmoured horsemen was to scout, pursue and probe. Armed with javelins and swords, the Thracian horsemen were not at their best in a formal charge. Their role at this point would have been to overtake and kill any Persian scouts that were spotted.

Next over were the Paeonians commanded by Arrhidaeus, a man with a solidly Macedonian name. These light horsemen, like the Thracians were equipped with javelins and swords. Arrhidaeus commanded not only the Paeonians, but also the Podoromai. They would soon take up station alongside the Paeonians, but presumably arrived a bit later from their scattered duties. Some of the prodromoi sent out to more distant places may not have arrived in time to take part in the battle at all.

Finally would have come the cavalry of the Greek states, commanded by Philip. Nothing is known of this man's background except that he was a Macedonian nobleman who was admired by Alexander more for his administrative abilities than his skills in battle. No doubt he was

Companion Cavalry and Hypaspists
1

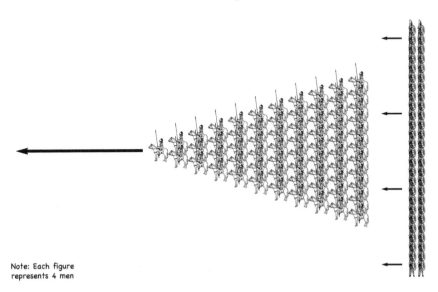

Note: Each figure
represents 4 men

Companion Cavalry and Hypaspist

This series of drawings shows the tactics used by Companion cavalry when advancing in co-operation with Hypaspist infantry. None of the ancient writers explains these tactics in detail, but they do seem to have been designed to allow the cavalry to reform after delivering an attack that failed. They were also used if the horsemen needed to reform during the pursuit of a defeated enemy formation, for instance if a new enemy phalanx appeared. The Hypaspists are shown here two ranks deep for clarity, though in reality they fought in 8 deep formations. The Companion wedge is similarly shown smaller than was the case in reality, again for clarity.

(1) A squadron of companion cavalry is advancing in wedge formation, with a unit of hypaspists following behind in phalanx. The hypaspists seem to have been divided into units 1,000 men strong. A phalanx of this size would have a frontage of about 120 metres, rather wider than the rear of a companion squadron in wedge. When close enough to the enemy, the companion cavalry charge.

175

Companion Cavalry and Hypaspists
2

Note: Each figure
represents 4 men

(2) While the companion cavalry deliver their attack, the Hypaspists continue to advance. These men were trained to move quickly, probably at a jog trot, for extended periods. Running in full armour was one of the sports at the ancient Olympic games. We know of one Hypaspist who kept up a jog during a pursuit for 5km, thought this seems to be exceptional.

given command of the Allied cavalry to stop some Greek commander taking it into his head to be disloyal. Each of the units under Philip's command did, however, have a commander from their own home city.

At some point, the elite hypaspist infantry crossed over among the cavalry. These superb infantry were commanded by Nicanor, another son of Parmenio. They frequently co-operated with the companion cavalry, so perhaps they crossed the river at the same time as those horsemen. Nicanor seems to have been older than his brother Philotas, who led the companion cavalry.

Then came the pezhetairoi, the foot companions, with their enormously long sarissas and heavy armour. These men were divided into six units, or lochus. The first was led by Perdiccas, a young Macedonian nobleman who was particularly close to Alexander. The second was commanded by Coenus about whom little is known other than that he was married

Companion Cavalry and Hypaspists
3

Note: Each figure
represents 4 men

(3) Seeing that the cavalry charge has failed, the Hypaspists come to a halt. The officers dress the ranks to ensure that the phalanx is solid and offers no weak spots to the enemy. The retreating companion cavalry ride around the flanks of the phalanx and come to a halt immediately behind the infantry. At once the officers start trying to reform the cavalry.

to a daughter of Parmenio. The third unit was commanded by Amyntas, son of Andromenes and the fourth was led by Philip, son of a different Amyntas, both men from Upper Macedonia. The fifth by Meleager, another younger nobleman from the mountains of inland Macedonia. The sixth unit of the foot companions came under Craterus, another upland nobleman.

At some point in proceedings, probably when the sun was already up, one of the mounted men sent out by Memnon during the course of the night came across the scene. He put his spurs to his horse and galloped back toward the Persian camp.

When they got the news that thousands of men were crossing the Granicus some distance away, the Persians eyed Alexander's camp on the far side of the Granicus. To all appearances it had been occupied throughout the night.

Companion Cavalry and Hypaspists
4

Note: Each figure
represents 4 men

(4) *The companion cavalry are now reformed into a wedge formation, though it is now smaller due to the casualties suffered during the abortive charge. Persian light cavalry pursuing the Companion horsemen now come up. They are halted by the Hypaspist phalanx. After some desultory throwing of javelins, the light cavalry retreat. The companion cavalry are now ready to renew their assault, or to fall back while being covered by the Hypaspists as circumstances dictate.*

Memnon was in a quandary. His scout had come in to report the Macedonians crossing several kilometres away, but others reported the bulk of the enemy were still just across the river. The flanking move might simply be a ruse designed to get the Persians to abandon their strong position so that the Macedonians could cross in peace. Or it might be a force that was aiming to come crashing down to launch a flank attack on the Persian defenders as the Macedonians began to attack over the river. Or it might indeed be the main Macedonian army.

Memnon would have wanted to be sure of where Alexander was before he committed himself. Perhaps he got the men with the keenest eyes to study the Macedonian camp from the river bank. Perhaps he sent a column of cavalry over to brush aside the Macedonian scouts and inspect the camp at close quarters. Whatever he did, Memnon was soon convinced that the camp was all but abandoned. The bulk of Alexander's army was crossing the river. Memnon at once realised that he had no time to lose.

Memnon had never wanted to fight the Macedonians in the open on equal terms. If he was still to avoid that fate, he had to move fast. His only chance was to get to the new crossing point before Alexander had most of his army over and formed up.

Leading the Persian and mercenary Greek cavalry out of the camp at top speed, Memnon and the satraps left orders for the infantry to follow as quickly as possible. Then they put spurs to their horses and set off to battle.

CHAPTER ELEVEN

The Granicus, Day Two

The various accounts of the different sources come together again at dawn on the second day on the Granicus. For those drawing on Macedonian sources, the main battle followed on directly from Alexander's cavalry only assault the evening before and took place at the same site. Those accounts seen from the Persian side have the main battle fought early the following morning close to the new crossing point.

Whichever time and site is given, the accounts of the battle open with the Macedonian army drawn up ready for battle and waiting calmly for the action to begin. Diodorus tells us that Alexander 'brought his army across the river and deployed in good order before the Persians could stop him'. Arrian has Alexander carefully organising and dressing the ranks before sending Parmenio to command on the left while he himself went to command the right.

The line of battle of the Macedonians was close to that which was standard for the Macedonian army. Clearly Alexander had had plenty of time to get his army into a fighting organisation – perhaps it was now two hours of so after dawn.

On the extreme right were the 500 Cretan archers and 500 Agrianian javelin men. It has been suggested that they might have been drawn up along the river bank. Perhaps they were to keep an eye on the riverbed in case any Persian units tried to sneak along the river to emerge and attack the Macedonians in the rear. If this were the case it would mean that Alexander had gone down stream to find his new crossing place.

Next to the Cretans and Agrianians were positioned the eight squadrons of companion cavalry, 1,800 men in all. To their left were the 200 or so Paeonian cavalry and such of the prodromoi that had arrived, maybe around 600 men. On their left were the hypaspists, some 3,000 strong.

Then came the vast mass of the foot companion pezhetairoi phalanx. The six lochus took it in turns to perform different duties on a roster that changed tasks daily. This day the lochus of Perdiccas had the task of being ready for instant battle, and was therefore stationed on the right of the phalanx. His unit was followed, going from right to left, by those of Coenus, Amyntas, Philip, Meleager and Craterus.

Beyond the massive phalanx were put the light Thracian cavalry, about 250 strong. Then came the 600 Allied Greek cavalry. Finally the elite 1,800 Thessalian horsemen formed up on the far left wing.

The brief statement by Arrian of the division of the Macedonian army into two wings under the youthful king and the elderly general has led to considerable debate. Some have suggested that the central phalanx came under Alexander on the right, others that it fell to Parmenio on the left and a few have suggested that it might have been divided into two phalanxes with part under Parmenio and part under Alexander. Such debates miss the essential basic battle plan of the Macedonian army.

As developed under Philip, the Macedonian army was designed to fight on a battle plan that in modern parlance is known as the attack in oblique order. The genius of Alexander was to be flexible in his application of this basic pattern, adapting it to the conditions of each battle and even changing his battle plan in mid fight while commanding from the saddle. It was a rare and special talent that was first put into action on the Granicus.

Put simply, the Macedonian battle plan centred on the pezhetairoi phalanx. This would be put into motion, moving forward at a steady walking pace. The slow, grinding advance of the massed phalanx was designed to put increasing pressure on the centre of the enemy line. With their long sarissa spears, the foot companions could afford to walk into the attack, unlike conventional hoplites who ran. Their job was not to break through the enemy centre, but to exert gradually but inexorably increasing pressure. This kept the enemy's attention focussed on the centre.

On the right, meanwhile, the right wing cavalry would be searching for a weakness. If one could be found the companion cavalry would be launched in a battering ram charge designed to smash a path through the enemy formations. Once through, the companion cavalry would fan out to attack the enemy units from flank and rear. If this plan were conducted properly, the enemy centre would be assaulted from the rear by the companion cavalry just as it was coming under maximum frontal pressure from the Macedonian phalanx. The enemy troops might be annihilated where they stood, or pursued and cut down as they ran.

The left wing cavalry was there to stop the massed phalanx from being outflanked by the enemy on that wing. Their secondary role was to keep the enemy troops facing them concentrating on what was going on in their own area and so stop them from interfering with what the companion cavalry were up to until it was too late. Once the enemy broke the left wing cavalry would surge forward to join the pursuit and the killing.

Companion Cavalry vs Persian heavy infantry
1

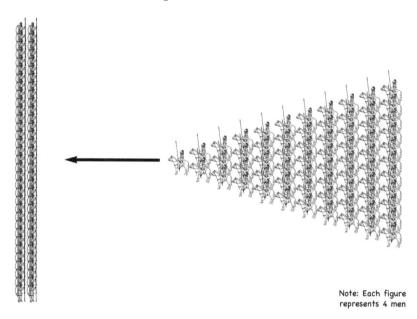

Note: Each figure
represents 4 men

Companion Cavalry vs Persian heavy infantry

This series of drawings shows the tactics used by Companion cavalry when assaulting a phalanx of formed heavy infantry. The Persian heavy infantry were armed in a similar fashion to Greek hoplites and formed up either 6 or 8 ranks deep. They are shown here two ranks deep for clarity. The Companion wedge is similarly shown smaller than was the case in reality, again for clarity.

(1) In wedge formation, a squadron of the Companion Cavalry canter toward the enemy phalanx. At this point poorly trained infantry, or those low in morale or which had already taken casualties, might prove unable to face the attack. The men at the point of impact might break ranks and flee. Assuming this did not happen, the cavalry would close to the attack.

Companion Cavalry vs Persian heavy infantry
2

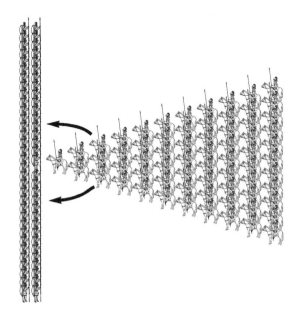

Note: Each figure
represents 4 men

(2) The leading horseman reaches the Persian ranks. Horses will not run straight into solid obstacles, so the lead horses would slow to a walk as they actually reached the enemy. The flankers on the ranks behind the leaders would continue forward until they too came into contact with the enemy. The horsemen would then use their long xyston lances to outreach the dory spears of the infantry. A few men on both sides would become casualties.

Companion Cavalry vs Persian heavy infantry
3

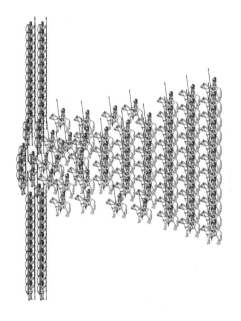

Note: Each figure
represents 4 men

(3) The front ranks of the cavalry unit are hustled forward by those behind, causing the infantry phalanx to begin to bow backward at the point of impact. The frontage of the engagement widens as the flank riders from ranks further back begin to engage with the infantry.

Companion Cavalry vs Persian heavy infantry
4

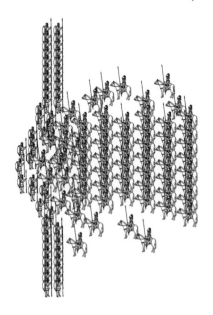

Note: Each figure
represents 4 men

(4) *The momentum of the horsemen continues to push back the infantry around the point of impact, while flank riders continue to widen the section of the phalanx coming under attack. The conditions at the centre of the front sections of the cavalry formation now become increasingly crowded and confused as the horsemen push and shove forward, trying to build up a momentum of movement. The infantry give ground. As they move back the bulge means that the line to be defended becomes longer just as the numbers of men to hold it are being reduced by casualties. The depth of the phalanx at this point was initially 8 men, but may now be down to four or even fewer.*

Companion Cavalry vs Persian heavy infantry
5

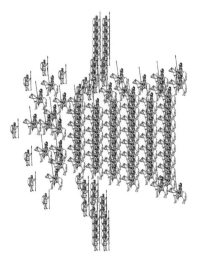

Note: Each figure
represents 4 men

(5) Eventually the thinning ranks of the phalanx give way completely. The companion cavalry burst through. As the resistance to the front collapses, the succeeding ranks are free to pour through the gap. The horsemen then fan out to either side to attack the infantry from the rear. The phalanx collapses into a mob of fleeing men.

It can be seen that the commanders of the two flanking cavalry forces had to be able to make lightning fast decisions, reacting quickly to a rapidly changing battle situation. They might have to get involved in hand to hand fighting, lead charges or send their horsemen on great sweeping manoeuvres. Such a task would be enough for any man.

By contrast, the job of the massed phalanx was simply to advance slowly and steadily. It was a tough, gruelling and demanding job, but not one that called for much in the way of rapid thinking or swift decision-making. So far as we know there was no overall commander of the foot companions. On the other hand there did not really need to be. Each lochus would lock itself firmly into that next to it to become a solid mass of armed men. The only co-operation between the lochus that was needed was remarkably simple: stay in line.

It is most likely that Alexander commanded the mobile elements on the right wing, from the Cretans to the hypaspists, and that Parmenio commanded the comparable units on the left wing from the Thessalians to the Thracians. The central phalanx could be left to get on with its job.

All accounts agree that having taken up his position at the head of the 300 strong lead squadron of the companion cavalry, Alexander donned a special helmet. It was usual practice among the Macedonians to indicate rank by decorations on the helmet. Plutarch describes it in some detail.

It was a bronze helmet of the Boeotian style, as was usual for companion cavalry. Standing up from the top of the helmet and running from front to back was a large crest. Contemporary usage would indicate that this was made up of hundreds of stiff, upright bristles about 15cm long. From the rear of the crest a tuft of longer hairs taken from a horse tail fell down Alexander's back in a cascade of carefully crimped waves. What made Alexander's helmet unique, however, were the two large feathered plumes of a dazzling whiteness. One of these impressive additions stuck up vertically on either side of the crest at the top of the helmet.

This helmet, combined with the top quality armour that Alexander wore, made him a conspicuous and easily identified figure. According to Plutarch the satraps of Persia decided that their best chance of winning the battle was to kill Alexander. He would at least be easy to find.

It was this sight that greeted Memnon and the satraps as they rode down the river bank with their cavalry. Clearly they were already too late to stop Alexander from the getting across the river and forming up. The Persians, at this stage, had only their horsemen with them. The infantry were hurrying along but it would be some time before they could reach the field of battle.

While they were waiting, the Persians formed themselves up into a line facing that of the Macedonians. Diodorus tells us that Memnon put himself and his small unit of elite mercenary cavalry on the left wing, facing directly toward Alexander with his showy helmet. Beside Memnon was Arsamenes and his men, probably the Phrygians. Memnon's unit would have numbered no more than a few hundred, but Arsamenes may have had as many as 2,000 with him. To their right were positioned Arsites with his Paphlagonian cavalry, perhaps another 2,000 men or so. To their right were the best cavalry of this left wing, the 2,000 Hyrcanians of the royal army led by Spithridates.

The Persian centre was made up of the assorted satrapal bodyguards and other small units that had arrived by the day of the battle. Diodorus does not mention any overall commander of this central mass, so it may have been rather disjointed from a command structure point of view. This would make sense as the Persians had not expected to fight an open battle of this kind. In any case, the centre would conventionally be filled by the infantry – but they were still hurrying up from the rear. Presumably this positioning of a group of small units to face the Macedonian phalanx was a merely temporary measure.

On the right wing the Persians had their best troops: the cavalry of the royal army. These were composed of 1,000 Medes and 2,000 others under Rheomithras plus getting on for 3,000 Bactrians. These Bactrians should have been commanded by Mithridates, but Diodorus does not say that he commanded these men at the outset of the battle. Indeed, no account mentions him until the fighting was well underway. Perhaps he was hurrying the infantry along.

Arrian tells us that 'there was a profound hush as both armies stood for a while motionless as if in awe of what was to come'.

This period of silence and waiting does make sense. Having failed to arrive before the Macedonians were over the river, the Persians will have been waiting for their infantry to arrive and would be unwilling to begin the battle until the tens of thousands of foot soldiers had turned up. They had nothing to gain by starting things early.

Alexander, on the other hand, had just seen the vast mass of Persian horsemen come trotting forwards in an apparent rush to begin the fighting. They would have come to a halt in a great swirl of dust. Then there would have been a scene of movement and apparent confusion as the cavalry units moved and swirled about taking up their positions. Wondering what the enemy were up to, Alexander would have waited until the dust settled. When it did, the Persians were revealed as having adopted a most extraordinary formation.

We have no other record from any battle fought around this time of an army drawing up for battle with its front line composed entirely of cavalry. Alexander was not to know the reasons for this, though he might have guessed in due course. The profound hush noted by Arrian ensued.

After some time, we don't know how long, Alexander decided that it was time to get things moving. His aim had not changed now that he was over the Granicus. He wanted to inflict a defeat on the Persian forces so decisive that they would be unable to interfere with him for some weeks, or better still months, to come. He wanted the Greek cities of Asia Minor no longer to be afraid of the vengeance of the Persians and so open their gates willingly. He needed to crush this army facing him.

The course of the battle that followed is fairly easy to pick out from the various sources. However, the fact that they are each looking at the battle from a slightly different point of view means that they put a different emphasis on events, with unavoidable discrepancies between the various accounts.

A key question that cannot readily be answered is precisely when the Persian infantry arrived. According to Arrian they did not arrive until after

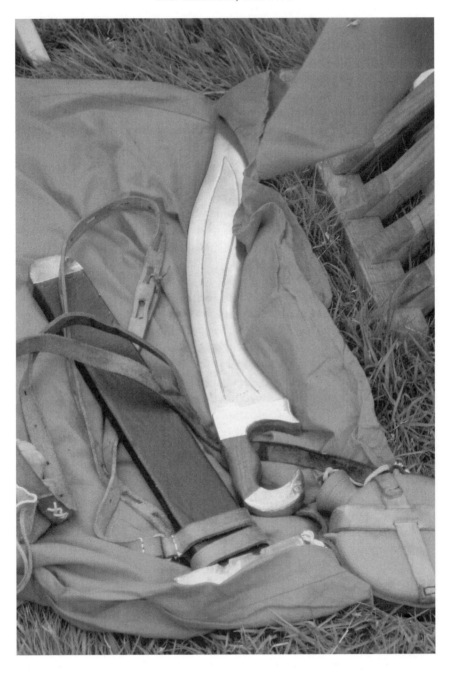

A kopis style sword, as used by the Persians during the Granicus campaign. The weapon had a single cutting edge and widened out near the tip to give added momentum to the blade when used in a slashing motion. (With thanks to the Hoplite Association.

the cavalry had finished fighting. Plutarch describes the infantry battle as beginning while the cavalry on the Macedonian right wing were at the critical point of their action. Diodorus, who usually appears to know most about what was happening on the Persian side, is vague saying that the infantry battle ended soon after that of the cavalry. On balance it would seem that the Persian infantry, or at least some of them, entered the fray while most of the senior commanders had their attention elsewhere.

What follows is an account drawn from all the available sources. At no point do any of the sources flatly contradict the others regarding what happened, though there are some confusions about timing and sequence. These have been ironed out by comparing the wording of the different accounts and, in the final analysis of particularly difficult issues, on the basis of what seems most probable taking into account how battles were usually fought in that distant age and the abilities of the troops involved.

The battle began, as usual, with some probing by the cavalry on the Macedonian right wing. Like lochus of the foot companions, the squadrons of the cavalry companions also took it in turns to perform different duties. This day it was the task of the squadron led by Ptolemy to take the lead in battle. There were several Ptolemies serving as officers in the Macedonian army and it is not entirely clear which was the man in question here. However, it seems most likely that this Ptolemy was the Ptolemy who is usually described as 'son of Lagos'.

As the squadron of 210 companion cavalry trotted forward they were accompanied by the Paeonians and prodromoi. The gap left in the Macedonian line would have been filled by the hypaspists. Their main role was to serve as a mobile link between the main phalanx and the right wing cavalry. Now they altered their formation to spread out right and close the gap.

The purpose of this initial attack was to probe the Persian left wing for weaknesses, test its cohesion and, with luck, clear the way for a devastating charge by the bulk of the companion cavalry led by Alexander himself.

The Paeonians will have mounted swirling advances, throwing their javelins into the Persian ranks, then wheeling aside and retreating. The prodromoi would have likewise hurled javelins at the Persians, but may have closed to fight with their lances for a while before they too broke off and galloped away. All the time Ptolemy's companion cavalry squadron was hovering on the edges of the action looking for an opening into which they could charge.

The Persians would not have taken all this standing still. The essence of cavalry actions in any age is rapid, fluid movement in an effort to put the opponent at a disadvantage. As the Paeonians and prodromoi were swirling and wheeling so too were their opponents.

The Persian unit directly opposite Ptolemy's units were the Paphlagonians. It must be assumed that these were the main target of the Macedonian assaults. These men traditionally went to war armed in a fashion not too dissimilar to the prodromoi they now faced. They had two javelins and a heavy thrusting spear. Their helmets were of hardened leather, not metal like the Macedonians, but they did carry a small round shield about 50cm in diameter.

It was not in the nature of these men to fight standing still. They too would have been formed into squadrons. Although most of the men were militia, their leaders are more likely to have been noblemen who had undergone some formal training. Sent forwards in small units by their overall commander, the satrap Arsites, the Paphlagonians plunged into the dust kicked up by the wheeling Macedonian horsemen. Showers of javelins flew in all directions as the groups of horsemen swirled around.

Pushing the units forward and back was a deadly dance of great skill. It was a complex, confusing and ever changing pattern of combat, but both Ptolemy and Arsites were professionals. These attacks were not designed to win the battle, nor even to begin that process. Their purpose was to allow the commanders to gauge the quality of the men in the opposing army, and to test the mettle of the opposing commanders. Ptolemy and Arsites were looking for signs of nervousness among the opposing units that had not yet joined the fray, and for fatigue or fear among those that had. And behind them Alexander and Memnon were likewise studying the opposition to see how well the men fought, and how cleverly they were moved by their commanders. They were testing the skills of each other, with the lives of their warriors.

Over on the Macedonian left wing, meanwhile, it was the Persians who were doing the attacking. We have much less idea of what was happening in this area of the battlefield. Alexander was on the right and most writers wanted to concentrate on his actions. It is clear, however, that Rheomithras was attacking with some skill.

Conventionally a Persian cavalry assault would have begun with their light cavalry, just as the Macedonians were doing on the other wing. These would have been the enigmatic '2,000 horsemen' mentioned by Diodorus. Armed with javelins, or perhaps with light bows, these men would have surged forward to deliver exactly the same kind of sweeping, swirling attacks being made by Ptolemy. Again, they were looking for weaknesses and seeking to demoralise or disorder their opponents.

Persian Light Cavalry in Skirmish Order

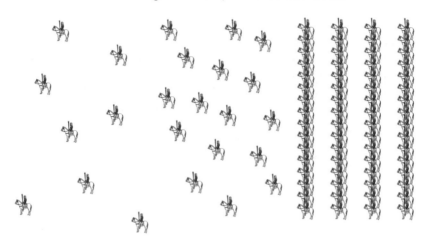

Persian Light Cavalry in Skirmish Order

Greek sources describe Persian light cavalry operating both in formed bodies and as masses of individual riders. Shown here are both formations. It may be that men formed in ranks were preceded into battle by a cloud of individuals. In either case, the light cavalry would charge toward the enemy, wheeling aside at the last minute as the men hurled their javelins into the opposing formation. Light cavalry seem to have operated in smaller units of about 100 men, though this is uncertain.

Those opponents were the Thessalian, Greek and Thracian cavalry led by Parmenio. The task given to Parmenio was simple to express, but could be very complicated to carry out. He was to keep the enemy right wing in play, stop it from getting on to the flank or rear of the main foot companion phalanx and stop it from moving off to intervene in Alexander's activities on the other side of the battlefield.

Actually doing this was another matter entirely. The Bactrians were drawn from the Persian Royal Army. They were every bit as elite and professional as were the Thessalians. Operating in small units, the Bactrians would charge forward, feint to one side, withdraw only to charge and feint again. It is difficult to describe the fast-moving combat conditions of this sort of combat between well trained, missile-armed cavalry. It called for quick wits, superb horsemanship and steady nerves. Fortunately for the Macedonian army, Parmenio and his Thessalians were highly skilled at this type of combat.

Coming up behind the Persian light cavalry were the more heavily armed units of Medes and Bactrians. The Medes were the most heavily

Persian Heavy Cavalry in Attack Column

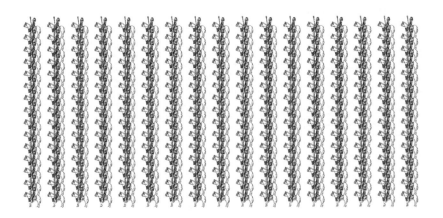

Persian Heavy Cavalry in Attack Column

No military manuals from the Persian Empire have survived, so we are reliant on Greek accounts for our information. These tend to report what they saw when fighting the Persians and may or may not be entirely accurate. It seems that the armoured cavalry units of the Persian army formed up in squadrons about 250 strong. When charging they adopted a column formation with a flat front that was at least four times as deep as it was wide. The unit shown here is 15 riders wide and 17 deep, giving a total strength of 255 men. This formation gave the advantages of depth and momentum, but tended to dissipate the impact over the wider frontage.

armed cavalry in the Persian army. They had helmets, body armour and leg armour of bronze, while even their horses had armour protecting their heads and chests. They were armed with javelins, but also with swords with which they were trained to fight at close quarters. Rheomithras who led these men would not unleash them until he was confident that a charge by big men on big horses was going to smash the enemy formation and so open the way to victory.

Until then he would have been using his Bactrians. These men, too, were comparatively heavily armoured with body and leg armour, though there are no records of horse armour. They also had javelins and swords and could be used in a concerted charge to drive deep into the enemy.

For now, however, Rheomithras and Parmenio were engaged in a classic light cavalry action of sweeping charges, retreats, sudden halts and abrupt changes of direction as each tried to secure an advantage over the other. At some point, the Persian light cavalry began to move to their right, seeking to outflank the Macedonian army. The Thessalians

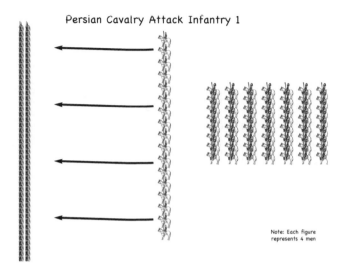

Persian Cavalry Attack Infantry 1

Note: Each figure represents 4 men

Persian Cavalry attack Infantry

This series of drawings shows the tactics used by Persian cavalry when attacking infantry. The infantry shown here are Macedonian Hypaspists, but the same tactics would be used whatever type of infantry were being attacked. The Hypaspists usually formed up 8 ranks deep. They are shown here two ranks deep for clarity. The Persian horse formation is similarly shown smaller than was the case in reality, again for clarity.

(1) The Persian heavy cavalry advance in their usual attack column formation, preceded by a force of light cavalry. When the Persians are about 200 metres from the enemy infantry, half of the light cavalry gallop forward to attack.

were equal to the task, however, extending out to cover the danger without opening up a fatal gap on their right.

It was while these two cavalry actions were going on that the Persian infantry began to make their presence felt. The faster moving units seem to have been arriving even before the cavalry fighting began. Both Arrian and Diodorus report some infantry being present, but held back behind the cavalry. No doubt this was because they had not yet arrived in sufficient numbers to take a place in the battle line.

They had now come up in sufficient numbers to be used effectively. The mixed group of cavalry that had been holding the centre of the Persian line now moved aside. Although the accounts are not altogether clear, they seem to have divided as they let the infantry through. We know that some of the central units moved to the left to join the wing being attacked by Alexander. Perhaps most of them did. The Persians had, by this time, recognised Alexander's helmet and correctly guessed that he would be leading the elite units of the Macedonian army.

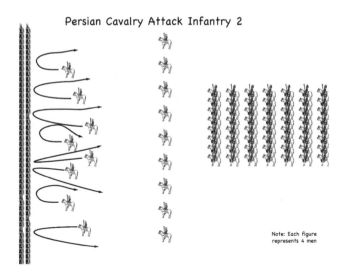

Persian Cavalry Attack Infantry 2

Note: Each figure represents 4 men

(2) The first wave of light cavalry ride up to the enemy, hurl their javelins into the enemy phalanx, then wheel aside and gallop away. They continue to make such attacks until their supply of javelins is used up.

It is unfortunate that, at this critical point in the battle, we do not know where either Memnon or Mithridates were, nor what they were doing. As we have seen, Mithridates was absent as the battle began, but he was soon to play a role in its progress. In contrast, Memnon was present on the Persian left wing when the battle began, but is scarcely heard of thereafter.

It is impossible to be sure, but it is difficult to resist the conclusion that Mithridates at least, and possibly Memnon as well, was organising the arrival of their infantry. Getting the infantry into line called for a reorganisation of the battle order of the Persian army. Such a task is never easy, but doing so once battle had been joined was a difficult and dangerous task.

If the infantry were now moving into position, there must have been enough of them to shoulder the task of holding the centre. If that had previously been held by 10,000 or so cavalry, we should expect there to be at least 30,000 infantry to fill the same space. It must be admitted that just as we are uncertain how many Persian infantry were camped on the Granicus the day before, we are equally ignorant of how many foot soldiers had managed to reach the scene of the battle by this point.

Certainly Memnon would have left some men to guard the camp, and others to watch the river crossing opposite the Macedonian camp.

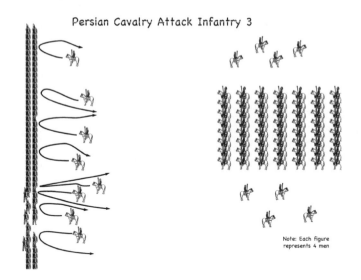

(3) *The first wave of light cavalry ride back to halt beside the heavy cavalry, out of their way. The second wave of light cavalry now go forward to deliver a similar series of javelin assaults. seeing that a developing weak spot in the enemy formation, some of the light Cavalry concentrate there, though others continue to attack all along the line.*

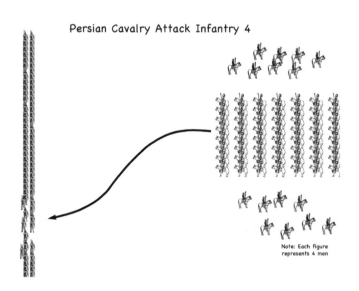

(4) *As the second wave of light cavalry pull back, the column of heavy cavalry canters forward to the attack. They make for the weaker section of the enemy line which has been disordered by the javelin attacks. Seconds before they impact the leading ranks hurl their javelins at the infantry.*

Persian Cavalry Attack Infantry 5

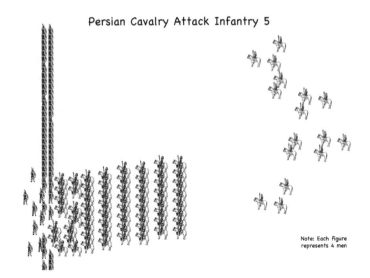

Note: Each figure represents 4 men

(5) The column of heavy cavalry strikes the enemy phalanx at its weakest point. The lead ranks are brought to a halt as their horses will not run into solid ranks of men. Throwing their remaining javelins, then drawing swords, the horsemen barge and push their way forwards into the thinning ranks of the infantry. As the rear ranks of the column join the scrum of men and mounts they too push and shove to build up an irresistible momentum that drives forward..

Persian Cavalry Attack Infantry 6

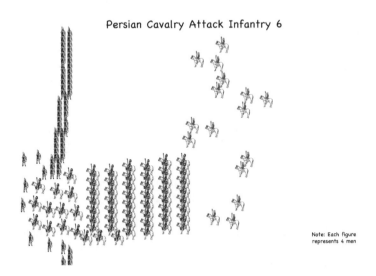

Note: Each figure represents 4 men

(6) Eventually the enemy infantry phalanx gives way in front of the point of heavy cavalry impact. With all resistance gone, the column of heavy cavalry can surge forward to burst through the enemy line. The horsemen can then fan out to attack the remainder of the phalanx in the rear. The enemy formation breaks down into a disorganised mob of fleeing fugitives. The Persian light cavalry draw their swords and come forward to join the pursuit.

It would not be beyond the wily Greeks to have kept a small force hidden in or near their camp to march over the ford as soon as it was abandoned. These were responsible tasks, so Memnon would have given the job to either some of his own Greek mercenaries or to a unit of satrapal guards. It is unlikely that any of the satraps would have wanted to hand over their men to Memnon's control, so it is probably best to suppose some of the 5,000 Greek mercenaries were left behind to do this task.

The infantry arriving on the battlefield would have been composed mainly of local levies from the satrapies of Paphlagonia and Phrygia, though with the satrapal guards and Memnon's remaining Greek mercenaries as well. None of our sources record how the Persian infantry were drawn up as they entered the Battle of the Granicus, but we do know how they were used on other occasions. This information, together with a few scraps of fact about where the different units moved to at later stages of the battle, can be used to put together a likely scenario for their opening positions.

The usual formation was to put the most reliable and heavily armed infantry in the centre. On either side of these men were positioned the second best, but still solid heavy infantry. In front of these men were put units of men armed with missiles – which could have been javelins, slings or bows. Most Persian armies had numbers of poorly trained and poorly armed men who were useful for digging latrines, excavating siege works or improving fords. These men were little better than armed servants and were not expected to do any serious fighting. They could, however, be useful if used to pursue the enemy when the better troops were tired from all the fighting. They were usually stationed behind the heavy infantry.

In the context of the Battle of the Granicus, the heavy infantry would have comprised the Greek mercenaries and the satrapal guards. There were probably around 4,000 Greeks marching down to join the battle. How many satrapal guards were present is pure conjecture. Each satrap certainly had a corps of professional infantry to serve as the bedrock of his satrapal army. No doubt they acted as drill masters and battle commanders to the levies, as well as forming up as a distinct unit. A satrap would be unlikely to have fewer than 500 such men in his employ, and may have had as many as 2,000.

There were, we know, six satraps present at the battle. They were unlikely to have brought all their infantry with them to the meeting at Zeleia. It would have made sense to leave some behind at home to organise the raising of levies, the manning of key fortresses and other duties. Perhaps there were between 5,000 and 8,000 of these men at the Granicus.

Satrapal infantry guards were armed and equipped as were men of Darius's own guard units. This was, effectively, a Persian version of the equipment of one of the more lightly armed Greek hoplites. They carried

Persian infantry
in Phalanx

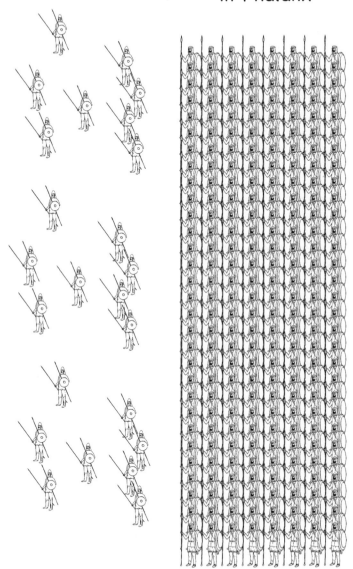

Persian infantry in phalanx

This illustration shows a phalanx of heavy infantry drawn from either the royal army or a satrapal guard. They are preceded by light infantry armed with throwing javelins. The more lightly equipped men would run ahead of the phalanx to hurl their javelins into enemy formations. They would then run aside to get out of the way before the phalanx advanced to crash into the enemy. The light infantry shown here are Mysian militia.

199

a large, round shield of similar construction to that of the Greeks. The spear was also similar to that of the Greeks, though it had a rounded counterweight at the butt end instead of a pointed spike. They had swords at their hips to use if their spears broke.

It is thought that these men did not wear armour, but this is not certain. We have no detailed records of their equipment. They do appear in Persian stone reliefs where they are shown dressed in tunics and trousers with a loose cloth head gear rather similar to a balaclava helmet. It is possible that these often voluminous garments may have concealed some form of armour. They may, indeed, have been made of some form of quilted fabric. If stuffed with enough densely packed fibres and rags, quilting can act as a surprisingly effective light armour. Certainly, however, these men were trained by this date to fight in a dense phalanx similar to that of the Greek hoplites.

The bulk of the Persian infantry that would have made it to the battlefield were levies raised from Paphlagonia and Phrygia. These men had throwing javelins and a heavier thrusting spear. Their shields were small and their only armour a helmet of leather. It is unlikely that these men could form a dense phalanx, or that they could face up to heavily armed infantry if they did.

We should, perhaps, see the infantry formation that Mithridates and Memnon were pushing into the line as being composed in this fashion. The front line was made up of a loose mass of local levies. Their task would be to shower the Macedonian phalanx with javelins in an attempt to break up its formation, weaken its discipline and affect is morale. They would then fall back to await the outcome of the main clash. As the levies dispersed, they would have revealed behind them the Greek mercenaries and satrapal guards in dense phalanx. It was they who would be intended to face the Macedonian foot companions.

While the Persian infantry were getting organised, the cavalry skirmishes had been continuing without either side being able to achieve a clear advantage. It may have been the arrival of the Persian infantry that, indirectly, precipitated the crisis of the battle.

The massed phalanx of the Macedonian foot companions, the pezhetairoi, had remained stationary so long as it was faced by the thin ranks of the mixed Persian cavalry units. The phalanx was well able to defend itself against a frontal cavalry assault, but was not itself trained or designed to attack cavalry. It was, however, beautifully prepared for attacking infantry. Now that the Persian infantry were revealed, it was time for the phalanx to advance.

Giving voice to their famous battle cry of 'ala la la la la lai', and stamping their feet to the beat of the chant, the foot companions began to advance. The enormously long sarissas were brought forward from

An infantryman of the type that would have served in the royal army or the satrapal guard units. By this date the Persians had adopted the Greek-style equipment of large shield and heavy thrusting spear. This man wears no helmet, which seems to have been typical, and no body armour. These men were trained to fight in phalanx, as were the Greek hoplites.

the upright carrying stance to point forwards toward the enemy. No doubt those who held their great pikes over the heads of the others, set their weapons swinging rhythymicaly from side to side as they advanced chanting. It was a formidable sight, designed to strike awe and fear into the hearts of the enemy. Moving forward with a slow and remorseless tread, the mighty phalanx was terrifying to behold.

The Persian levies braced themselves to dash forward and hurl their javelins into the serried ranks advancing upon them. The mercenaries and satrapal guards behind them prepared to meet the awesome phalanx.

But it was Spithridates, the Persian satrap heading the Hyrcanian cavalry, who was watching the Macedonian formation with the keenest interest. Thus far Spithridates had kept his men in check. These were men of the royal army and as such were probably the best on the Persian left wing. Spithridates had been holding back until he saw an opportunity to use his tough, skilled men to best effect.

It was now that he saw it. We don't know exactly what it was that he saw. Maybe a gap opened up between the phalanx and the hypaspists. Perhaps an opening grew between the hypaspists and the companion cavalry. Or it maybe that the hypaspists got disordered themselves. We don't really know. What we do know is that Spithridates now charged at the hypaspists.

According to Diodorus, this assault was made not only by the Hyrcanians, but also by a group of 40 'Royal Relatives' and 'a large body of cavalry'. This large body of cavalry would certainly have included the Hyrcanians, but may have included some of the smaller units that had previously comprised the centre of the Persian front line. It would have been natural for these smaller bodies to follow the lead of a large force of professional soldiers led by one of the satraps.

The 40 Royal Relatives were not, it must be said, all blood kin of the Persian emperor Darius. The title was an honourary one that could be bestowed by the emperor on anyone he liked. Traditionally the title went to men from the nobility of the Medes or the Persians, the two ethnic groups that ruled the empire. It was sometimes awarded for bravery in battle or for some other outstanding service performed by the recipient. It might sometimes be conferred as a mere symbol of rank or favour, but this seems to have been unusual. Diodorus says that these men were 'all of outstanding valour', so presumably they were given their titles for military reasons.

The charge went well, crashing home and inflicting casualties. The Persian horse began jostling and crushing their way into the Macedonian formation.

This sudden attack by Spithridates was seen by Alexander. According to Diodorus, Alexander was deeply worried by the impact the Persian attack had. According to Plutarch and Arrian, he was seized by a desire to attack. In these two statements it is easy to see the prejudices of the men who the two writers used as a source. Ptolemy, whose lost work lurks behind that of Plutarch and Arrian, seeks to emphasise the gallantry of Alexander and play down the impact of the Persian attack. The anonymous mercenary drawn on by Diodorus was more willing to talk up the success of Spithridates.

Whatever the truth of Alexander's motives, his actions were clear enough. Riding at the head of the royal squadron of the companion cavalry, and followed by the rest, Alexander led a charge that slammed into the flank of the horsemen following Spithridates. The crashing impact of Alexander's elite horsemen ploughing into a force of 2,000 cavalry already closely engaged with the 3,000 hypaspists was shuddering.

According to Arrian 'it was a cavalry battle with, as it were, infantry tactics: horse against horse, man against man, locked together'. Certainly it was very different from the fluid, swiftly changing combats that had raged so far. But it was exactly this sort of close combat for which the companion cavalry were trained. It was their job to hack a path through the enemy formations. Nevertheless it was hard going.

> During the fight Alexander's spear was broken. He called on Aretis for another, but Aretis was himself in difficulties for the same reason, though still fighting gallantly enough with the remaining half of his weapon. Showing it to Alexander, he called out to him to ask someone else, and Demaratus the Corinthian – one of Alexander's own men – gave him his spear.

This incident, told by Arrian, shows just how cramped and confused the combat was as it raged around Alexander. Nevertheless, the key importance of the xyston cavalry lance to Macedonian horsemen cannot be missed. All these men had swords, but they preferred the xyston. Even when the head was broken off his xyston, Aretis preferred to turn it around and use the butt spike to fight with rather than draw his sword.

According to Diodorus, the cavalry melee was about to get even more dramatic. Spithridates spotted Alexander's distinctive helmet over the fray and spurred his horse toward it.

> To the Persian it seemed as if this opportunity for a single combat was god-given. He hoped that by his individual gallantry, Asia might be relieved of its terrible menace, the renowned daring of Alexander arrested by his own hands and the glory of the Persians saved from disgrace.

This was no idle hope. At this date the stability of kingdoms and states very often depended on the well being of the ruler. When Philip died, the Kingdom of Macedon was effectively paralysed for weeks until Alexander managed to secure his grip on the throne. That struggle was followed by more months of uncertainty as Alexander was forced to put down rebellions and enforce the same rigid control over the northern tribes and the Greek states that his father had enjoyed.

If Spithridates could kill Alexander now, in the heat of battle, it was very likely that a similar bout of dynastic feuding and murderous intrigue would break out. As a satrap, Spithridates will have known that the original Persian plan of campaign had envisaged the sending of an expeditionary force to Greece to aid rebellions against Macedonian rule. That force had been halted by the need to keep the soldiers in Asia Minor to face Alexander. But with Alexander dead, that force could head for Athens or Sparta within a few days. Greece would collapse into internecine warfare, and Persia would be secure.

There would be the added advantage that with Alexander slain, his army itself might break up. The troops from the Allied Greek states would be keen to head home as quickly as possible. The Macedonians would be uncertain whom to obey and might well head back home to sort out the dynastic succession. Alexander, after all, had no children at the time of the Granicus. He had disposed of his half-brothers. That left no obvious heir, only a number of nobles each with a claim no better than that of the others. Civil war would be almost inevitable.

All this Spithridates would have known when he spotted the distinctive white plumes of Alexander's helmet over the heads of the struggling mass of men. It might even be that the death of Alexander was one of the agreed aims of the battle on the Persian side.

Whatever the case, Spithridates urged his horse toward Alexander. Diodorus continues: 'He hurled his javelin at Alexander with so mighty an impulse and so powerful a throw that it pierced Alexander's shield and right epomis [shoulder strap] and drove through the breastplate.' This was an impressive blow indeed, and shows that the satrap and king must have been fairly close when this occurred.

Incidentally, this comment by Diodorus is the only reference to Alexander, or any of the companions, carrying a shield. It has caused a great deal of debate over the years. Some think that the shield referred to might have been the one that Alexander had acquired during his visit to Troy. Others that Diodorus was mistaken, Arrian's rather briefer account of this same event makes no mention of a shield.

The blow might have been impressive, but it did not wound Alexander. The point of the javelin stuck in the royal breastplate, but did not penetrate. Alexander yanked the javelin out, then gripped his xyston and urged his horse on. The javelin thrown by Spithridates had had a longer reach than Alexander's thrusting xyston, but now the xyston had a greater reach than the Persian's sword. Diodorus continues, saying that Alexander:

> drove his lance squarely into the satrap's chest. At this, adjacent ranks in both armies cried out at the superlative display of prowess. The point of the spear, however, snapped off against the breastplate and the broken shaft recoiled. The Persian drew his sword and drove at Alexander. But the king recovered his grip upon his lance in time to thrust at the man's face and drive the blow home. Spithridates fell. But just at this moment, Rhosaces, his brother, galloping up brought his sword down on Alexander head with such a fearsome blow that it split his helmet and inflicted a slight scalp wound. As Rhosaces aimed another blow at the broken helmet, Cleitus the Black dashed up on his horse and cut off the Persian's arm.

Alexander had had a very lucky escape in this savage little episode. The Cleitus who saved his life was a Macedonian nobleman aged somewhere in his forties. Although not of royal blood, Cleitus had been very close to Philip and had lived in the royal palace for most of his life. He was probably one of the soldiers in the royal squadron of the companion cavalry and may even have been its commander.

But although Spithridates and Rhosaces were both now dead, neither Alexander nor Cleitus were safe. Diodorus recounts what happened next.

> The Royal Relatives now pressed in a solid body about the two fallen men. At first they rained their javelins on Alexander, then closing went all out to slay the king. But exposed as he was to many and fierce attacks, Alexander nevertheless was not overborne by the numbers of the foe. Though he took two blows on the breastplate, one on the helmet and three on the shield, he still did not give in but borne up by an exaltation of spirit surmounted every danger.

Arrian adds a detail at this point that is missing from Diodorus, that 'Alexander's party was being steadily reinforced by the mounted troops'. These were, presumably, the remaining squadrons of the companion cavalry. They must have been piling into the melee as they rode over from the Macedonian right.

While this critical episode was taking place on the Macedonian right, the events on the left went largely unrecorded by the ancient writers. We know that at some point Rheomithras made an attempt to turn the flank of Parmenio's horsemen. The wily old commander was, however, equal to his task and managed to contain the move. After the battle, Parmenio was singled out for praise by Alexander for the way he conducted this holding action. The fact that the left wing cavalry needed to keep contact with the advance pezhetairoi phalanx as well as drive off the Persian attacks made their task all the more difficult. The Thessalians, Diodorus notes, won a great reputation in this battle for their skilfull manoeuvring and for courage. It was well deserved.

Meanwhile, the infantry had been getting to grips with each other in the centre. The action would have begun with the Phrygians and Paphlagonians dashing forward to hurl their javelins at the slowly advancing phalanx of foot companions. The shower of missiles these men unleashed was awesome. In less than two minutes some 30,000 javelins must have rained down onto the phalanx.

These javelins were dangerous weapons. They were able to pierce unprotected flesh with ease and could frequently prove fatal. The pezhetairoi were not, however, unarmoured. Their first line of defence was the network of sarissa shafts that formed a mesh roof over the entire formation. The incoming javelins were sharp, but light. They could be easily diverted or their momentum lost if they struck even a glancing blow against a Macedonian pike shaft. Many of those that got past this line of defence would have bounced off helmets or shields.

Nevertheless some foot companions did go down to javelins. It was now that the fearsome discipline of the Macedonian infantry came into play. Each man knew his job was to step forward into the place of any man ahead of him who fell. The more senior men would have been shouting and pushing their juniors to get them to take up position. And all the time to the sound of the 'ala la la la la lai' chant, the phalanx was remorselessly grinding forward.

Their javelins thrown, the Phrygians and Paphlagonian infantry would have turned and run. Their prime job was done. Now they had the task of getting back behind the main phalanx of hoplites. From there they would watch the battle unfold. If the Persians won, these militia would draw their swords and join the pursuit. They would be fresh, while those who had been in the phalanx would be tired. They would be better able to pursue the enemy. But if the Persians lost, they would join the retreat. If the retreat was conducted carefully and with skill, these men might be drawn up to act as some form of rearguard. They did, after all, carry thrusting spears and shields. They do not seem to have been trained to fight in massed phalanx and, in any case, their shields were small, but they could have been useful to delay and frustrate the pursuit.

With the Phrygians and Paphlagonians out of the way, the two phalanxes could come together to settle the issue. The hoplites on the Persian side were at a disadvantage when it came to the reach of the weapons. The Macedonian sarissa could hit the hoplites before the hoplite dory spears could reach the Macedonians. Moreover the entire front of the Macedonian phalanx was bristling with overlapping spear points. And they were all being driven relentlessly forward by the sheer momentum of the Macedonian formation.

It was not all one way, however. Awesomely effective as it was, the Macedonian phalanx was now some years old as a tactic of war. The novelty of its power and force was wearing off. Enemy commanders and veterans were beginning to gauge its weaknesses as well as its strengths. The Persian satrapal guards may not have had to face up to this tactic of war before, but Memnon had seen it in action and so had some of his men. They will have known two things about the weakness of the phalanx.

The first was that the men armed with the sarissas were very difficult to tackle from the front, but were highly vulnerable to a flank attack. If the Persian horsemen on either flank managed to get through their opponents and charge the Macedonian phalanx from side or rear the apparently irresistible advance of the formation would collapse. They also knew that the frontal power of the formation depended entirely on the ability of the Macedonians to keep strictly in formation and to march forward with steady, measured tread.

There was not much that the hoplites could do about the phalanx's vulnerability to a flank attack, except to try to keep the phalanx in play and retain their own formation long enough for the Persian cavalry to break through. They could, however, hope to do something about disrupting the formation and advance of the phalanx. The javelins will have inflicted some casualties, and might have served to create a few gaps in the bristling hedge of spears. If the hoplites now sought to hack off the heads of the Macedonian sarissas or to duck underneath their points they might yet achieve something. They could not hope to defeat the phalanx, but they might cause it to slow down. If parts of it slowed down, but others did not, it would begin to lose its all important cohesion. Once that happened, the phalanx might become vulnerable.

It was not to be.

Back on the right of the Macedonian army, Alexander was getting the upper hand. Arrian tells us:

> The Persians were now in a bad way: there was no escape for horse or rider
> from the thrust of the Macedonian spears. They were being forced back from
> their position and, in addition to the weight of the main attack, they were

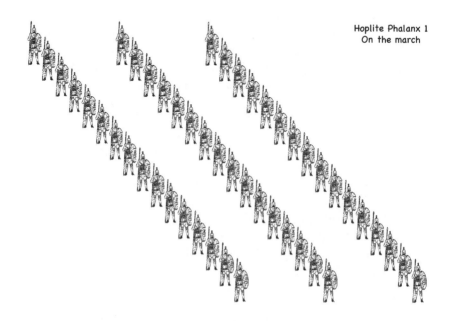

Hoplite Phalanx 1
On the march

Hoplite

Greek hoplites fought on both sides during the Granicus campaign. They were equipped and trained in an identical fashion. These formations might have been used by Memnon's men in the Persian army or by Alexander's Greek Allies. The Persian heavy infantry that were equipped in similar fashion adopted similar tactics.

Phalanx 1

This illustration shows six files of a traditional 8 deep phalanx advancing to battle. There are wide gaps between the files to allow the men to flow around obstacles such as ditches, bushes or rocks as they march. It was usual for two files to line up behind each other, as shown here, but three or four might be put behind each other when passing over rough ground.

Phalanx 2
Standard Phalanx

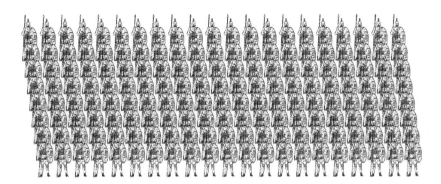

Phalanx 2

A standard phalanx drew up eight men deep and with about one metre of frontage per man. When battle was imminent, the men would shift their shields so that they were held in front of their bodies to form a solid wall of shields. The dory type spears were held in the overarm position to stab down over the top of the shields at the enemy.

Phalanx 3
Extended Phalanx

Phalanx 3

When a unit needed to cover a wider frontage than could be achieved by the standard 8 deep phalanx the ranks could be thinned out to as little as four men deep. This was a risky move with anything but the most reliable of men as much of the strength of the formation came from its depth. The mercenaries serving with Memnon were probably trained well enough and had high enough morale to be able to adopt such a thin formation, but Alexander's allies would probably not have risked it. Conversely, when shorter frontage was to be covered the phalanx could be deepened to 12 or 16 ranks.

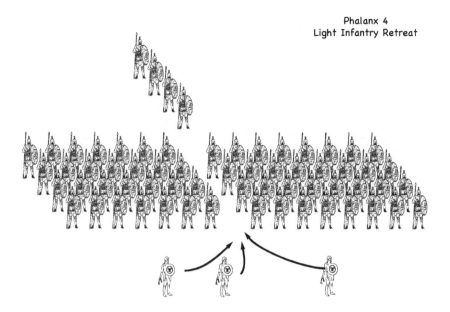

Phalanx 4
Light Infantry Retreat

Phalanx 4

This shows how the Greek infantry co-operated with light infantry, in this case slingers. At intervals along the phalanx a file of men would be withdrawn to form a narrow lane through the formation. The light infantry would hurl their missiles at an advancing enemy, then dash back through this gap. The file of men would then advance back into position so that the phalanx was, once again solid.

suffering considerable damage from the lightly armed troops who had forced their way in among the cavalry. The Persians began to break just at the point where Alexander in person was bearing the brunt of things.

The fact that there were infantry mixed in with the companion cavalry should come as no surprise. This was a traditional role for the hypaspists. They were getting in among the crumbling Hyrcanian formation to despatch enemy horsemen with spears and swords.

Suddenly the Hyrcanians broke and fled. This was the decisive moment for which Alexander had been striving. The iron discipline of the companion cavalry allowed them to be formed up into compact squadrons that could then fan out to chase up the retreating enemy horsemen. It is little wonder that in the confusion of these fast moving events things got jumbled and ill reported. What happened to Memnon and his mercenary Greek cavalry during this disaster is quite unknown – except for the fact that they got away. Presumably, Memnon had seen the collapse of the Hyrcanians as it began to unfold and realised what was about to happen. Diodorus tells us that:

Hypaspists protect flank of Foot Companions
1

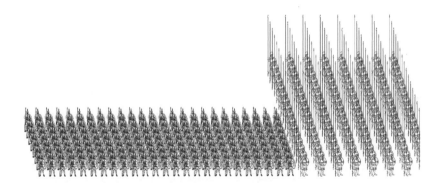

Hypaspists protect flank of Foot Companions
This series of drawings shows the tactics used by Hypaspist infantry when they were on the defensive and covering the vulnerable flanks of the Foot Companion phalanx. Alexander began all his major battles with the Hypaspists in this location. He moved them forward or sideways only when he was certain that his Foot Companions were not in a position to be outflanked.

(1) At the start of a battle the Foot Companions were drawn up 16 ranks deep and with about 1.5 metres of frontage per man. This gave them room to manoeuvre their long pikes when the front five ranks lowered them to the horizontal. The Hypaspists formed up 8 ranks deep and with only 1 metre per man. They used their shorter spears in the overarm position and only the front two ranks could use their weapons at a time, so they did not need to be so widely spaced.

Hypaspists protect flank of Foot Companions
2

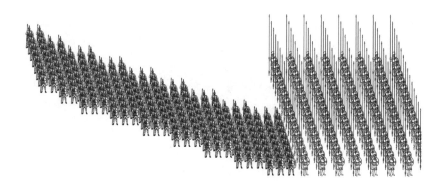

(2) Seeing a threat developing on the flank, the Hypaspist commander orders his men to begin to fall back in echelon. This preserves a fighting front, but pulls it back away from the immediate threat while still covering the flanks of the Foot Companions.

Hypaspists protect flank of Foot Companions
3

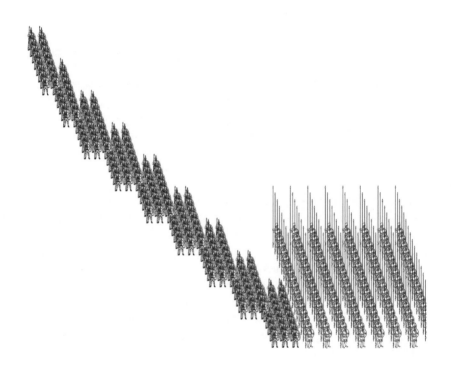

(3) As the flank threat develops, the Hypaspists continue to fall back in echelon. If needs be the Hypaspists could wheel to present a phalanx facing at right angles to the Foot Companions and trailing back for some 400 metres. We know of no instance of this being done in battle by Alexander, on each occasion the echeloning back was enough to cover the emergency. The elite Hypaspists were trained to alter formation at the run, so they could adopt this flanking formation faster than any enemy infantry could advance.

After this, several of the other noble Persians fighting against Alexander fell. Now that many of their commanders had been slain and all the Persian squadrons were worsted by the Macedonians, those facing Alexander were put to flight.

Arrian describes the moment Mithridates entered the fray.

Alexander caught sight of Mithridates, Darius's son-in-law, riding with a squadron of horse in wedge formation out on their own. Instantly he galloped out in front of his men, struck Mithridates with his spear and hurled him to the ground.

The Persian left wing was disintegrating as formations broke up and men fled. Now might have seemed the time for the pursuit to begin. For the cavalry to be unleashed to chase the fugitives, harry them and give them no chance to regroup. But Alexander knew better. He might have won a convincing victory on his right wing, but the battle was not yet over. The Macedonian phalanx in the centre was making its usual steady progress, but the enemy hoplites were as yet in unbroken phalanx, while away on the left Parmenio was still struggling to contain Rheomithras and his horsemen.

At this point Alexander showed that he was a commander of genius who in all circumstances kept in mind the ultimate aim of the battle. It was not enough simply to defeat the enemy, the Persian army had to be crushed so thoroughly that it could not again take the field against Alexander. The Macedonians needed to be undisputed masters of not only the battlefield, but of Asia Minor in its entirety. Only then would the Greek cities welcome him as he wanted.

Not only did Alexander keep his head, so did his men. Victorious cavalry are notoriously prone to go galloping off after their defeated opponents. The prospect of an enemy with his back turned and spurring from the field is almost irresistible. More than one cavalry force has won its immediate combat, only to find that it has lost the battle by riding off the field in a premature pursuit. Not so the Companions and other Macedonian horsemen. A few shrill blasts on the trumpet were enough to get them to break off the pursuit.

The Macedonian cavalry began reforming their ranks. Alexander intended to use them to attack the flanks and rear of the Persian units still in the field.

The collapse of the Persian left wing and the ominous sight of Alexander preparing his men to charge proved to be decisive. The militia infantry behind the main phalanx in the centre simply turned and ran from the battlefield.

Omares, the commander of the Greek mercenary infantry, quickly realised that the position of his men was becoming untenable. Looking round for some route of escape, he fixed on a hillock that lay some distance behind the Persian front lines. Disengaging from the Macedonian phalanx, Omares led his men for the hill. Perhaps he hoped to get clean away, but he was to be disappointed.

The satrapal guards fell back with the Greek mercenaries for a time, then they too broke and fled. Out on the far right wing of the Persians, Rheomithras saw what was happening. His units were still largely intact, though losses had been considerable. He turned them away from the river and trotted them off toward Dascylium. Rheomithras knew that his men would be needed again. The battle might be lost, but the war was only just beginning.

The abrupt collapse of the Persian army meant that Omares and his men had no way out. If they tried to run they would be cut down by the Macedonian horsemen. If they tried to march out as a formed unit they would fare little better. The only choice was to negotiate a surrender.

For men in their position, this was not usually too difficult. Mercenaries were highly regarded in the ancient world, and often highly paid. Mercenaries were expected to fight loyally and doggedly for their paymasters, but not to die to the last man. Cut off and helpless, it was usual for mercenaries to negotiate some sort of deal with the commander who had bested them. This might involve the men being ordered not to serve as mercenaries for a set period of time. More often the victorious commander would seek to hire the mercenaries himself. Given the strength of the respective negotiating positions, a general could hope to get himself a bargain. The defeated men were in no position to hold out for high wages.

Accordingly, Omares sent a delegation down from his hillock asking Alexander for his terms. What nobody could have been expecting was what Alexander did next. Plutarch tells us:

> Alexander, influenced by anger more than by reason, charged foremost upon them and lost his horse, which was smitten through the ribs with a sword. And most of the Macedonians who were slain or wounded fought or fell there since they came to close quarters with men who knew how to fight and were desperate.

Arrian confirms 'Ordering a combined assault by infantry and cavalry, Alexander quickly had them surrounded and butchered to a man'.

In fact, not all the Greek mercenaries were killed, as Arrian suggests, though it would seem that all those surrounded with Omares were slaughtered. Certainly Omares was among the dead. A total of 2,000 Greek mercenaries were captured by the Macedonians. These might have included those left back at the Persian camp and the original ford by Memnon as well as any fugitives who ran rather than retreating in good order with Omares.

The fate of these men was not much better than that of the dead. They were clapped into chains and marched off back to Macedonia. They were condemned to work on state-owned farms and in royal mines in the most appaling conditions of hard slave labour. The sentence was for life, with no prospect of release or remission.

This was an astonishing action by Alexander, against the accepted rules of warfare of the time, and requires some explanation. Ordering his men to kill the mercenaries with Omares had cost the Macedonians dearly in terms of men and horses. Plutarch alleges that Alexander was angry, and he probably was. Throughout his career, Alexander was prone to violent bouts of rage that cost the lives of many men, including some of his close friends.

But that was not the whole answer. Alexander was claiming to be fighting a campaign to free the Greek cities of Asia Minor from Persian brutality and to be exacting revenge on the Persians for the injuries done by previous Persian invasions of Greece. And yet here were Greeks fighting on the side of Persia.

Of course, Alexander's pretensions were not entirely accurate. During the Persian invasion of Greece in 480BC, Macedon had been neutral. And his army included many men from Thrace who were not Greek at all, as well as Macedonians whom most Greeks thought be half foreign. It is possible that the very weakness of Alexander's claims made him all the more determined to enforce them.

Be that as it may, the mercenaries were killed or enslaved so that Alexander could make his point.

Then the pursuit could begin in earnest. Alexander let his horsemen loose to chase, harry and kill the fleeing fugitives. The Macedonian horsemen did their job well. Rheomithras got his cavalry units away safely, so successfully in fact that Alexander did not know where they had gone. That apart, however, the Persian forces ceased to exist as a fighting force. Alexander had won his battle in the convincing fashion that he so badly needed.

Now he had the task of exploiting his victory.

CHAPTER TWELVE

The Fruits of Victory

Alexander was never a man to put off actions that would save him time and effort in the long run. As soon as the battle was over, he began gathering the fruits of victory.

Many of his cavalrymen were off pursuing the Persian fugitives, but there was one task that had to be taken care of by a responsible and competent commander. Alexander sent for Parmenio. The satrapal capital of Dascylium was a key target. It was not that it was a large city, but that it was the administrative centre for the satrapy of Paphlagonia. Backed up by a strong column of cavalry, probably the Thessalians, Parmenio set off.

Parmenio rode fast. But he was too late. When he arrived it was to find that somebody, probably Rheomithras, had got there first. The satrapal palace was abandoned, its treasury and chambers empty. There were clear signs that the place had been abandoned in a hurry. There had been no attempts to destroy the fortress or its contents. The place was ready for the Macedonians to move in, but the money had gone.

Back at the Granicus, Alexander was visiting the wounded Macedonians. Arrian tells us that:

> For the wounded he showed deep concern. He visited them all and examined their wounds, asking each man how and in what circumstances his wound was received, and allowing him to tell his story and exaggerate as much as he pleased.

Alexander's visit to the wounded was good for morale, but there is plenty of evidence that he genuinely cared for the men under his command. On other occasions he was to take great pains over their welfare. It seems that his actions after the Granicus were perfectly genuine, and in part explain why his men loved him so much.

The plight of the wounded in the wake of a battle at this date were not as dire as popular imagination might have it. The ancient doctors lacked modern drugs and had no knowledge of germs, infection or advanced medicines. They did have, however, a vast amount of experience on which to draw, and they were considerably skilled in treating the sort of wounds that the weapons of the day produced.

Alexander had taken with him a number of doctors to minister to his troops, and no doubt they were now pushed into action. These doctors would have been trained at one of the great medical schools of the Greek world, perhaps at Kos, Epidavros or Cnidus. These schools taught anatomy with some skill, and had a basic understanding of the importance of hygiene. They also understood that diseases and infections could spread from one person to the next, though they did not know why, and some of their steps for preventing such spread undoubtedly worked.

The Greeks had an extensive knowledge of the medicinal properties of various plants. They knew, for instance, that oil of cinnamon would curb infection of an open wound, while burned resin in wine would relieve swelling. For more surgical procedures, the average Greek doctor would have had a probe, forceps, saws, retractor, cauterising iron, bandages, shears, sponge, at least six different sorts of scalpel, cupping vessels and much more. And there were numerous needles for stitching up wounds. The juice of wild poppies – which contained opium – was used to alleviate the pain suffered by wounded men.

The god of doctors was Asclepius, a son of the greater god Apollo by a human woman. The religious rites at the temples of Asclepius were as important, to a Greek doctor, as any medicines or surgery he might undertake. Asclepius was generally in favour of rest and bathing for the sick or ill, both of which will have done them some good, as well as dreaming and making sacrifices, neither of which would have done much harm.

No doubt the assorted rituals inspired confidence in the patients, which alone could help to effect cures. Today the placebo effect is well known, though poorly understood. If a patient is told that he is being given a strong medicine, even if the concoction is only flavoured water, he will often improve and may even be cured. All in all, the doctors of Alexander's day had an impressive array of skills and abilities. So long as a wound was clean and had not touched a major organ, the prospects of survival were fairly good.

It must be said, however, that the care of the wounded had its brutal side. Some wounded were deemed beyond help, and the experienced military doctor would have been as able to identify these unfortunates then as effectively as they can today. Such men might be dosed with poppy juice to ease their pain, but a slit throat was more usual.

The enemy wounded could expect even less mercy. Important men were usually kept alive if at all possible since they might be useful in negotiations or for extorting a ransom. Among the rank and file, those that might recover to be useful slaves were helped. The rest were killed out of hand.

Having dealt with the wounded, Alexander next turned his attention to the dead. Clearing up after a battle was a gruesome business, but an important one. It was well understood that the bodies had to be buried or burned quickly to stop disease spreading. It was also important to strip the dead of any weapons, armour or valuables that might be of use to the victors, or that could be sold for profit. It was considered a mark of great respect to the dead to bury them with their weapons. Only heroes who had impressed all those present with their courage and skills were usually accorded this honour.

Alexander began his treatment of the Macedonian dead by ordering that all of them should be buried with their weapons. It was an unprecedented move. He then went further by exempting the parents and children of the fallen from all local and property taxation as well as from the requirement to serve the king in certain circumstances.

Alexander's generosity to the Macedonian dead went further. The 25 men who had been killed during his abortive first assault over the river the previous evening were singled out for special treatment. Alexander ordered that a statue should be made of each and put up in the city of Dium. Not only that, but the statues were to be made in bronze, then an expensive medium, by the royal sculptor Lysippus. The decision to have Lysippus produce statues of the fallen men was a mark of the most special favour indeed.

At the time Lysippus was a young man, he was to live until 270BC, but he was already famous for his skills in bronze. Alexander had hired Lysippus during the preparations for the Persian expedition because of his ability to make convincingly accurate portraits. He had been commissioned to produce an official likeness of Alexander the king that would serve as the basis for portraits on coins, in paintings and all other mediums while Alexander was absent. It was the first instance we know of when a ruler commissioned an official portrait of this type. The official portrait statue has not survived, nor have any copies, but written sources tell us that it showed Alexander in full armour wielding a spear over his head. No doubt a very dramatic and martial representation of the young king in all his glory.

Exactly how many men from the Macedonian army were killed at the Granicus is not clear. Arrian says that in addition to the 25 men killed on the first day, a further 60 horsemen and 30 infantry died during the main battle. Plutarch says that only 34 men were killed during the fighting. Neither writer says how many men were wounded. These figures are almost certainly too low.

The battle had been a hard fought contest. The opening cavalry skirmishes on either flank had lasted some considerable time, while the climactic clash between Alexander's companions and Spithridates Hyrcanians had been a real slogging match in which neither side gained an advantage for some time. Common sense would indicate that Alexander's losses must have amounted to several hundred, but of this we cannot be certain.

Nor can we be certain of the Persian losses. Arrian says only that the Persians lost 1,000 cavalry during the battle. Plutarch says that the Persian losses totalled 20,000 infantry and 2,500 cavalry. Diodorus, as usual probably drawing on the account of the anonymous mercenary, says that more than 10,000 Persian infantry were killed along with more than 2,000 cavalry. He also says that 20,000 were taken prisoner.

We already know that Alexander ordered the deaths of the Greek mercenaries gathered around Omares at the end of the battle – perhaps around 2,000 to 3,000 men. If Plutarch is right and 1,000 cavalry were killed in the battle, the deaths of another 1,500 in the pursuit to get to the totals given by Plutarch and Diodorus is not out of the question. The figures for the infantry losses are probably best viewed as estimates. Counting thousands of bodies is not a pleasant task, and given the need to dispose of the bodies it may well have been rushed. And Alexander had an obvious motive for overestimating the numbers of the dead for propaganda purposes. In any case, the Persian army had ceased to exist as a functioning body of troops. Many of the local levies that survived the pursuit probably simply walked home.

What is certain is that the Persians had lost very heavily in terms of senior military and civilian commanders. Mithridates, son in law of Darius was among the dead and so were the satraps Spithridates and Mithrobuzanes. Pharnaces, a brother in law of Darius was also killed and so was Darius's nephew Arbupales. Niphates, Petines and Rhosaces are also among the named dead of the Persian high command.

One prominent survivor was Arsites, who had led the Paphlagonian cavalry. He blamed himself for the defeat and committed suicide a few days later. He may have been fearful of the revenge of Darius and thought that a swift death was better than a slow one. It is an interesting question as to why Arsites felt that he was to blame. His unit was stationed beside that of Spithridates when that satrap had launched his charge on the Macedonian ranks. Clearly Arsites had not led his men to join that charge, nor had he tried to intervene when Alexander in turn attacked Spithridates.

In order to get from his initial position on the far right wing of the Macedonian army to close with Spithridates, Alexander would have had to lead his men across the front of the unit commanded by Arsites. It is usually assumed that the men led forward earlier by Ptolemy – including one squadron of companion cavalry plus the Paeonians and prodromoi – had kept the men led by Arsites in check. But these Macedonian horsemen were also faced by the units led by Memnon and Arsamenes. It seems likely from the drastic action taken by Arsites that he had had the chance to attack Alexander, but that he had missed it. Why, we will never know. We do know that his death not only saved him from experiencing the wrath of Darius, it also left his satrapy of Phrygia without a leader.

The Persian dead were not simply corpses to be stripped of anything useful and buried, they were also a source of propaganda benefit for Alexander. Whether or not Alexander had his writers exaggerate the number of the dead, he certainly now engaged in a clever bit of publicity. Most of what was not needed by the army was packed up to be sent back to Macedon for sale or to be stored against future use.

However, 300 of the finest sets of armour stripped from the bodies of the Persian dead was packed and shipped off to Athens. They were dedicated to the Temple of Athene, and tradition demanded that they should be hung as trophies in the temple precincts. Alexander sent with the armour a written message. It read: 'Alexander, son of Philip, and the Greeks (except the Spartans) dedicate these spoils that were taken from the Persians who dwell in Asia'.

The wording was very clever. Alexander described himself modestly as merely 'son of Philip', using none of his official titles. He was not a king or a leader, merely a man like any others. And his fellow dedicators of the spoil were the Greeks. In fact there were precious few actual Greeks on Alexander's side at the Granicus. Most of those that were with his army were absent, only the 600 cavalry being present. The rest of the army was made up of Thessalians, Macedonians, Agrianians and others.

If this were not clever enough, Alexander added the words 'except the Spartans'. This was a dig at Sparta, the only city state that had refused point blank to join the crusade against Persia. Sparta famously fielded the finest soldiers in Greece, but this great victory had been won without them. And Alexander knew that many city states in Greece, including Athens, had suffered at the hands of the Spartans before. It would do no harm at all to remind them that Alexander was not on good terms with the Spartans.

Then the dedication goes on to say that the spoils were taken from the Persians. In fact the enemy army had included many Greeks, possibly more than were actually in Alexander's army on the day of battle. It did not pay to remind people back home of that uncomfortable fact, so Alexander spoke only of the Persians.

Perhaps the most important death at the Granicus for the immediate future was that of Spithridates. It had left his satrapy of Lydia without a leader to co-ordinate resistance. That was important, for it was to Lydia that Alexander now marched.

Before leaving the Granicus, however, Alexander took a step that was rich with meaning for the future. This was not land thickly settled by Greek colonists nor with much in the way of Greek cities or culture. It was not, therefore, covered by Alexander's promise of bringing liberty. Alexander sent Callas, the commander who had taken over Parmenio's advance guard the previous year, to occupy Dascylium.

Callas had orders to rebuild the administration of the area along the lines of the former Persian satrapy. He was to charge taxes exactly as before and to employ the same administrators, so far as that was possible, as had the departed Persians. Alexander also ordered his men not to loot and plunder. Whatever Alexander intended for the Greek cities, he clearly wanted to take over the role of the Persian emperor in the non-Greek areas. Alexander was adding new provinces to the Kingdom of Macedon.

Now that the Persian army was destroyed, the towns and cities of the region could be relied upon to open their gates to Alexander. The Macedonians were short on food, so it was important for Alexander to take his army to those cities in order to gather supplies. If any cities were inclined not to surrender, the arrival of the army could be guaranteed to overawe them.

One of the first to surrender was Zeleia. Alexander ostentatiously gave all the citizens of Zeleia a free pardon for any actions that they had taken in recent months. 'He knew that they had fought with the Persians only under pressure,' records Arrian. There were plenty of other Greek, and non-Greek, cities that had to some extent or another helped the Persian war effort. Alexander was giving them a way out. So long as they surrendered promptly, claiming that they had helped the Persians only because they were forced to do so, they could expect mercy and friendship. This was in stark contrast to the way Alexander had treated the Greek mercenaries who, it must be supposed, had chosen to serve Darius rather than having been forced to do so.

Presumably one of the first cities to take advantage of Alexander's new mood of leniency was Lampsakos that had turned him away just a few short days earlier. Also rushing to make their peace with the new ruler were the hill tribes of the interior. Alexander greeted them well, then sent them home. Also allowed to go home were those Persian fugitives not yet captured. Arrian says 'all the men who came out of hiding and surrendered, he allowed to go home'.

Meanwhile the Macedonian cavalry were ranging widely across the area. They found no sign of Memnon and his surviving Greek mercenaries, nor of Rheomithras and his royal cavalry units. Both commanders and their forces had abandoned the area. It is not clear if Alexander knew where they had gone. Presumably his riders were able to pick up rumours of where these fairly substantial groups of men had passed by, but if so Alexander made no serious attempts to chase them. They were gone, that was all he cared about.

Having settled the local affairs, with himself as the new ruler, Alexander could afford to move on. He had secured the immediate bridgehead into Asia and could advance without worrying about what was going on behind him.

Alexander had two routes open to him on his march to Lydia. He could take the direct route over the Mount Ida massif to the coast near Astyra. However this road was steep and poorly surfaced. More significantly it did not go past any towns or cities from which Alexander could gather supplies and cash paid as an advance on taxes or tribute.

It is far more likely that Alexander now led his army back along the route that they had come. As he passed Troy once more, Alexander decided to found the first of many cities to which he gave his name: Alexandria. This town was to be called Alexandria Troas, for obvious reasons. It grew to be a prosperous little seaport in a non spectacular sort of a way. Although he probably chose the site and may even have sketched out the plan, Alexander did not do much to build the town. It was not until 310BC that Antigonus, one of his generals, started the main building work.

From the site of the future city, Alexander and his army headed south along the coast to pass the cities of Sigeum, Thymbra, Neandria and Assus to reach Astyra. He then pushed on through Klila and Thebe to Adramyttium (now Edremit). At each city he fed his army from local supplies, drank the local waters and gratefully accepted whatever cash gift the city felt like donating to him. Alexander also took steps to secure the ports against the Persian navy. The Persian ships had still not put in an appearance, but their absence could not be taken for granted. By blocking these bases to them, Alexander was ensuring that they could not operate in his rear.

South of Adramyttium, Alexander led his army along the narrow road that squeezes between the sea and the Madra Mountains to reach the wide, fertile plains around the city of Pergamon (now Bergama). These farmlands are the richest and most productive in all Asia Minor. Supplying the Macedonian army with food was no longer a problem. At Myrina (now Smyrna) the army turned inland to march up the river valley past Magnesia.

Alexander was heading for the large, populous and wealthy city of Sardis. Not only was this an important target in its own right, but it was also the capital of the satrapy of Lydia. The fortifications of the city and its inner fortress were famously strong. It had formerly been the capital of the Kingdom of Lydia and had held out for months against the invading Persians in 546BC.

Alexander and his men must have been wary as they began their final march toward this near impregnable fortress city. Unlike the Greek cities along their route, Sardis had sent out no messengers or delegates to welcome Alexander with gifts and promises of tribute. From Sardis there was only an ominous silence. But the death of Spithridates on the Granicus was about to pay dividends.

About 10km from the city the Macedonians met a small group of richly dressed men waiting in the road. Leading the group was a Persian bureaucrat named Mithrines. This was the man who had been left behind by Spithridates with orders to get the crops in, muster the local levies and then await further orders. No further orders had ever come. With Mithrines were the leading citizens of Sardis. These men were not Greeks, they were Lydians. Although the Lydians had adopted many Greek customs, they were a distinct nationality with their own gods and their own language. As yet, nobody knew how Alexander was going to treat such peoples.

Mithrines came with a tempting offer. He and the citizens of Sardis offered to change sides, recognising Alexander as the true ruler of Lydia. They could hand over to him not only the city and fortress of Sardis, but also the vast treasury of the Lydian satrapy. All the Lydians wanted in return was to be permitted to carry on their lives as before. Mithrines would, presumably, be happy to get away with his life.

Alexander was inclined to accept this stroke of good fortune. Instead of being sat outside Sardis for weeks, perhaps months, he could occupy the city and then move on south. But he was nothing if not careful. Alexander marched on to the junction of the Hermos and Gediz rivers. Sardis was visible just 5km away.

Alexander and his army pitched camp by the river confluence. Mithrines and the citizens of Sardis were kept in Alexander's camp.

Ostensibly they were being treated as honoured guests, being invited a banquet and amused with entertainments. But there was no hiding the fact that they were effectively hostages.

Meanwhile, Amyntas, son of the Andromenes, was sent forward with an armed guard. This Macedonian nobleman had commanded the third lochus of foot companions at the Granicus, so his escort was presumably made up of these infantrymen. Amyntas and his men moved warily. The gates of the city were opened peacefully enough, so Amyntas and his men went in to be met by some equally wary citizens. These men escorted the Macedonians up to the central fortress. The gates there were also opened, by a small garrison only too grateful to have their lives spared.

Amyntas rode back to camp to announce that there was no trap. Sardis was theirs for the taking.

Alexander himself now rode to Sardis. He went up to the citadel, now securely in the hands of Amyntas's men. Alexander surveyed the triple walls and precipitous slopes and gave thanks to Zeus for having the place delivered in to his hands in peace. Alexander decided to erect a shrine to Zeus and was looking around for a site, when a sudden summer thunderstorm blew up. The storm lashed the city with rain, and sent a thunderbolt down to strike the ground close to the old palace of the Lydian kings. Alexander believed that this meant that Zeus himself had chosen the site for the shrine, and gave his orders accordingly.

Alexander decided to stay in Sardis for a few days while he made arrangements to take Lydia into the rapidly growing Macedonian empire. Unlike at Dascylium, Alexander decided against simply taking the existing Persian administrative system and incorporating it into Macedon.

Instead of appointing a satrap to have powers over the civil, judicial and military administration, Alexander appointed three different men. Alexander gave command of the fortress of Sardis, and the garrison of Greek hoplites that he left there, to Pausanias, an officer in the companion cavalry. The business of collecting taxes and tribute was handed to a man named Nicias, who is otherwise unknown. Presumably he was a bureaucrat from the staff of Eumenes. Asander, brother of Parmenio, was given the task of actually governing the province.

This triple division of authority might indicate that Alexander did not believe that Lydia was fully content with accepting Macedonian rule. He may have thought the task of looking after Lydia was beyond any one man. Alternatively, he may have been aware of the fact that more than one satrap had become too rich and mighty to accept that he was a mere provincial governor and had rebelled against the Persian monarch. Macedonian nobles were a traditionally touchy and quarrelsome lot. Maybe Alexander was wary of giving any one of them too much power.

Whatever the case, Alexander took some swift steps to try to win over the Lydians to his cause. His first move was to announce that the Lydians would no longer be bound by the judicial system and laws of the Persians. Nor were they to be forced to accept those of Macedon. Instead the old laws of the Lydian kings were reintroduced, presumably under native judges and systems of administration.

Alexander, as so often, also showed that he had a keen sense of history. He came to Asia promising to restore the liberty of the Greek cities, but at Sardis this promise was potentially more of a handicap than a help. Back in 499BC those Greek cities had risen in rebellion against the Persian monarch. Their armies had made straight for Sardis, the much-hated satrapal capital from which they were ruled. The citadel had held out, but the city had been captured and thoroughly looted. Among the buildings that had gone up in flames was the great Temple of Artemis that stood a kilometre or so outside the city walls. It had never been repaired, the successive Zoroastrian Persian satraps having no time for such pagan foolishness.

Now Alexander announced that the Temple of Artemis was to be rebuilt. The money, presumably, was to come from the treasury handed over by Mithrines. At a stroke Alexander emphasised that he was neither Persian nor Greek, but was prepared to let the Lydians worship their gods as they pleased. The temple was later rebuilt in grander style by the Romans after an earthquake, but several columns from Alexander's structure were incorporated. The temple was abandoned when Christianity took over and fell into ruins. It has since been excavated and 13 columns, found fallen but intact, have been re-erected.

As Alexander had marched down the coast, then up the river to Sardis, it had become clear that his old enemy Memnon the mercenary from Rhodes was up to something. At every city or town that the Macedonian army reached they found that the garrison of Greek mercenaries had gone. Always the townsfolk told a similar story: A dusty and travel-stained messenger had galloped in and headed for the garrison commander. The commander read whatever message the man had brought. Then the mercenaries had packed up and left in a great hurry. Where they had gone, nobody knew.

Alexander and his officers had much respect for Memnon as a military commander. If Memnon was busy, it could not possibly bode well for the Macedonians. Alexander therefore formed up his Allied Greek units and put them under the command of a Macedonian nobleman, Alexander son of Aeropos. Aeropos had been a successful general under Philip, but his career ended in disgrace when Philip caught him being entertained by a female musician when he should have been on duty. Perhaps his son was redeeming the family honour.

This separate force was sent up the valley to make its way to the estates owned by Memnon. Perhaps Alexander thought that Memnon might have fallen back to his home ground to regroup and prepare to renew the struggle. Or perhaps Alexander simply wanted to occupy his opponent's base to stop it sending assistance to him. We do not know where Memnon's home was, but the expeditionary force was gone for some days. When it returned it could report only that Memnon was not at home and that nobody seemed to know where he was.

Alexander then set out for the large and wealthy city of Ephesos. It took him three days to get there. This was by far the biggest and most important city that he had yet reached. More importantly it was completely Greek, and was in a state of civic turmoil as a result of Persian rule. Sorting out the government here was potentially going to be much more difficult than anything Alexander had yet encountered.

Ephesos had been, in theory at least, a free Greek city within the Persian Empire. This should have meant that its only duties to the Persian monarch consisted of paying an annual cash tribute and refraining from making any treaties or foreign agreements without the permission of the local satrap in Sardis. The internal government, justice system, trade policy and other matters should have been up to the Ephesians themselves.

As so often, however, this was not the case. Successive satraps had been unable to resist the temptation of getting involved in the affairs of the rich city. There was too much money about waiting to be pocketed. At Ephesos, and many other cities that had been under the control of the satrap Spithridates, this meant that the Persians had actively controlled who was in charge. They had set up a dictatorship run by a small number of men who could be trusted to be utterly loyal to the Persian monarchy, and to slip Spithridates a helpful gift every now and then. The old democratic forms of government had, it seems, been left in place but only a few men were allowed to hold office. The system had been enforced, if need be, by Persian spears. More often the mere fact that everybody knew that the Satrapal army was willing to intervene had ensured that it had no cause to do so.

Now that power in the region was falling to Alexander, things were bound to change. As elsewhere, the mercenaries left by Memnon departed hurriedly, this time by sea. At once, men who had been exiled by the ruling elite – the democrats called them tyrants – came hurrying back to

Ephesos. Soon street fights and riots broke out. The tyrants and their families were set upon by the democrats, their homes looted.

One of the tyrants, a man named Syrphax, took refuge in the Temple of Artemis that stood in partial ruins outside the city. Syrphax had with him his son Pelagon and some other relatives. When the mob learned where he was they surged out of the city and along the sacred road that led to the temple. Syrphax and Pelagon were dragged out of the sacred precincts by the mob and butchered.

It was at this dramatic and bloody moment that Alexander arrived at Ephesos. Alexander had no taste for anarchy or for mob rule; he was a king after all. The Macedonian troops were sent into break up the crowd and impose martial law on the city. Arrian tells us that this was because Alexander knew that if mobs were not stopped they would 'continue the hunt for guilty men and, indulging its lust for revenge, would out of personal hatred or greed kill many who were innocent as well'. He was right.

As soon as the army had restored order by the simple expedient of clearing the streets, Alexander marched into Ephesos and sat down in the city's council chamber. He summoned to appear before him all the leading citizens of both factions. Alexander sternly told them that he was not going to tolerate any further riots or disorder. He then announced that he was granting to Ephesos a democratic constitution and would allow it to run its own affairs. At the same time the private property of all citizens, including the 'tyrants', was to be respected.

Alexander went on to announce that he was abolishing the annual tribute that the city had paid to the Persian satrap. Before the Ephesians got too excited, however, Alexander told them that they had to pay the money to the Chief Priest of the Temple of Artemis instead. It was a move of startling political and religious importance.

Not only had the Temple of Artemis been the scene of the murder of Syrphax and Pelagon, but the Chief Priest was a Persian. And although the Temple of Artemis was the most famous building in the area, the goddess herself was not Greek, but a native deity of Asia Minor that the Greek colonists had adopted when they settled there a few centuries earlier.

Not only that, but the Temple of Artemis at Ephesos had a very curious link with Alexander himself. There is no doubt that this sanctuary of Artemis was one of the most ancient sacred sites in the world. It was also one of the most prosperous, serving as a sophisticated and effective bank for the local merchants. It also had formal powers of sanctuary, though this had not saved the hapless Syrphax and Pelagon.

What form the earlier temples took, we don't know. But in about 560BC the temple was rebuilt in magnificent form by a famous architect named Chersiphron. He is credited with having invented the idea of having beautifully carved reliefs around the lower part of the columns. These became famous, and the surviving examples are now in the British Museum.

But on 21 July 356BC a lunatic named Herostratus burst into the temple and set fire to the wooden roof. The blaze spread quickly to engulf the entire structure. Although the stone walls and columns remained, they were badly burned and many of them needed replacing. The link to Alexander is that he had been born on exactly the same day. Legend soon stated that Artemis had been unable to intervene to stop the lunatic Herostratus as she had been busy in Macedonia supervising the birth of Alexander. He was, in part at least, responsible for the burning of the old temple.

Alexander instructed the Chief Priest to use the tribute money to rebuild the temple to be more magnificent than ever. Alexander then suggested that since he had made possible the rebuilding it might be a good idea to have his name carved on the new temple. The Chief Priest smiled and bowed, but he refused. 'It is not fitting for one god to do honour to another,' he said tactfully.

This episode was remembered for various reasons. First the money was used to rebuild the temple in such a dramatic and magnificent style that it became one of the Seven Wonders of the World. It remained so until AD401 when a mob of rampaging Christians led by St John Chrysostom tore it down. Some of the better carvings and statues were then carted off to decorate the imperial palace at Constantinople. The site was excavated in the 19th century. The foundations and one column alone remain on site today.

The other reason the exchange between Alexander and the priest of Artemis was remembered is that it was the first time that anyone referred to Alexander as a god. This was not as bizarre as it might appear. The ancients regarded their minor deities much as a modern Christian might regard a saint. It was perfectly possible for a human to become a minor god if he displayed the necessary talents, gifts and deeds. For the Greeks, it was not normally done, however, for a person to be declared a god until after they died. In the East, however, declaring a living person to be a god of some kind was not unheard of, though it was rare. Later in his career, Alexander would be declared a god more than once. Much modern academic debate has centred on how seriously he took these statements. And it all began at Ephesos.

Religious matters aside, Alexander's actions at Ephesos were widely applauded and did much to smooth his path in other Greek cities. It was no longer necessary for Alexander and his army to turn up. Now city after city threw their gates open to the first Macedonian to arrive. A lone diplomat was enough to get a city to surrender.

Then Alexander got a letter from the ruler of the great port city of Miletus. He was willing to join Alexander. It was as dazzling a prize as Sardis. Pausing only to gather together the men not engaged on other tasks, Alexander leapt into the saddle and headed for Miletus.

Things were not to go the way he planned.

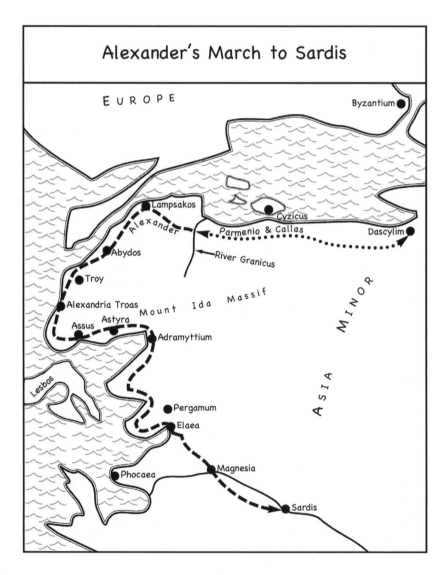

CHAPTER THIRTEEN

The Sieges

When Alexander arrived at Miletus it was to find the gates of the city closed against him. For the first time on the long march from the River Granicus, the Macedonians found that the city's garrison of Greek mercenaries had not left. Their commander, Hegistratos – who was probably from Ephesos – looked down on Alexander from the walls with defiance.

The reason for the refusal of the garrison to flee or the city to surrender was soon revealed to Alexander by local peasants. One of those ubiquitous messengers from Memnon had arrived a few days earlier with a message for Hegistratos. As soon as he had read the note, Hegistratos had begun preparing for a siege, and he had ordered the port authorities to clear the harbour of ships and prepare to be very busy. It could mean only one thing. The much feared and long awaited Persian war fleet was about to arrive.

As usual, Alexander did not hesitate. He sent a messenger to alert his own warships to the news and order them up to Miletus. The ships arrived next day and took up positions on the island of Lade, just off the coast, that effectively blocked access to the port of Miletus from the open sea. On land, Alexander had realised that the outer city and the acropolis were not manned, so he had seized them both. Hegistratos was clearly intending to defend only the inner city, which had shorter and more impressive defences, and to rely on the Persian fleet for supplies.

When the Persian fleet of 400 warships did arrive, its commander got close enough to see the Macedonian fleet at Lade, then pulled back. He moved off to Mycale on a headland facing the island of Samos, the nearest suitable anchorage with a reliable supply of fresh water. Scout ships were sent out to inspect the Macedonian positions, but the Persians made no move to attack.

And then an eagle came down and landed on the beach on Lade where Alexander's own flagship was pulled up, waiting for the Persian fleet to arrive. The eagle sat there for quite some time, while the men watched. Then it gave a harsh cry and flew up to disappear into the sky. As soon as it was gone the men began discussing this strange event, and a ship was sent to carry the news to Alexander. The reason for the excitement was not just that eagles very rarely landed on beaches, it was that the eagle was the bird sacred to Zeus. The eagles were the eyes and ears of the great god, and their behaviour was thought to indicate omens sent by Zeus. The question was, what did this omen mean?

Alexander seems to have been in conference with his commanders when the news about the eagle arrived. Parmenio suggested that it meant that Zeus had confidence in the Greek fleet, so a naval battle should be fought without delay. Alexander objected. He pointed out that the eagle had come to rest on the land, indicating that a land assault should be planned.

The debate was still continuing when a citizen of Miletus named Glaucippus arrived. He was ushered into the officers' conference. Glaucippus made a flowery and well written speech filled with flattery and historical allusions. Stripped of these fripperies, however, Glaucippus was stating that Miletus had never really been part of the Persian Empire and had decided to stay neutral in the current war between Alexander and Darius. He went on that Miletus was willing to allow both the Persians and Macedonians to use the city's facilities.

It is not clear whether Hegistratos had been consulted by the city council about this offer, probably not. The Council had probably acted once it became clear that the Persian fleet could not get access to the harbour.

Alexander eyed Glaucippus coldly. 'Get back to your friends,' he said, meaning Hegistratos and the mercenaries. 'Tell them to get ready to defend themselves.'

The reason why Alexander had refused the offer of Glaucippus was that he had already decided to close all ports to the Persians. By doing this he could pen the enemy ships into an ever shrinking area of sea. If Miletus remained open to the Persian ships, they would be able to range freely behind Alexander's army as it advanced down the coast. That could not be allowed to happen, so Miletus had to be captured if it did not surrender willingly.

The problem facing Alexander was that Miletus not only had strong walls, but was sited beautifully for defensive purposes. It stood on a rocky headland that jutted out into the sea. The sea has since retreated by several miles, so the site now juts out into a fertile plain. The land around the headland was just as rocky and barren as the site of the city itself. There were no fresh water springs in the immediate vicinity where the Macedonians could drink and no prosperous farms from which to gather food. Supplying the Macedonian siege forces was going to be a tricky and time consuming operation.

Alexander soon found out just how difficult it was going to be keeping his army supplied when a detachment sent out to collect water from a distant spring was ambushed by a small force sent out from Miletus. The Macedonians were slaughtered, and the army went thirsty for a night. If Alexander tried to starve the city into surrender, it was by no means certain that it would run short of food before his own army did. Alexander decided on assault.

The components of the siege engines were sent for, and timber to make them up into complete weapons was acquired. Within a few days Alexander had several battering rams ready. These were pushed up against the walls while the Cretan archers and field artillery swept the ramparts with missiles to keep the mercenaries from fighting back.

After a few days of this treatment, the walls of Miletus began to crumble. Alexander massed his assault troops out of bow range of the walls and gave them orders to attack as soon as the battering rams had brought down enough of the walls to make getting inside a reasonable proposition. Arrian suggests that it was the Agrianians and Thracians who were used for the assault, although Alexander also had four squadrons of the companion cavalry present. Nicanor, the Macedonian admiral, left his base on Lade and brought his ships close inshore off Miletus. He was taking no chances that any Persian relief might sneak in. In the event, no Persian ships made the effort, though Nicanor did intercept and capture some fishing boats leaving Miletus carrying those men and their families who had been ruling Miletus on behalf of the Persians.

Eventually a section of walls came crashing down. The Agrianians and Thracians surged into the town. There followed the scenes of mayhem and brutality that usually followed the fall of a city. Civilians were killed, their houses robbed and their women raped. But it did not last long. Alexander wanted Miletus intact. Soon he and his officers were inside Miletus, restoring some sort of order. The fact that they succeeded quickly is shown by the fact that none of the central public buildings down by the harbour were damaged in any way. Alexander must have got his troops under control quickly. In any case, the fighting was not yet over.

A group of about 300 of Hegistratos' mercenaries had swum from the city to a small island offshore. The island was tall and rocky, its sheer sides being almost as impressive defences as the walls of Miletus had been. Alexander ordered scaling ladders to be loaded on to a number of ships along with a mass of infantry. The ships moved forward to begin the assault on the island. The mercenaries on the island, assuming that they were about to face the same fate as their colleagues had met at the Granicus, prepared to fight to the death. They would have begun to sing the old war songs of the hoplites as they brandished their weapons at the approaching Macedonians.

Then Alexander suddenly ordered his ships to halt and back water. Arrian tells us that 'he was moved to pity by their courage and loyalty'. Alexander now sent forward a messenger to shout terms up to the mercenaries on their rock. If they joined his army, at a cheap rate of pay of course, and promised to serve Alexander as loyally as they had served Darius, their lives would be spared. The mercenaries readily agreed.

This was a change of policy for Alexander. At the Granicus he had treated the Greek mercenaries in Persion employ severely. Now he was being merciful, as he would remain for the rest of the war. It may be that he realised that he was going to keep on meeting these men and it would be better if they surrendered easily than if they fought hard to the death.

The fighting was over; Alexander had won Miletus. But the area was not yet secure. The Persian fleet was still at Mycale. The day after the fall of Miletus, the Persian fleet put to sea and came racing toward the Greek ships. A group of Persian ships veered off at the last minute and headed toward Miletus harbour as if they were about to land a force of marines in the city. Nicanor reacted swiftly, sending a squadron to block the harbour mouth, while he manoeuvred his ships to keep out of the clutches of the Persian fleet that outnumbered his ships by three to one. Next day the Persians tried again, adopting a different battle plan. The third day saw the Persians come again, using yet another ploy to try to lure Nicanor into open water where they could use their superior numbers.

In response Alexander sent Philotas, son of Parmenio, with the squadrons of companion cavalry and a force of infantry to march to Mycale. Once there, the Macedonians seized the sources of fresh water and dug in. The marines on the Persian ships were too lightly armoured to stand much chance against Philotas and his men. The Persian ships abandoned Mycale. The Persian ships put out to sea and vanished over the horizon. Alexander no more knew where they had gone than he knew where Memnon was.

As the Persian ships slipped away, Alexander called Nicanor to see him. Alexander had decided to disband most of his fleet. He was keeping only 20 warships and a few merchant vessels. These would be used to keep him in touch with cities up and down the coast, carry messages back to Macedon or Greece, and carry supplies of grain to the army when necessary. The rest of the fleet was to be sent home. The events at Miletus had convinced Alexander that he could negate the power of the Persian fleet by capturing the seaports and securing the sources of fresh water.

Now that he had gained control of the main cities of Ionia and Lydia, Alexander was assured of a ready and permanent supply of food for his men. He no longer needed such a large fleet. Ships and the men to crew them were expensive, and Alexander was still short of ready funds.

With Miletus captured, Alexander set about settling a new governmental order for the area. He began by giving the city a democratic constitution and recalling the exiles from abroad, as he had done at Ephesos and elsewhere. The citizens of Miletus responded by electing Alexander to be head of the city council for the coming year. Alexander graciously accepted the offer. Then he set off along the Sacred Way that led from Miletus to the nearby Temple of Apollo at Didyma.

This was one of the greatest Greek religious sites in Asia Minor. Unlike the temples at Ephesos or Sardis, Didyma was dedicated to a thoroughly Greek god and officiated over by Greek priests. Moreover, it had a resonant history of which Alexander wanted to take full advantage. Didyma had, like Delphi, long been an oracle of Apollo, a place where humans could come to get a message direct from the gods. The oracle had centred around an ancient cult statue of Apollo set over a sacred spring of pure, sweet water.

Back in 500BC, the local Greek cities had risen in revolt against rule by the Persians. The oracle at Didyma had issued a message that indicated that Apollo supported the rebels. When the rebellion was put down, the Persians came to Didyma to exact revenge on the god. As good Zoroastrians, the Persians did not believe that Apollo existed, but they knew that the Greeks did and that was what was important. The cult statue was ripped from its pedestal and dragged away, perhaps to the satrapal palace at Sardis, as a prisoner of war. The sacred spring was blocked up. Although the temple remained open to worshippers, the oracle was closed.

As Alexander arrived at Didyma along the Sacred Way, he ordered that the spring should be unblocked. The water again flowed as pure as before. He had brought with him the cult statue and he had this re-erected. The priest was allowed once again to perform the rites of oracle. The message was suitably encouraging for Alexander.

Alexander ordered that the old temple should be torn down and a magnificent new one begun. He set his team of architects to work drawing up plans for a most astonishing structure. The cost of the projected temple was vast, and the building work was not finished until several generations after Alexander's time. It was, however, a truly wonderful structure. It was abandoned when Christianity ousted paganism,

The sacred road from Miletus to Didyma. It was along this paved road that Alexander walked to consult the oracle of Apollo at Didyma after he had visited Ephesus.

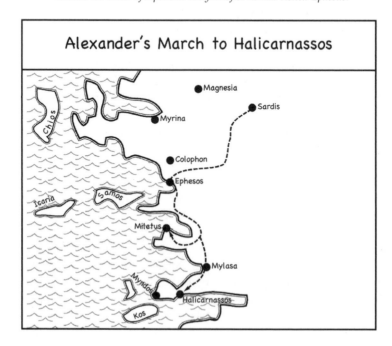

and most of it was brought down by a medieval earthquake. Modern excavations have restored much of the building.

The symbol of the Temple of Apollo at Didyma was traditionally a winged gorgon's head. Carvings of this symbol can be found littering the site to this day. Later statues, reliefs and mosaics often depict Alexander with the same symbol on his breastplate. Presumably he adopted the symbol after his visit here.

From Miletus, Alexander headed on south. It was now getting on towards autumn and he was keen to complete the Granicus campaigning season having captured as much territory as possible. South of the hills lay Caria. This was a satrapy within the Persian Empire that retained its own royal family. The constitutional arrangements are obscure, but it seems that the Persian monarch appointed the head of the royal family as satrap. Thus Caria retained its own laws and own rulers while being formally part of the Persian Empire. It was not entirely clear how the rulers of Caria would react to the new power in the land.

The current Satrap-King was a Persian named Orontobates who had married the daughter of the previous king, Pixodaros. Pixodaros had long been on friendly terms with King Philip, so the marriage may have been a way for the Persians to be more certain of his loyalty. He had died the previous year, so Orontobates had taken over the seat of power. There was, however, another potential heir in the shape of Ada, aunt to Pixodoros. She was childless, but was of pure Carian royal blood.

As Alexander advanced he sent messengers on ahead to Orontobates, but received no reply. Nor did he receive a reply from Ada. He received a visit from Ada herself. The lady came with an offer. She would turn over to Alexander her estates and its fortress if, in return, Alexander would recognise her as the Queen of Caria and confirm that she would be allowed to rule the kingdom under the same terms as her family had done under the Persians. She added that she would adopt Alexander as her son, effectively making him her heir and guaranteeing that he would inherit the kingdom direct when she died.

Alexander jumped at the offer. He could now pose as the champion of a claimant to the throne instead of as a foreign invader. He would also be spared any awkward negotiations with the few, small Greek cities along the coast. They had not been covered by the original promise of Greek liberty made by Philip when he began preparing for the war, but might reasonably be hoping for some sort of generous treatment from Alexander. Any such hopes were now dashed. Though, to be fair, those Greek cities were ruled with a light hand by the Carians.

Ada also brought Alexander the one piece of information that he had most wanted. She knew where Memnon was and what he was doing.

The mercenary commander was in the Carian capital of Halicarnassos with Orontobates. Together the two men had been preparing the city to hold out against Alexander. She also told Alexander that Darius had now promoted Memnon so that he was superior to all the Satraps of Asia Minor and was in a position to issue orders to them, or directly to their men. He had also been made commander of the Persian fleet, which now lay off Halicarnassos.

The city of Halicarnassos (now Bodrum) was one of the most famous in the then known world. It had been founded by the kings of Caria to take advantage of the seaborne trade on which the Greek coastal cities were growing rich. It was deliberately constructed along Greek lines, with a formal grid street layout, an Agora and other Greek features. The Carians made great efforts to attract large numbers of Greek merchants and craftsmen to the city so that when Alexander arrived the city was largely Greek in culture and population. It remained, however, a creation of the Carian royal family and their personal property.

Large and wealthy the city may have been, but what really made it famous was a tomb. This was the great Mausoleum of Halicarnassos. Although the word mausoleum is now used for any large tomb, it was originally specific to this tomb as it was the last resting place of King Mausolos. Mausolos had died in 353BC, and the tomb was built by his widow Artemisia in the three years that followed.

Nobody had ever seen anything like it, and the Mausoleum soon became ranked as one of the Seven Wonders of the World. Over the grave of the king was raised a massive stone platform 38 by 32 metres square and 18 metres tall. On top of this rested 36 ionic columns, each about 9 metres tall. This colonnade was capped with a stone pyramid another 9 metres tall, topped off by a stone statue of Mausolos and Artemisia riding in a chariot pulled by four horses.

The structure was impressive in itself, but what astonished the Greeks that saw it was the sheer number and quality of the statues that adorned it. There was a battle scene of Greeks fighting Amazons around the base. A mass of Carian notables higher up, then another battle frieze, this time of Persian cavalry fighting steppe barbarians. The colonnade was topped by lions.

The structure remained standing until about 1250 when an earthquake brought the columns and pyramid crashing down. The stones of the ruin were subsequently used as a quarry by locals, and particularly by the Knights of St John when they were building the medieval castle that still stands at Bodrum. The broken statues were generally tossed aside. Some of these statues have survived to be recovered by modern archaeologists, mostly in broken form, but they confirm the great skill of the carvers.

When Alexander came over the hills northeast of the city along the road from Mylasa on his way from Miletus, he would have seen the Mausoleum towering over the city and dominating the view. However, he would have been more interested in the city's defences. Memnon had had plenty of time to work on these since his arrival here after the Battle of the Granicus. He had not been wasting his time.

The city walls were already strong, but Memnon had inspected them personally and ordered the repair of any defects and the strengthening of any weak points. He paid especial attention to the gates. He also ordered the digging, or perhaps the clearing, of a ditch right around the city. This ditch was positioned a few metres away from the foot of the wall. It was intended to stop Alexander from pushing any battering rams up to the base of the wall, while its position meant that any Macedonians trying to fill it in would be within easy reach of archers on the walls above. At 15 metres wide and 8 metres deep it was a formidable obstacle.

The entrance to the harbour was already defended by a strong fortress on a crag overlooking the eastern side of the harbour entrance. Thinking this was not enough to secure the port, Memnon separated out a section of the city known as Salmacis on the far side of the harbour entrance. A strong wall was built blocking access to Salmacis from the rest of the city. The civilians were expelled and the area was made into a mini fortress.

Finally, Memnon took the usual precautions of importing vast stores of food and ammunition, while at the same time evacuating all inhabitants who would not be needed during the siege. Halicarnassos was going to be a tough proposition for Alexander.

For the siege of Halicarnassos we have two different eyewitness sources, though each is third hand in the versions that have survived. The first is that found in Plutarch and Arrian that derive from the version written down by Ptolemy, son of Lagos, who was with the Macedonian army. The second comes from that anonymous mercenary who was serving with Memnon and who was inside Harlicarnassos during the siege. The two accounts do not often contradict each other and, when they do, it is most likely simply the different viewpoints that can explain the discrepancies.

The Macedonians decided to try speed and surprise. An assault on the Mylasa Gate was made within hours of Alexander arriving, but it was beaten off with comparative ease by Memnon's men. Alexander then established a permanent camp between the road to Mylasa and the sea. There he would be in a good defensive position if another Persian army arrived, but could stay in touch with the fleet and with his men who

Bodrum, the ancient Halicarnossos, from the southwest. Alexander's camp lay to the extreme right of this photo. The medieval castle, centre right, stands on the site of the ancient fortress. The current town clusters around the harbour much as did the ancient city. (David Jones)

were absent on other missions or were stationed in the cities that had come over to him.

While Alexander had his engineers prepare the siege engines, traffic along the road to Mylasa was brisk. Most of these travellers were representatives of the various Greek cities coming to surrender in person and hand over gifts of money or golden crowns. But one group came from the small town of Myndus (now Turgutrels). This town had not yet surrendered and was held by a garrison of Memnon's mercenaries. It stood west of Halicarnassos on the end of the peninsula on which Harlicarnassos stood. Its position was important as it dominated the narrow straits between the mainland and the island of Kos which formed the western sea approaches to Halicarnassos. Whoever held the city could block that approach.

The delegation told Alexander that most of the Greek inhabitants wanted to change side, but that they could not do so because of the mercenaries. They said that if Alexander sent a force to Myndus they would try to overpower the guards on a small side gate, then throw it open at midnight to admit the Macedonians. Alexander was so excited by the prospect of capturing Myndus without much effort that he chose to lead the assault force himself.

Alexander arrived just before midnight and led a small group of men in utter silence up to the gate. The rest of the force held back, but had orders to storm forward as soon as Alexander and his men had secured the gate. Midnight came and nothing happened. The time passed, and there was no sign of activity from within Myndus. The mercenaries must have been more alert than the citizens had thought.

With dawn approaching, Alexander decided to try a surprise assault. He had not brought with him any scaling ladders, still less any heavy equipment, but he sent his infantry into the attack anyway. These men seem to have been the hypaspists, the elite of the infantry. The men managed to get into a strongpoint and capture it, but the mercenaries fought back with determination and the Macedonians were unable to get any further.

As the cold light of dawn crept over the scene, Alexander saw ships hurrying up from Halicarnassos loaded down with reinforcements. He abandoned the attempt to take Myndos and trailed back to the larger city.

After a delay of several days, the engineers got the siege engines completed. As at Miletus there were battering rams, but there were also heavy catapults with which to bombard the walls. The engineers had also constructed at least three siege towers. Teams of infantrymen, presumably pezhetairoi foot companions had meanwhile been advancing under cover of wooden sheds on wheels to tip rubble into a section of the ditch in front of the walls north of the great Triple Gate. The task was finished after several days and the siege towers trundled forward ready to begin a dawn assault the next day (see page 250).

Memnon, however, was not one to remain passive in the face of danger. That very night he led a sally from the city. The mercenaries overwhelmed the Macedonian patrols and set fire to the siege towers. Memnon and his men formed a defensive ring around the burning towers. They held off the Macedonians who came hurrying from their camp for just long enough for the flames to get a good hold, then they retreated back to the city. Arrian claims that Memnon lost 170 men in this raid, which may be true. He also says that Alexander lost 300, though he claims that only 16 of them were killed and that the rest were wounded.

With his siege towers gone, Alexander reverted to using battering rams and catapults to bring down the walls. It was a long, slow and tedious job that involved a great deal of hard work and some degree of danger for the men on both sides. The attackers were, however, making progress. Cracks and fissures began to appear in the stone walls of Harlicarnassos and it seemed to be only a matter of time before a section of them came tumbling down.

That, at least, was clearly the view of Memnon. He set his men to build a second wall in a semi-circular shape behind the section of wall on which

Alexander's men were working. The space between the two was cleared of all buildings. His plan was that when Alexander mounted an assault, the mercenaries should at once abandon the front line defences and take up positions on the second wall. Alexander's men would be faced with crossing an open killing ground swept by arrows and sling shot from both the second wall and the tower on the front wall. It would, if all went well, be a slaughter that would gain Alexander nothing.

But wine was to intervene first.

The siege lines were manned by units from the pezhetairoi, the lochus of which took it in turns to be on duty on different days. On a day when Perdiccas men were on duty two sentries at the very edge of the filled in ditch managed to sneak a flask of wine past their officers. The two men were getting slowly tipsy as they discussed the progress of the siege. By this time two towers had been brought down, along with the stretch of wall between them. The pile of rubble was still a difficult obstacle, but it was not as sheer as the wall had been. Regarding the state of the ruins in front of them, the men delivered themselves of the opinion that Alexander would soon order an assault as the rubble was almost climbable. The wine flowed and soon the two men were arguing about who was better able to clamber up the walls. Then they set off to prove their boasts.

The sentries on the crumbling walls were alert and saw the drunken pair coming. They alerted their officer, who in turn sent a message to summon his superior while he led a few men out of a side gate to intercept the drinkers. The sallying force killed the two men, but the noise brought forward the rest of Perdiccas' sentries. This led to a fight, which escalated as more mercenaries came out to support their fellows. Perdiccas now sent a message to Alexander, and formed up his entire force to attack.

The charging pezhetairoi were met by even more mercenaries pouring out of the city. It seems that by this point Memnon was on the spot. He launched a renewed attack that tumbled Perdiccas' men back into the ditch. But when Alexander himself was seen to arrive at the head of reinforcements, Memnon ordered a withdrawal.

Dawn revealed a scene of carnage. Most of the fighting had taken place around the ditch, which was within easy reach of the archers on the walls of Halicarnassos. Memnon sent his men out to collect their dead and wounded, but the Macedonians could not do likewise without risking being shot. Alexander was forced into what was probably the most humiliating action of his entire life. He had to send forward a herald to ask permission to recover his dead and wounded. According to the rules of war of the time, only a defeated commander had to ask for such permission, and doing so was an open acknowledgement of failure. This was the only time that Alexander ever did this.

The request led to a heated debate inside Halicarnassos. Among the mercenary officers were two Athenians named Ephialtes and Thrasybulus. These were former generals of the Athenian army who had long opposed Macedonian rule in Greece. Before setting out for Persia, Alexander had sent a message to Athens demanding that these two men should be handed over to him so that they could be put in prison for the duration of the campaign. They had fled Athens, and this is the first time that they re-enter the story. They advised that Alexander's request should be refused. Perhaps they wanted to flaunt the Macedonian defeat in Alexander's face. Memnon, however, overruled them and allowed the Macedonians to take away their dead. Memnon was a professional doing a professional's job. Unlike the Athenians he did not have a personal stake in the quarrel.

Again the two forces settled down to the dreary danger of siege works. Alexander's engineers cleared a path through the rubble of the fallen outer wall. Through this were pushed two or more battering rams to start on the demolition of Memnon's second wall. This wall was tall and thick, but had been hurriedly put up using the bricks from the demolished houses. It would not stand as long as the original wall. The days passed, but the eventual collapse of the wall was certain.

Memnon called a conference of his commanders. Ephialtes the Athenian suggested that they should try to destroy the battering rams and heavy catapults, just as they had burned the siege towers some weeks earlier. It seemed the only way that the siege might be broken. However, the Macedonians had been taken by surprise on the earlier occasion, but now all the remaining siege engines were well guarded at night. That much was clear to all, so Ephialtes came up with a daring plan: attack them in daylight.

The idea certainly had the advantage that it would take the Macedonians by surprise, but it was incredibly risky. Memnon insisted on careful planning and thorough preparation. In its final form it was a sophisticated scheme. The attack began when all three of the gates of Halicarnassos were thrown open at dawn. Hundreds of men streamed out of the Myndos Gate screaming and shouting, alarming the Macedonians set to watch that stretch of the defences. Another force poured out of the Mylasa Gate and headed for Alexander's camp as if intent on launching a surprise assault.

These were only feints. The main assault was made through the Triple Gate. Ephialtes led out 2,000 hoplites. Half of them turned to the right to assault the men working the siege engines. These hapless Macedonians were quickly killed and the mercenaries then tried to set fire to the siege engines. This proved to be more difficult than expected. Perhaps Alexander, learning from the loss of his siege towers, had soaked the wood or covered it in wet leather to make the engines less flammable.

Meanwhile, Ephialtes had formed the hoplites up in a phalanx and was attacking the main body of pezhetairoi in the siege lines. The Macedonians did not have time to adopt their irresistible sarissa phalanx before the hoplites were upon them. In small groups, the Macedonians stood little chance. They were pushed back and cut down as they fled.

Alexander had not been on the spot when the assault began, but was not far away. He sent off messengers to the other pezhetairoi to hurry to join the fight, while sending his bodyguard into action. This is one of the few occasions on which these bodyguards are known to have fought in battle as a formed unit, and obviously were doing so here only to meet an emergency. They brought Ephialtes men to a halt.

Ephialtes began to fall back, but it was only a ruse. As the battle line fell back toward the Triple Gate a harsh trumpet blast rang out. Memnon now charged forward at the head of a fresh phalanx of men. They crashed into the fray, and among the men they killed was the commander of the Macedonian royal guard, a nobleman named Ptolemy.

It was at this point that Alexander was saved by a scratch body of men. These were the older veterans among the pezhetairoi. These older men had been spared the arduous digging and construction work in the siege lines and had been on other duties nearby. Seeing the moment of great peril engulfing their comrades, the old men grabbed their sarissas and their shields. Forming up into a solid phalanx they came hurrying forward. Faced by this new intervention, Memnon ordered a retreat.

When the action was over Ephialtes was found dead, killed fighting at the head of his men as they met Alexander's guards. It was also clear that although several of Alexander's siege engines had been damaged, they had not been destroyed. Memnon called another council of war with his commanders.

Memnon declared that it was time to go. The city, he said, should be abandoned. He believed that Alexander was keen to capture the capital of Caria so that it could serve as the seat of the new government under Queen Ada. It was unlikely that Alexander would destroy the city or sell its inhabitants into slavery. Memnon could go with a clear conscience. But Orontobates objected. He was, after all, the reigning King of Caria and saw no reason to abandon his kingdom. He thought that he could hold out in the Royal Fortress and in the newly fortified section of city at Salmacis, so long as he had enough men and the Persian fleet could

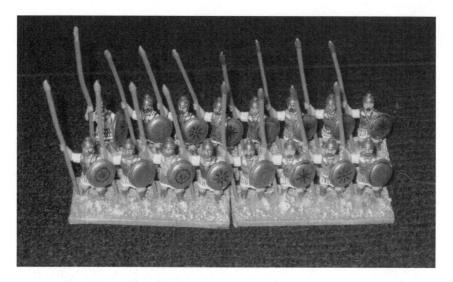

The campaigns of Alexander the Great continue to excite the imaginations of the world. These model phalangites were produced for use in modern wargames.

supply him by sea. Memnon agreed. The move would, at any rate, mean that Alexander could not use the harbour.

As soon as it got dark, the work began of shifting supplies and weaponry into the areas to be held. About four hours after dark, Memnon loaded his men on to the Persian ships and left for the island of Kos. The stores that could not be moved were set on fire. Several houses also went up in flames, though whether this was deliberate or not is unclear.

As soon as the flames were seen Alexander guessed what they meant. He ordered a force to smash a way into the city and gave them orders to kill anyone they saw setting fire to anything, but to spare everyone else. There was to be no sack of Halicarnassos.

Alexander himself entered the city about dawn next day. He was surprised, and not a little annoyed to find that Orontobates still held out in the two fortresses. Alexander was keen to move on before the winter weather closed in, but now could not do so. He began by ordering that all houses close to the walls of the two fortresses were to be demolished. He then gave 3,000 infantry to the command of Ptolemy, son of Lagos, and ordered him to keep the two strongholds under close watch. Alexander told Ptolemy that he was to take no risks, but was to blockade Orontobates into surrender. Given that the garrisons could be supplied by sea this promised to be a long job. In the event it took more than a year.

Alexander then realised that the approach of winter made it unlikely that the Persians would try anything until the following year. The

Granicus Campaign was drawing to a close. Alexander sent those men who had married only recently back to Macedonia to spend the winter with their wives. Among them was the young officer who had married Parmenio's daughter just before the campaign began. It proved to be a highly popular move both at home and with the army. Parmenio was sent back to Sardis with one half of the army, perhaps to reduce the pressure n the local food supply.

Alexander then marched off south and east. If fighting was now out of the question for some months to come, not all activity was impossible. Alexander moved along the coast accepting the defection or surrender of cities that were unable to hold out against him. The Granicus campaign ended with Alexander in a commanding position. But the war was not yet won. Memnon had, once again, eluded Alexander and had got away with most of his army intact. Even more ominous was the knowledge that Darius himself was likely now to take a hand. And he would be coming with all the vast resources of the Persian Empire at his command.

It was going to be a long war.

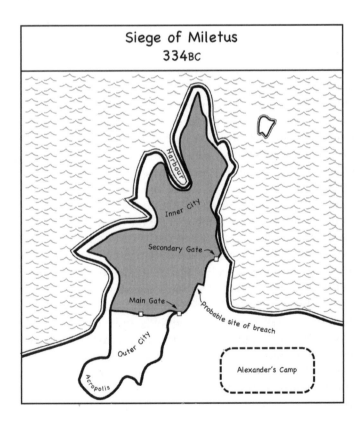

CHAPTER FOURTEEN

What Happened Next

After the Granicus Campaign the war between Macedon, its allies and the Persian Empire continued for some years. It ended with the defeat of the Persian Empire. The fates of the individuals, when known, are as follows:

Ada remained Queen of Caria for the rest of her life. Her date of death is unknown.

Agathon was later appointed Governor of Babylon by Alexander. It is not known how long he held this position nor when he died.

Alexander went on to conquer the Persian Empire, then to lead his army into India to make more conquests. He died in 323BC. His vast empire was subsequently divided up among his generals, who proceeded to war against each other.

Aristoboulos remained with Alexander until his death, then returned home and spent the rest of his life writing books on geography.

Aristotle returned to Athens to found his famous school the Lyceum. He was later forced into exile when an anti-Macedonian faction took power in Athens after Alexander's death. He died in Chalcis at the age of 62.

Arrhidaeus, the son of Philip II, was appointed joint king on the death of Alexander. He was later murdered by Olympia.

Asander died campaigning north of the River Oxus in 327BC.

Callas held various positions in the army. He died sometime after 315BC.

Callisthenes continued to accompany the Macedonian army, writing up his account of the expedition. In 328BC he fell out with Alexander after he began introducing criticisms of Alexander's actions into his book. He was put in prison, where he died.

Cleitus the Black was promoted by Alexander and became commander of the Companion Cavalry. In the spring of 328 he attended a banquet and he and Alexander both got drunk. The two men argued, apparently about the relative merits of the Philip's older veterans, of which Cleitus was one, and newer recruits. In a fit of anger Alexander killed Cleitus with a spear.

Coenus remained an officer of the Foot Companions. He died of disease in 325BC.

Craterus continued to hold high military office and came to be greatly trusted by Alexander. After Alexander's death he sided with Antipater against Eumenes and was killed in battle in 321BC.

Darius III came to Asia Minor to fight Alexander in person the year after the Granicus and was defeated at the Battle of Issus. He was defeated again at Gaugamela in 331BC. Darius fled to the eastern provinces of the empire to raise a new army, but was murdered by Bessus, Satrap of Bactria.

Eumenes held his post as head bureaucrat throughout Alexander's life. After Alexander's death he seized power in Paphlogonia, but in 316BC was defeated and killed by Antigonus.

Hephaistion later obtained senior commands in Alexander's army. He died of a sudden disease in 324BC.

Lysippus went on to become one of the richest and most widely admired sculptors of his time. He died in 270BC.

Memnon of Rhodes moved his surviving armies east after evacuating Halicarnassos. He marched to meet Darius the following spring, but died of disease before the two armies joined.

Nicanor died fighting in Hyrcania the year after the Campaign.

Olympia remained in Macedonia while Alexander conquered the Persian Empire. After Alexander's death she supported Antigonus. In 316 she was besieged in Pydna by Cassander and, on being captured, was killed.

Orontobates held out in Halicarnossos for a year. He and his men were then evacuated by sea. His eventual fate is unknown.

Parmenio remained second in command of the army until 330BC when he was murdered on the orders of Alexander after his son, Philotas, had been convicted of treason.

Pausanias who commanded one of the squadrons of the Companion Cavalry was later appointed governor of Sardis.

Perdiccas, commander of one of the lochus of the Foot Companions, rose to be one of Alexander's most trusted generals. After Alexander's death he attempted to set himself up as an independent ruler, but was murdered by his own soldiers.

Philotas, son of Parmenio, rose to a position of high command. In 330BC he plotted to murder Alexander after two of his brothers died in battle. The plot was uncovered and Philotas was executed.

Ptolemy, son of Lagos, remained with Alexander to the end. He made himself ruler of Egypt where he wisely had himself made pharaoh and honoured Egyptian gods and customs. He died in 283BC and his descendants ruled Egypt until the country was conquered by Rome in 30BC.

Rheomithras skillfully led his Cavalry units out of Alexander's reach, heading southeast toward the Euphrates. He joined Darius late in 334BC. In 333BC he was killed fighting Alexander at the Battle of Issus.

Bibliography

There are more books written about Alexander the Great than about almost any other figure of the ancient world. Some are biographies; others look at his military skills while others focus on other aspects of his life or on his place in the wider hellenistic world.

Of these many dozens of books, *Alexander the Great* by Robin Lane Fox and published by Penguin is probably the best all round biography, though it can be a bit light on military matters and covers the Battle of the Granicus in just half a dozen pages. *Alexander the Great: The Hunt for a New Past* by Paul Cartledge and published by Pan gives a rather different overall perspective and spends some time trying to get to the bottom of some of the various disputes about Alexander and his life. *In the Footsteps of Alexander the Great* by Michael Wood and published by BBC Books is a highly illustrated and easily read look at the route taken by Alexander on the course of his conquests, but it spends relatively little time on the enigmatic figure of Alexander himself.

Of the ancient sources the writings of Arrian, Curtius and Plutarch are generally available in a number of different editions. The others are not so easy to find, but can be tracked down with a bit of luck. Given that Alexander was himself so obsessed with Homer it is worthwhile reading the *Iliad* by that great poet – again it is easily available in a number of editions.

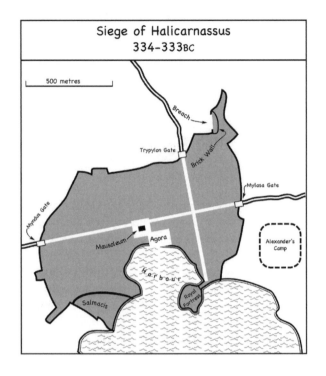

Siege of Halicarnassus
334–333BC

500 metres

Breach

Trypylon Gate

Brick Wall

Mylasa Gate

Myndus Gate

Mausoleum

Agora

Alexander's Camp

Harbour

Salmacis

Royal Fortress

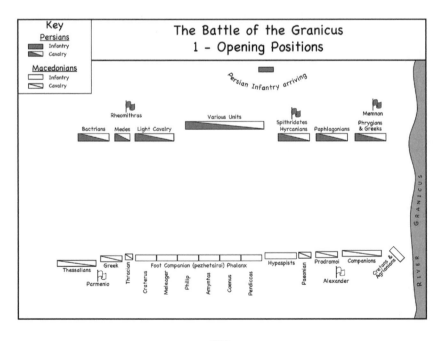

The Battle of the Granicus
1 – Opening Positions

Key

Persians
Infantry
Cavalry

Macedonians
Infantry
Cavalry

Persian Infantry arriving

Rheomithras

Various Units

Spithridates
Hyrcanians

Memnon

Paphlagonians

Phrygians & Greeks

Bactrians   Medes   Light Cavalry

Thessalians   Greek   Thracian   Foot Companion (pezhetairoi) Phalanx   Hypaspists   Prodromoi   Companions   Cretans & Agrianians

Parmenio   Craterus   Meleager   Philip   Amyntas   Coenus   Perdiccas   Paeonian   Alexander

RIVER GRANICUS

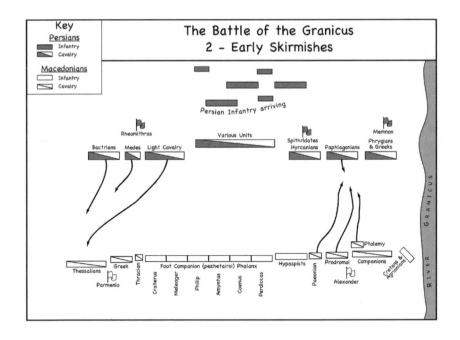

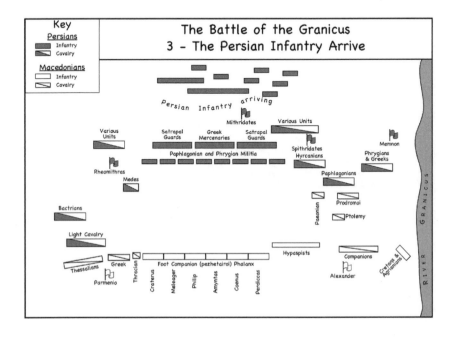

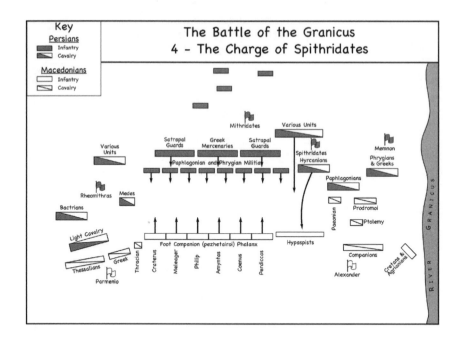

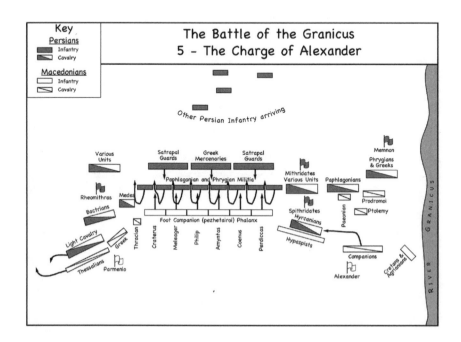

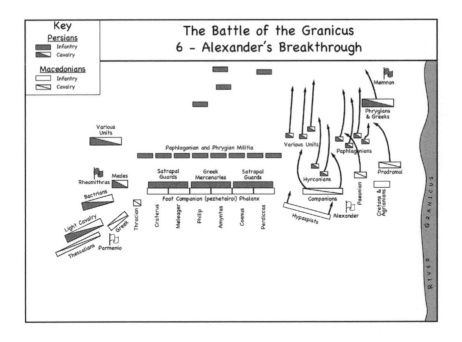

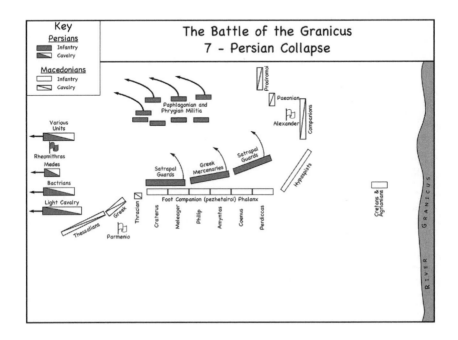

Index

254